Counseling Tools For Nonprofessionals

Counseling Tools For Nonprofessionals

PRACTICAL MENTAL HEALTH STRATEGIES WITH A CHRISTIAN PERSPECTIVE

Gretchen Jacobs, MA, MS, Chaplain

Counseling Tools for Nonprofessionals:
Practical Mental Health Strategies with a Christian Perspective
First Edition
Copyright © 2016 Gretchen Jacobs, MA, MS, Chaplain. All rights reserved. It is illegal to copy this book, post it to a website, or distribute it by any other means without permission from the author. No portion of this book may be reproduced or transmitted in any form or by any means, electronic or mechanical, including photocopying, recording, scanning, or by any other storage or retrieval system, without prior permission from the author.

However, the "Tools for Counselors to Use as Homework for Clients" section of the appendix may be copied by the original purchaser only for his/her exclusive use in his/her ministry or job and are not to be copied for others' use.
It is my request that the user say a prayer that the "Tools" and the contents of this book contribute to both the user and the recipient so that both grow in devotion and obedience to Christ. Thank you.

Unless otherwise noted, all quoted scripture is taken from the New American Standard Bible®, Copyright © 1960, 1962, 1963, 1968, 1971, 1972, 1973, 1975, 1977, 1995 by The Lockman Foundation. Used by permission.
Scripture noted nkjv is taken from the New King James Version®. Copyright © 1982 by Thomas Nelson. Used by permission. All rights reserved.
Scripture noted niv is taken from the Holy Bible, New International Version®, NIV® Copyright © 1973, 1978, 1984, 2011 by Biblica, Inc.® Used by permission. All rights reserved worldwide.
Scripture noted tlb is taken from The Living Bible copyright © 1971 by Tyndale House Foundation. Used by permission of Tyndale House Publishers Inc., Carol Stream, Illinois 60188. All rights reserved. The Living Bible, TLB, and The Living Bible logo are registered trademarks of Tyndale House Publishers.
Scripture noted hcsb is taken from the Holman Christian Standard Bible® Copyright © 1999, 2000, 2002, 2003, 2009 by Holman Bible Publishers. Used with permission by Holman Bible Publishers, Nashville, Tennessee. All rights reserved.
ISBN: 0692682783
ISBN 13: 9780692682784
Library of Congress Control Number: 2016908955
Gloria Gretchen Jacobs, Mesa, AZ

Disclaimers

The author and/or publisher offer(s) no guarantees that anyone following these techniques, tools, suggestions, or strategies will become successful. The author and/or publisher shall have neither liability nor responsibility to anyone with respect to any loss or damage caused, or alleged to be caused, directly or indirectly by the information contained in this book.

The author and/or publisher offer(s) no guarantees with respect to the accuracy, application methods, or completeness of the contents of this book. The author does not take responsibility for any loss or damage incurred by using the information within the e-book or hard copy editions. The reader should take advice from her/his lawyer, tax accounting specialist, or other professional source of legal/financial aid to become aware of any potential liability concerns.

All links are provided as a resource, and I, Gloria Gretchen Jacobs, take no responsibility for their accuracy.

All cases and illustrations are fictional.

Gloria Gretchen Jacobs, MA, MS, Chaplain / LLC
www.gretchenjacobscounselor.com

Dedication

To our Father, who lets us be redeemed despite our failings, thank You for letting me take the lessons I have learned and put them to use. May You be glorified by this work and the lives it touches.

Introduction

Why Was This Book Written?

This book was written to help train nonprofessionals who are in a position of providing counseling to do so skillfully and only when appropriate, and, most importantly, to encourage helpers to rely on God to work *through* them.

It is also written to encourage people who are seeking change that change is possible through information, application, and surrender of one's problems to God. Psychology offers change strategies, but only God can permanently change one's heart and behaviors.

People who would benefit from counseling are everywhere. Many are grievers suffering through a divorce, lifestyle changes, addictions, natural calamities, betrayals, financial hardship, and so forth. This book addresses how to begin to help most people—if they seek help. Many do not, or they do not sustain the changes at which they worked hard, because they have not truly surrendered their will, mind, and heart.

Some people fear seeing a professional counselor and may feel more comfortable talking to certain people they already know (for example, their pastor, a ministry worker, or a deacon). If you are responsible to help, these guidelines will enable you to assess if it is appropriate for you as a nonprofessional to provide counsel, or if you should refer them to a professional.

If you feel you lack sufficient counseling skills or want to improve your skills, hopefully your toolbox will be better equipped with these guidelines.

Most of the chapters are relevant to ministry servants, church leaders, chaplains, and nonprofessional counselors, although parents, close friends, and troubled individuals themselves may also find select chapters helpful (although reading the entire book is recommended).

Notes

The content is Christian faith based and is nondenominational.

This information is a guideline and is not meant to teach everything one needs to know on the subject of counseling.

A user-friendly style was used to accommodate a variety of readers.

Prior training on some level in counseling is ideal but not essential.

For additional skill building and spiritual growth, see the appendix for Suggested Reading.

Although some social-support services are identified, that type of information is not the purpose of these guidelines.

All client case examples are fictional.

For writing ease, *he* and *she* are used interchangeably, with most situations applying to either gender. No bias is intended. *Client* is used for the counselee.

I have repeated certain material throughout the book knowing that some people will read only select chapters, shortchanging themselves on learning much of the applicable material.

Contents

	Introduction	ix
	Notes	xi
Section I	**The Hurting and the Helpers**	**1**
Chapter 1	To Whom Do Hurting People Turn?	3
Chapter 2	Strengths and Characteristics of a Counselor	5
Chapter 3	Qualities of an Effective Counselor	6
Chapter 4	Vulnerabilities of a Counselor	7
Section II	**Potential Clients**	**11**
Chapter 5	Who Seeks Help and Whom to Accept	13
Section III	**Foundational Material to Know before You Begin: Potential Contributing Causes of Problems and Clients' Reactions to Counseling**	**17**
Chapter 6	Assessing the Problem: Potential Contributing Causes of Problems (Health, Heart, and Fear Issues)	19
Chapter 7	Assessing the Problem: Understanding Clients' Feelings and Reactions	23
Chapter 8	Assessing the Presenting Problem: Family and Historical Factors	34
Chapter 9	Assessing the Client's Experience with Counseling	36

Chapter 10 Understanding Clients' Coping Mechanisms and Boundaries · · · · · · · · · · · 41

Chapter 11 Understanding Clients' Defenses · 47

Section IV Preparation for the Meeting/Session · **57**

Chapter 12 Preparation · 59

Chapter 13 Getting Started and Setting Goals · 68

Chapter 14 Counseling Strategies and Tools for Clients · 71

Chapter 15 Types of Questions to Ask and a Strategy to Ask Them · · · · · · · · · · · · · · · · 81

Section V Foundational Information and Strategies for Managing Common Issues · · · · · · · **89**

Chapter 16 Sexual, Physical, and Emotional Abuse, and Anxiety · · · · · · · · · · · · · · · · · · 91

Chapter 17 Why People Stay in or Return to Abusive Relationships · · · · · · · · · · · · · · · 98

Chapter 18 A Perspective on Our Family of Origin's Influence · · · · · · · · · · · · · · · · · · · 101

Chapter 19 Marital and Relational Issues · 108

Chapter 20 Parent and In-Law Issues (and Part of the Marital Assessment) · · · · · · · · · 127

Chapter 21 Managing Arguments (and Part of the Marital Assessment) · · · · · · · · · · · · 131

Chapter 22 Anger Management · 138

Chapter 23 Addiction and Other Issues · 142

Chapter 24 Codependency · 164

Chapter 25 Twelve-Step Recovery Groups: An Overview · 175

Chapter 26 Grief and Depression · 177

Section VI Closure Material and Strategies for Growth · **189**

Chapter 27 Encouragement · 191

Chapter 28 Our Need for Confession · 195

| Chapter 29 | Forgiveness | 198 |
| Chapter 30 | Spiritual Issues and Personal Growth for Counselors and Clients | 203 |

Section VII   **Considerations for Helpers in Noncounseling Settings and Situations** **211**

| Chapter 31 | How to Handle Problematic Situations Outside of a Counseling Office and Case Examples | 213 |

Section VIII   **Professional and Liability Concerns** **225**

| Chapter 32 | Administrative and Legal Reminders | 227 |

Section IX   **Next Steps** **233**

| Chapter 33 | Preparations | 235 |

Appendix **237**

Reader's Knowledge Test **239**

Tools For Counselors to Use as Homework for Clients **247**

    Oreo Cookie Strategy 249

    Getting Back on Track 253

    Communication Tool: The Table Meeting 257

    What I Want in a Partner Worksheet (Husband/Wife) 263

    What I Offer a Partner Worksheet (or What I Bring to the Relationship and What My Triggers Are) 265

    Ways to Improve Communication 267

    Summary of Communication Tips from Ways to Improve Communication 273

    Life Lessons Learned 275

Suggested Reading	277
Reader's Knowledge Test Answers	281
Acknowledgements	283
Index	285
About the Author	289

SECTION I
The Hurting and the Helpers

CHAPTER 1
To Whom Do Hurting People Turn?

Besides professionals, hurting people seek sympathetic listeners, who might be family, friends, neighbors, clergy, social service workers, or others with whom they are comfortable. Sometimes faith-based wisdom is offered and sometimes not. This material targets those who are in faith-based helping ministries, including church leaders, ministry leaders, and nonprofessional counselors. However, parts of the content will educate anyone who is in a position to help others.

What Challenges Do You as a Nonprofessional Counselor Face, and What Are Your Training Needs?

Church Leaders

Those of you who are church leaders (pastors, deacons, elders, ministry and twelve-step/support group leaders) may be seen as the go-to person for the entire church. You are expected to address or solve members' needs, personal crises, and complaints. In addition, you may be asked or told to counsel someone. You may or may not have the expertise or time to help. You need to seek guidelines to conduct an appropriate assessment, gracefully set boundaries about how you can or cannot help, provide initial support, and/or refer clients in-house or elsewhere. This book will guide you.

Moses's father-in-law, Jethro, wisely counseled Moses to educate leaders to help him with his responsibilities so "they will bear the burden with you." Be encouraged and delegate when appropriate.

Nonprofessional Counselors in the Mercy Ministries

You provide help with basic needs, like food, shelter, and clothing. As a worker, you probably encounter the emotional and behavioral problems that your clients face, problems that need attention. Your challenge is that you may feel frustrated if you don't know how to handle their problems or behaviors while still honoring the boundaries of your ministry and job. Another challenge is that you may struggle with resentment as you witness clients' attempts to manipulate the system, detect rebellious attitudes, or encounter constant emergencies. This book will help with the training needed to deal with these struggles.

Nonprofessional Counselors Providing Informal or Lay Counseling

Some nonprofessional counselors volunteer to counsel those in need on a "first tier" or lay level. If you are among these, you may long for guidelines to help you determine when to refer clients, how to handle problem clients and clients' problems, and how to professionalize your service and grow your skills.

Additionally, **Professional Counselors** may find some helpful tools for their toolbox.

Parents, Couples, and Close Friends

If you are in this group, you may desire tools to heal relationships, communicate better, and encourage those in trouble to seek the right level of assistance—especially if they refuse help. You do not have to be a counselor to provide healthy guidance and comfort.

Note: If someone close to you needs counseling, sometimes it is appropriate to offer it. Other times it is best to wait to be asked. Of course, parents always have the responsibility to instruct, train, correct, and discipline.

> **"Train up a child in the way he should go, even when he is old he will not depart from it" (Proverbs 22:6).**

You may wish to scan the contents to see which section is applicable to your situation; however, reading the entire book will be the most helpful.

CHAPTER 2
Strengths and Characteristics of a Counselor

Do You See Yourself as a Counselor (Servant)?

As people of faith, we are called by God to be used as vessels for His glory. We are called to be servants who honor one another with humility, unselfishness, giving, and compassion. It is a beautiful compliment to be told you have a servant's heart, for that is the heart of Christ.

Having a servant's heart may be demonstrated in *everything* that anyone does—cleaning the house willingly, taking care of the car, picking up roadside trash when walking, or giving someone a treat when making or buying one for oneself. Serving is an *attitude of the heart* more than an action. It is giving from the heart, knowing you are honoring God with your efforts, regardless of how hard, sad, or painful serving can be and whether or not it is acknowledged. This is noted because counseling is indeed hard and painful, and one's work may go unnoticed.

There are many types of servants, and by using the gifts God gave you, there are many ways to serve and develop even more Christlike characteristics. For example, hospice work was an option when I was seeking volunteer work. I did not think it was my gift. However, the recruiter challenged me by suggesting I take the training; I could try it and leave if it did not work for me. Serving God faithfully for the past seven years in hospice work has grown the gift of compassion in me—well beyond my expectations. God puts opportunities in our path to stretch our abilities. Counseling will grow in you the fruit of the Holy Spirit: love, joy, peace, patience, kindness, goodness, faithfulness, gentleness, and self-control. These qualities are all needed to be an effective counselor.

Some of us have a more compassionate heart and feel the pain and suffering of others more deeply. We don't want others to suffer. That is an asset, but it can also make us vulnerable. Some people may take advantage of compassionate people; their generous efforts are unappreciated, especially when the giver stops giving. Counselors and servants are not doormats, nor do they let others take what they receive for granted. They set boundaries when helping others—not only to feed them, but also to teach them to fish. Some of us have more discernment than others and can see when a person is attempting to use the provider or the system. A careful, discerning counselor can spot a person's heart and motives quickly. Then he or she makes an informed decision about how to help, or if helping the client is the best option. You will learn tools in this manual to aid in your discernment.

(See the sections on "Emotional Manipulation" and "Boundaries" in chapter 7, "Assessing the Problem: Understanding Clients' Feelings and Reactions.")

CHAPTER 3
Qualities of an Effective Counselor

1. Invests in helping others with emotional issues

2. Listens carefully and has empathy

3. Is nonjudgmental and patient

4. Surrenders both successes and disappointments willingly to the Lord

5. Loves first and then corrects and counsels in love

6. Is aware of and teaches boundaries that need to be honored

7. Enlightens and honors the level of insight, self-awareness, and self-honesty of those with whom he or she works (God will open their eyes and hearts as they surrender their issues to Him)

8. Objectively assesses one's own life journey; admits failures and successes

9. Is a person of faith

10. Is always willing to grow and learn

11. Is genuine and authentic

12. Is willing to grow in his or her skills and faith, since a counselor can take people only as far as the counselor has come

CHAPTER 4
Vulnerabilities of a Counselor

Assess if you have any of the following vulnerabilities. If so, seek help. Otherwise, your counseling will be hindered, and you may even cause damage. Be honest and seek counseling as needed. Additionally, most professional counselors are supervised and often also may see a therapist periodically to assist them with their own problems. Nonprofessional counselors are encouraged to do the same.

Some of the following vulnerabilities may also be witnessed in your clients or are work-related problems for them as they may also be for you. (Where applicable, consider suggesting the recovery strategies below as initial goals for your clients.)

In this book, the content as well as the tools in the appendix address many of the following vulnerabilities. Please check the contents, the appendix, and the index.

1. **Not maintaining a balance or staying in the center of a servant's spiritual gift/characteristic.**
We all have assets, but taken to the extreme, they become deficits, weaknesses, or liabilities. Boundary work is needed as well as someone to hold you accountable to keep that balance. For example, being compassionate is godly, but being a rescuer is not.

Let your accountability partner honestly share observations about how you are doing and what she sees as your strengths and weaknesses.

2. **Having a savior mentality.**
This is when someone feels he or she needs to save the world—that he or she is solely responsible—regardless of his or her other responsibilities. These people burn out and use up their resources helping others, not realizing that most often needy people need to help themselves. Figure out why you avoid investing in other areas in your life and overinvest in saving others. Assess if you acquire your worth from "doing it all." If so, you need to talk to a counselor.

Believe that God knows your intent and He will manage things when you are not there. Focus on building a godly lifestyle that includes not only work, but also the willingness to delegate and encourage others to assume responsibility.

3. **Overidentifying with the client and becoming too emotionally involved.**
This issue suggests that you have not finished working on yourself. It is not good role modeling; it is potentially an ethical issue and is definitely a boundary issue. Counseling is needed.

Clients need to see your confidence and strength based on the Word of God and your growth. You do not want them to see you as their rescuer. If you overreact to a situation and feel you have to fix it, it may be a trigger that reflects your own unfinished business. This is very different from empathy, where you are *with* another person in his or her pain.

4. **Creating dependency by not letting people grow.**
Get counseling and see why you need to be needed.

Delegate, let people learn from their mistakes, and give them the respect and confidence to make their own choices.

5. **Feeling you have to do it all.**
This involves thinking that no one can do it as well as you. You may not recognize another's potential ability to learn, help, or take over their own lives. This vulnerability does not acknowledge that we all learn from our mistakes—a good lesson that leads us to depend on God to get us through. Submit to counseling to determine why your self-worth is contingent on what you *do* versus who you *are* in Christ.

6. **Creating dependence in order to feel needed/useful because of other voids in your life.**
Consider counseling to help figure out why you choose not to develop or have a fulfilling life of your own. Sometimes your own lack of confidence or control in any number of areas may cause you to focus on your work as a source of usefulness.

7. **Not having godly accountability from supervisors or peers.**
Supervision and accountability are critical and ethical. Insist on quality and regular supervision. Also, take a personal inventory of your motives—daily if needed. Find a mentor whom you respect and who will stretch your abilities.

8. **Not being able to download/decompress.**
The cause could be the confidentiality of the work, the lack of helpful listeners, or the desire to not burden others. This is an occupational hazard. A supervisor or a peer support group can meet this need. Prayer is also essential as you share your burdens with our Father.

9. **Not receiving support from supervisors', or not listening to instruction or training.**
Let your needs be known. Read and study so you feel as equipped as you possibly can. This will add confidence and reassurance. Continue to seek support.

10. **Allowing yourself to be taken advantage of by clients or supervisors and bowing to pressures from the church to participate.**

If *you* cannot say no, you can't teach your clients to set boundaries. When you say yes, you could wind up saying no to something God intentionally put in your growth path.

Being a complaining, overly busy victim is not good modeling, and complaining tells others that your busyness is really your choice. You will not get sympathy. Create a life that will inspire others rather than annoy them.

11. **Allowing yourself to be manipulated because of your naïveté or the skills of master manipulators.**
Study the section on "Emotional Manipulation" in chapter 7, "Assessing the Problem: Understanding Clients' Feelings and Reactions," and see the applicable book under "Suggested Reading" in the appendix.

Once you are aware of the tools of a manipulator, you will not be stressed and anxious. You will confidently manage the attempted manipulation to your advantage.

12. **Not being prepared/trained in what to watch for and how to respond.**
Study counseling material continuously and stay alert to clients' needs, fears, and manipulations.

Your confidence will grow, and you will feel secure, not anxious. Listen to the Holy Spirit coach you.

13. **Not realizing when a client is projecting (dumping his or her emotional problems on you) or exhibiting transference (seeing you as someone else).**
These behaviors may make you uncomfortable or defensive. The more you get to know a client, the more skilled you will be in recognizing and being open about these behaviors. In a transference situation you can say,

> *"I'm wondering if I remind you of someone in your life, maybe a parent."*
>
> *"Do I seem to have any of his or her behaviors?"*
>
> *"I sensed a shift in you just now. Did I say or do something that impacted you negatively?"*
>
> *"Did I do something that reminded you of someone?"*

Then explain transference and mutually agree that whenever this happens, it will be brought up and discussed openly.

14. **Experiencing secondary trauma.**
This is where reading, watching, or listening to a horrific, traumatizing situation—especially if a visual image comes to mind—stays with you and becomes emotionally distracting or very upsetting. You might not be able to dismiss the memory and may have nightmares. Sometimes even reading examples about trauma for educational purposes can sear the images into your mind.

Try not to focus on the visual imagery, and switch your thoughts to pleasant things. Try not to share your secondary trauma experience with someone else because you may then traumatize him or her. Consider discussing your trauma with a counselor. If secondary trauma affects you, you can imagine what your traumatized client is going through. This is why traumatized clients must be referred to professional counselors. It is difficult work.

15. **Experiencing burnout.**
One characteristic of burnout is a loss of patience and kindness. Remember that Christ died for that hard-to-love person/client. He loves him or her as much as He loves you. He wants us to love others even when they are temporarily unlovable.

Be sure to nurture your own spiritual journey and physical and emotional health. Recall that Jesus Christ took time for Himself in prayer in isolation. (See also chapter 27, "Encouragement," and chapter 30, "Spiritual Issues and Personal Growth for Counselors and Clients.")

Counseling is hard work. It is emotionally draining, and it is often hard to leave the work at the office. Anyone who cares about others who are very troubled can become distracted and wonder how they are doing. Pray for them. It takes discipline to respect your time and thoughts. God will take care of what you cannot. Trust that He will provide.

You are to do what your schedule permits and not feel the need to do more. If the problems are not resolved, you have to let it go, knowing you did your best. There will be many times when you may have the opportunity to work extra hours to resolve a crisis. Assess if it can truly wait until tomorrow. Clients are typically very resourceful and will find a way to manage.

If you are being intimidated or made to feel guilty, see the section on "Manipulation," in chapter 7, "Assessing the Problem: Understanding Clients' Feelings and Reactions" and then manage your response.

Be sure to eat healthy, sleep enough, and not rely on caffeine or sugar to motivate you when you are exhausted.

Exercise regularly to release endorphins that help manage anxiety.

Jesus left hurting people and went on to other towns to do His ministry. They managed before He came, and they will manage without you. You are a servant, not a slave.

Respect your schedule and take time for yourself for prayer and study, listening to God coach you.

SECTION II
Potential Clients

CHAPTER 5
Who Seeks Help and Whom to Accept

People seek assistance for basic practical needs like housing and shelter, as well as assistance with emotional problems like grief, anxiety, anger, marital conflicts, or addictions.

People of all ages, social statuses, professions, and levels of education come for help. Everyone has issues regardless of his or her accomplishments in life or the amount of money he or she has. Do not feel intimidated by anyone; we are all brothers and sisters, and you have been placed in a person's life for a reason.

A partner may coerce an applicant to get help. Other applicants may be required by the courts to seek help, or they may come because of the threat of a divorce. Some people come voluntarily, while others come under pressure.

Either way, you can still be helpful as

- a seed planter to develop or grow anyone's faith,
- an attitude changer,
- a source of hope,
- an affirming voice, and
- a comfort in the storm.

Sometimes people who are pressured to seek help wind up appreciating the help, find it a relief and thrive.

Whom Should You Consider Helping?

That depends. Consider helping only clients you are comfortable handling and who are appropriate for your level of training and responsibility. If you have personal experience with a problem and have resolved it, that experience could prove very helpful. Be sure to give God the glory for your recovery if it is appropriate to share your recovery with a client.

If you are still struggling with an issue but are in counseling and/or a recovery program, that is also helpful as you will be wise to a client's defenses. You will need to be rigorous about your own supervision and accountability as your weaknesses may be triggered when listening to a client.

That said, Margaret Mead, the famed sociologist, said, "You don't have to be a horse to be a veterinarian." Therefore, you do not have to have experienced all of life's issues to help someone. Get smart. Be wise and discerning. Read about all of the issues addressed in this resource, and ideally read more elsewhere, preferably using Christian resources. (See the "Suggested Reading" section in the appendix.) Take an inventory of your own issues that may come up. Pray about specific client issues you would feel comfortable working with, and wait for God's confirmation.

Be prepared. Some issues are easier to handle than others are. For example, abuse issues are quite challenging.

The gamut of relational issues appears easy to resolve, but helping people to retain their new ways of relating can be frustrating.

Addictions can be manageable if the person is motivated and will attend support groups.

Codependency can be manageable because once people are able to see their issues, they are usually motivated to change, and they and others in their life can see changes quickly.

Grief is easier as you mostly need to be a good listener and help grievers put their feelings in perspective as to what is normal.

Remember you can and should refer a client elsewhere if at any point you feel in over your head.

Whom Should You Refer Elsewhere?

Again, take only clients you are comfortable handling and who are appropriate for your level of training and responsibility. Otherwise, refer those clients to a professional.

- People with certain disorders—for example, borderline personality disorder, bipolar disorder, admitted severe depression, anxiety disorders, schizophrenia, obsessive-compulsive disorder (OCD), and so forth—are extremely exhausting to work with. Even seasoned professionals are challenged by them.
- Clients who have a history of attending *any* type of inpatient programs are better suited to work with professional counselors.
- Clients who are "cutters" or admit to having active anorexia or bulimia are best referred to a professional.
- Clients who have suffered a trauma should be referred to a professional.
- Clients who speak of suicide in any manner should see a professional. Even if suicide attempts were in the past, still refer them to a licensed professional. If suicidal thoughts are current, tell them to go to a hospital immediately for an assessment. Call your supervisor and 911 or the suicide-prevention hotline if there is any suspicion that suicide might happen. Do not leave the client alone.

Other disorders that should be referred to professionals are too numerous to mention. Only accept what you are capable of handling. Otherwise, you can do more harm than good and be liable for the consequences. Better safe than sorry for you and better for the well-being of clients.

When someone contacts you initially (by phone), use that opportunity to assess if you are able or want to potentially work with this client. If not, say, "It's best to refer you elsewhere." Then give him or her two or three suggestions.

If you accept a client and find in the first session that you are not a match or cannot handle the issues, say that it's best to refer him or her elsewhere and give two suggestions.

SECTION III

Foundational Material to Know before You Begin: Potential Contributing Causes of Problems and Clients' Reactions to Counseling

CHAPTER 6

Assessing the Problem: Potential Contributing Causes of Problems (Health, Heart, and Fear Issues)

Health Issues as a Potential Cause

In the initial interview, ask for known health issues and ask how they are being treated. Health issues often contribute to emotional and behavioral issues, so it is essential to ensure this area is covered. The following are questions to ask your client:

"How long has it been since your last physical?"

"What were the results?"

"Are you taking any medications? Please list them by name and dosage."

"How long have you taken them? Any side effects?"

"Tell me about your diet."

"What do you eat, smoke, or drink that you know you shouldn't? How much and how often?" (Understand he may not tell the truth.)

"Have you taken or do you take medication for depression or anxiety?"

Conditions such as mood swings and health or medication issues may cause irritability and need to be assessed.

Physicals

Encourage clients to have a physical if needed, including lab work, a check of vital signs, a review of current medications, an examination of symptoms, an assessment of sleep deprivation, nutritional issues, and an assessment of whether any medications are needed. Urge them to talk to their doctor about any medication issues.

Medication Issues

One promedication argument for clients who need medication and are resistant to taking it is that medication takes care of a physical chemical imbalance. This results in clients having energy to work with their psychological problems like anxiety or depression. For example, an antidepressant for a depressed person is like insulin for a diabetic. The medication helps one's body when the body isn't making enough of a certain chemical. For those clients who refuse to take a doctor's recommendation, expect behavioral and emotional swings. You cannot force them to take medication and can only encourage them and help with their fears about taking it.

Some people will not tell a doctor about their negative medication issues. Instead, they just stop the prescribed medication when an adjustment might be all that was needed. Some medications need weeks to become effective, but some clients may not realize this. Ask if they are uncomfortable talking to their doctor, and work with them on any issues if they are uncomfortable expressing their needs.

Sexual Issues

Sexual dysfunction can be a medical and/or a psychological/emotional issue. Again, first rule out the medical issues. Some medications affect sexual desire and function as does aging.

Normalizing the sexual changes that take place in relationships and aging is often helpful and a relief for clients. Sometimes they do not talk about these issues with others—not even their physician. They do not know what is normal or repairable or that changes are part of the normal aging process, so be prepared to help them with this if you are comfortable and knowledgeable.

(See the section on "Sexual Issues" in chapter 19, "Marital and Relational Issues.")

Heart Issues as a Potential Cause

Heart Issues and Coping Mechanisms

Many issues clients present are heart issues, meaning they have emotional unrest because of something in their history or in the present that is extremely unsettling, disappointing, painful, and/or traumatic. As a result, they try to drown it out with things like drugs, alcohol, food, shopping, sex, or pornography.

Minimizing as a Coping Issue or Denial

For example, a victim of sexual or physical abuse may not recall any incident or may dismiss it as *"nothing"* or say that *"nothing was meant"* by it. This person's coping mechanism to minimize the abuse is kicking in, and you need to be extra gentle when asking if he or she will tell you more about it. Be very careful not to ask questions out of curiosity. Let the client set the pace as he or she talks about it.

God Reveals Issues in Time

Clients may or may not be aware of the source of their pain. It may be buried subconsciously and, if so, let it reside there. God will reveal the things He wants us to know, and you should work on His perfect timing. If He made all our faults and pains known to us at once, we would not be able to handle them. So if someone does not know or want to deal with the source, let it go. When he or she learns to trust you and does various homework exercises, he or she may open up. (See chapter 16, "Sexual, Physical, and Emotional Abuse, and Anxiety.)

You can ask,

> *"What expectations, dreams, or fantasies about your life didn't come true?"*

> *"What didn't or hasn't happened that you had envisioned?"*

Perhaps the answer will be a marriage, children, or a career.

Teaching Clients about Feelings and Managing Their Thoughts

"I felt this way, so it must be true." Clients rely on and give too much credibility to their feelings. Teach them the following:

- Feelings can be deceptive and distorted; thus, they should not dictate behavior.
- Your mind needs to dominate and filter your feelings, enabling you to make healthy behavioral choices.
- Managing unwanted thoughts: pray with full concentration, on your knees, and ask Jesus for His calming presence to hold you. Don't let any negative thoughts stay in your mind. Replace them with affirming ones like "Jesus will help me through this," then repeat it.

Some people have very good intuition and should be encouraged to trust it (depending on their track record).

Fear Issues as a Potential Cause

Fear is the root of many emotional stressors—fear of failing in areas such as being good enough or being liked, getting along or fitting in, doing well at school or work, being a parent, dating, or performing sexually. Fear is the devil's tool and needs to be attacked with confidence. Fear kills dreams. There is an acronym for fear:

False
Evidence
Appearing
Real

- Ask clients what fears they have and the basis of their fears.
- If they do not know, probe to see if there is a connection to their childhood or teen years.

We tend to carry unreasonable fears for decades. They can handicap us, even when we know they are unreasonable.

- Search for the payoff that motivates them to keep their fears. They may say, for example:

"If I learn to drive, my husband won't spend as much time with me."

"If I don't buy him beer, he will fight with me."

- Teach clients about codependency, boundaries, and how to assert themselves with "love and grace" (respect and gentleness).

(See chapter 24, "Codependency" and chapter 10, "Understanding Clients' Coping Mechanisms and Boundaries.")

Projecting into the future keeps people who are anxious in a state of fear.

Fearful people don't want to rock the boat. Ask,

"What are the anticipated or known consequences of this fear?"

"When did this fear begin?"

These two questions alone will take several sessions to address.

- Encourage clients with scripture:

"I sought the Lord, and He answered me, and delivered me from all my fears" (Psalm 34:4).

"And the peace of God, which surpasses all comprehension, will guard your hearts and your minds in Christ Jesus" (Philippians 4:7).
"Commit your works to the Lord and your thoughts will be established" (Proverbs 16:3).
"We are taking every thought captive to the obedience of Christ" (2 Corinthians 10:5).
"You will keep him in perfect peace, whose mind is stayed on You, because he trusts in You" (Isaiah 26:3 nkjv).

CHAPTER 7
Assessing the Problem:
Understanding Clients' Feelings and Reactions

Regardless of the problem a client presents, you need to understand the client's feelings about it, his or her reaction to it, and his or her emotions around changing him or herself as well as its impact on others.

Hurting people may experience a spectrum of emotions and live in overwhelming emotional pain. People who are homeless, live in a shelter, or live with severe abuse will each have one set of emotions, while people who are in marital conflict, grieving, or dying will have other sets of emotions.

In order to help anyone, **counselors** need to have the following:

- Empathy for the client's expressed feelings, even if they seem unreasonable. Empathy is putting yourself in another's shoes, understanding how *he or she* feels, and connecting as best as you can. Empathy is being in pain *with* someone. (On the other hand, sympathy is feeling sorry for someone without relating or connecting deeply to how he or she feels. Sympathy is feeling *for* someone).
- An appreciation for those issues that a client cannot (or does not) identify that contributes to his or her intense and dysfunctional feelings and behaviors.
- An understanding of normal or appropriate responses to life's trials and circumstances. This will allow you to educate and enable a client to put his or her emotional concerns in perspective.

Clients will need help in order to do the following:

- Recognize that when stress is increased, they may tend to withdraw socially. It is helpful for clients to be social and distracted from their cares. Encourage clients to socialize.
- Acknowledge bad habits and wrong thinking and track them in list form on paper in order to increase their awareness and then bring the list to the counseling sessions. This self-help tool is eye opening.
- Improve their quality of sleep (not necessarily the quantity), which helps lower anxiety and improves mental functioning. When clients' quality of sleep is poor, their felt pain is increased. They may benefit from a sleep study. Do they snore? Do their legs twitch? Do they wake frequently? They may have sleep apnea.
- Have three or four calming tools to help them relax: a comforting visual image, relaxation tapes, a deep-breathing exercise (always take longer to exhale), prayer, and physical exercise.

- Enlarge their use and self-recognition of feeling words. Wounded people often have had their feelings discounted, and they in turn minimize or dismiss them. Have clients drill down feeling words to see if they can reach the root words that truly express their feelings. For example, they may say "upset," "mad," or "furious." Just articulating one's feelings promotes relief.
- Learn that their feelings are not facts. Often, feelings are distortions of reality.

What Clients May Be Feeling

Fearing Change
One client mantra, spoken or unspoken, is "ABC" (Anything but Change). These clients have a lot of fear, and even though they may be faithful counseling attendees, they hardly change.

- Tell clients they *can* take steps. Do not accept "I'm not able." Everyone can do *something*.

Do not shame or guilt-trip clients into acknowledging their part or responsibility in the situation. They need to discover this on their own.

- Explore what their payoff is, whether it be staying the same or changing.

Totally Changing Themselves
It is not a complete overhaul. When a client defiantly says he does not want to have to change his whole personality, you can say,

"We're working on changing a behavior, not your core personality."

Understanding Their Choices
We make choices about how we behave with our employer, our coworkers, our friends, our family, and our partners. In addition, we often treat each differently. Sometimes we present ourselves *entirely* differently.

- Ask clients if they would react differently if, for example, they were responding to their boss rather than to their wife. This will show them that how they respond or react is always a *choice*.
- If you have a reticent client who isn't invested in doing what you are asking—investing in counseling, reading a book, or attending a twelve-step group for a period of time (as examples)—ask if he would do it for $1,000. He will probably say, "Sure." So say to him that it is obvious that behavior is a choice. He will have no choice but to agree.

This should set you up to hear a commitment to counseling.

Ask if he will commit to at least six weeks of counseling and working hard. Anyone who is on a diet or is training works consistently at his or her goal, not on and off. Counseling needs the same commitment.

- Be familiar with every type of problem listed in the contents so you will be prepared for whatever the client comes up with initially or later.

A List of Clients' Potential Feelings

Embarrassment, unworthiness, self-disrespect, shame, anger, rage, depression/sadness, desperation, guilt, and frustration. Additionally, addiction, dependence, alienation, anxiety, hopelessness, disillusionment, loss of faith, and grief are all possible answers.

Let's look at the potential causes of some of the feelings cited above.

Embarrassment and perhaps shame. These feelings often arise when asking for help, for not having or being able to use the skills or resources necessary to provide for those in one's care. This is especially true for people who are homeless or in shelters.

Depression. A person claiming to be experiencing depression is not usually truly clinically depressed. The client who claims depression may more accurately be experiencing intense sadness that is situational, though the symptoms may resemble those of depression (but to a much lesser degree). These clients may choose to hold on to their self-diagnosis of depression for attention and sympathy. Also, it offers an excuse for the person not doing enough with his or her life.

Clinical depression extends for weeks. The person doesn't pursue normal activities like eating, sleeping regularly, self-care, or socializing. The client would rather be alone or is terrified of being alone. Depressed people often look "detached" or "out of it."

(See chapter 26, "Grief and Depression.")

Disillusionment. This is the contrast between what we had expected and reality. Our unmet expectations may seriously affect us and be evidenced in physical ways.

- Couples, newlyweds, and those in marriages decades long may experience disillusionment that leads them to question if they made the right decision or if it is time to leave a marriage. They want to know if these feelings are normal and wonder if they can be managed in a healthy way to correct the relationship. These people need perspective to normalize their situations if that is the case or correction if there are behaviors and attitudes that need to change. (See chapter 19, "Marital and Relational Issues.")
- Anyone who belongs to an organization, church, club, or business may experience disappointment or disillusionment for various reasons. How the person voices that frustration is significant, and it is not always healthy or respectful. Disillusioned people need to learn to respect boundaries, surrender control, and assess whether they are focusing on their business issues instead of those in their personal life.

- Men may feel disillusioned or feel like failures as the providers or heads of their households. They may see themselves as less masculine (which can lead to sexual dysfunction) and express their disillusionment and frustration in anger.

Fear. This is one of the most paralyzing emotions and inhibitors to growth. Teaching clients how not to yield to fear requires patience and discipline. Help them take apart their fears by keeping them in the here and now rather than taking them into the past or into the future. Fear is the devil's most used tool and is the main cause of emotional distress. Fear will show up anywhere as a nuisance or as a gigantic obstacle to a client's ability to function. Fear can become an idol, preoccupying our minds and hearts. Fears need to be explored to discover

- where or how they originated;
- how long they have existed;
- how they show up in one's everyday life;
- how based in reality these fears are; and
- if the client has replaced a fear with something else once the fear was managed.

Some of the following fears people have in various situations are addressed more thoroughly elsewhere in chapter 6, "Assessing the Problem: Potential Contributing Causes of Problems (Health, Heart, and Fear Issues). Anticipate that fear may be admitted or not realized.

Women may fear for their safety and health as well as that of their children. This includes the impact of the situation on their children's behavior, schooling, and personality, and how they and their children will survive if they leave a relationship.

Parents may fear that their marital conflicts are influencing their children's behavior and the children's impressions about marriage, relationships, and conflicts. Learning where and how to respectfully argue is healthy for children to witness, giving them hope that conflicts can be worked out rather than thinking that marriage is about arguing, yelling, and being hurtful.

(See "Communication Tool: The Table Meeting" in the appendix for resolving conflicts; chapter 19, "Marital and Relational Issues"; and chapter 21, "Managing Arguments.")

Retirees may fear being of no value and therefore have a hard time adjusting to the loss of work or the status of their job, the lack of financial security, unfulfilling free time, and shifting spousal expectations. These issues can show up as anger, irritability, control issues, or depression-like symptoms.

Empty nesters may feel abandoned and fear a loss of investment from their children, they may have marital stress because of the current shift in attention to each other, or they may experience frustration in expectations about spending time and money.

The elderly may fear aging and health issues that could result in a loss of independence, driving ability, sexual performance, and attractiveness. They could also have fears about who will care for them, loneliness, and having sufficient money.

Children in a transient situation may feel fear due to the unstable lifestyle and lack of a routine, proper clothes, and bathing options. They may also have a fear of strangers. They may feel guilt, experience a loss of friends, and lack schooling or have excessive school absences. Some of these feelings also show up if they are being shuffled between separated or divorced parents, with the children also feeling resentment for the varying rules imposed in split households, and frustration from adjusting to new parent figures, stepsiblings, and new expectations.

Clients may fear being overwhelmed and devalued because of handicaps and accessibility issues. They may fear that they are unable to effectively communicate because of language issues or domestic and vocational skill deficits. They may have anxiety or fear because they have a limited or nonexistent support system, a lack of social skills, and a limited spiritual foundation.

Believers may fear losing their faith when they are overwhelmed with conflicts or when their faith is challenged. They may have serious concerns about what God is up to and His seeming lack of provision. They may fear their own anger at God.

(See chapter 30, "Spiritual Issues and Personal Growth for Counselors and Clients.")

Grievers may fear getting through a death, a sickness, or the loss of their home, their finances, or a job. They may fear facing a change in status because of retiring, moving, aging, or becoming an empty nester. They may also be grieving a marriage that has become boring or changes in sexual ability and satisfaction.

(See chapter 26, "Grief and Depression.")

Some exaggerated reactions clients may have and some techniques that may help:

Reacting. When we react rather than respond, it is usually unhealthy and unproductive. Some people like to be stuck in reactive responses because they gain attention. They do not want to think about options because they are not acceptable or they were always in crisis when they grew up, so reacting seems normal. People can get addicted to crisis.

- Teach clients how to respond by observing what manipulation is being attempted and strategizing an appropriate response.

Defeatism. Sometimes people overthink an issue and work themselves into thinking the worst. They do not see other options but only disaster, despite having sound evidence to the contrary. These people resist any suggestions and carry a defeatist attitude: "I tried that. Nothing will change." Typically, they have exhausted the patience of their family and friends and now seek counseling—a new listener or sympathizer.

- Listen to how they present the problem. Ask what potential solutions others may have suggested and what they thought of those solutions. This will give you an idea of their defense level and how to proceed.

Sometimes you can be direct and say,

"Sounds like you have been given some reasonable advice; I'm wondering why you haven't taken it?"

If they just offer more excuses, you can say,

"I'm not sure we can offer you anything much different from what you have been told."

"I'm sorry to say this, but I think you might consider the options already presented to you."

Regrets. Clients may include a lot of should'ves, could'ves, and would'ves in their description of what's bothering them. These descriptors are about regrets—wishes that things could have been different. Some people will own their part in the story; others will not. These descriptors let you know they are stuck and feel hopeless.

- Clients need to be taught a larger understanding of the past and the circumstances of their own lives when they made past decisions, as well as what was going on for others involved at the time. Then they can learn to accept the past and find peace. Focus on how these regrets affect them now. Also focus on the present and moving forward.

Catastrophizing is thinking the absolute worst will happen. You can say,

"I realize you are facing a serious problem [you are validating their feelings], *but thinking the worst is not the most helpful option. Let's consider other possible outcomes."*

Making everything an emergency when that is usually not the case. (Some things *can* wait.) A lack of planning can contribute to this. Help them plan. You can say,

"I appreciate that you feel this is an urgent situation [you are validating their feelings], *so let's talk about what we can address right now and what can wait."*

Dramatizing is using emotions to emphasize the situation with tears, loudness, and neediness—for example, asking for soothing measures like water, a little something to eat, to lie down, an aspirin, and so on. You can say,

"I can see this is affecting you emotionally [you are validating their feelings]." (Do not say "but.")

"Let's try to be clearheaded about this. Put your feelings aside, and try to brainstorm or think through solutions. I'm confident you can do this."

Your being in control will be calming. (This is different from a client who is genuinely grieving with sobbing and needs validation and comforting words.)

Forecasting is predicting the future with many what-ifs. It is assuming the worst, which does not evidence faith. You can say,

"I can appreciate that there are unknowns in your situation [you are validating the client's feelings], *so let's work with the here-and-now situations and options."*

Matthew 6:34 quotes Jesus as saying, **"So do not worry about tomorrow; for tomorrow will care for itself. Each day has enough trouble of its own."**

Mind reading/believing is when clients think they know what the other person is thinking. They are often wrong. Mind reading can also be a codependent behavior, with clients thinking they can anticipate what someone else needs or wants. In addition, a client's own suspicions may distort his or her perceptions. You can say,

"You are saying that you don't socialize because you think everyone is looking at you and talking about how overweight you are. You cannot assume that. They may be thinking that you are attractive or that they like your outfit or maybe they are just glancing around the room. When you think about it, believing people are looking at you is vain, and vanity is a sin. Try to just be concerned about how God sees you and not how others in your past or present see you. Let's talk about other reasons why you might not socialize."

Minimizing is not acknowledging the reality of a situation. Assess how the client sees other people. Is he or she too self-focused? You can say,

"Your reaction/words seem(s) like a fraction of what would be typical for anyone in your circumstances. Would you share why you think it was/is no big deal?"

Perfectionism is insisting everything has to be perfect: others, life, and oneself. This thinking is self-defeating because it can never be accomplished. It sets people up for failure and disappointment or a self-degrading confirmation that they "weren't ever any good" or "can't ever get it right." Sometimes people use this thinking to justify being stuck or their addiction. You can say,

"You say you spend a lot of time keeping the house spotless and that you are an admitted perfectionist. What is your fear if the house isn't perfect? Where did you get those very hard expectations of yourself?"

Denial is not acknowledging the reality of the situation or the consequences because it is too painful. The client may also be protecting an addiction. For him or her, the solution or way through the situation is incomprehensible. You can say:

"I hear your take on this, but I'm wondering if people have ever told you they see it differently?"

"What would you say about their way of seeing things?"

Blaming is when clients say their partner/spouse is the problem because he or she drinks, uses drugs, spends too much time with his or her family, is irresponsible, and so on. It typically is not about themselves and what they may be doing or not doing. Sometimes they will say they have tried everything and have come to counseling because they need another perspective or they want to leave the relationship, but they want to be sure they have tried everything to save it.

To those clients, you might say,

"If you will consider doing 100 percent for six months and come to counseling regularly, you will see a change in yourself and your partner. If those changes inspire you to continue working at your relationship, good. If not, you need to find another counselor and get his or her perspective on what has changed before you make up your mind to leave the relationship. If you decide to leave, you at least will be able to say you tried your best. God hates unjustified divorce, so it is important to work as hard as you can to save your marriage."

Other Challenges

An **entitlement mentality** describes people who think a person, organization, or a governmental entity is responsible for meeting their needs, and they have expectations regardless of their role or capability to contribute. They feel they are owed being taken care of and sometimes express this with arrogance. These clients are especially good at trying to make you feel guilty if you do not honor their request. They may say, "What kind of Christian are you?" If so, be on guard for their manipulations. Do not defend yourself. Keep your response simple by acknowledging what you see they are feeling and then state your position. You might say,

"I realize you are frustrated and disappointed [you are validating]. *I'm sorry we can't help you with that issue; unfortunately, that is the policy."* (Then refer to it.)

Simply repeat this again if needed. Hold your ground.

A **serious immediate threat to the client's safety or threatened abuse** may be present. If the person perceives a threat as serious and imminent, ask,

"Have you been in this situation before? What happened?"

"What are your supports?"

"What is your financial situation?"

"What are your transportation options?"

"Is there someone who could take care of the children temporarily?"

"What options have you considered for places to stay?"

"Have you ever used a restraining order? If so, what happened?"

Some clients have these life-threatening situations regularly, so it is important to learn their history.

For clients who have never been in such a situation, it is especially distressing emotionally. Help them take each issue gradually and *explore* the fears they have along the way. Try to help them with each of their fears by educating them about their options—what shelters can offer, how a restraining order works, counseling, and twelve-step program options.

(See chapter 16, "Sexual, Physical, and Emotional Abuse, and Anxiety.")

Emotional Manipulation

Emotional manipulation is when someone subtly or overtly tries to control another person with fear, obligation, guilt, flattery, mental confusion, exhaustion, distraction, criticism, or isolation. Some clients experience this, or they may be the manipulator/abuser. The abuser may try to manipulate you as well. Be on guard for hearing such remarks from clients or as told to them by spouses such as the following:

"What did you say your qualifications were for your position?" (Subtle criticism after you confront them on something.)
"Your family drains us, and it is not good for us to spend so much time with them." (Validating their reasoning for their partner's isolation.)
"Who taught you how to cook?" (Criticism.)
"I don't mind spending the holiday alone. I'll be able to catch up on my sleep." (Attempted guilt.)

They are very critical and cannot be pleased, resulting in the exhaustion and frustration of others. Other typical manipulative comments are:

"If you really loved me, you would…"

"After all I've done for you, you…"

"I thought you were a Christian."

They may smile and look directly at you the whole time they are talking, making you feel obligated to listen. They are controlling, or they are being controlled. They may buy their partner an expensive gift they both cannot afford and then criticize them for being ungrateful.

The remedy is to educate the abused client, so she

- recognizes the manipulation instead of defending herself or her decision;
- responds with the truth as she sees it—for example, "I'm sorry you don't like my cooking. Perhaps tomorrow you can cook"; and
- returns their question with a question.

(See chapter 14, "Counseling Strategies and Tools for Clients.")

And you can say in response to a client,

> *"It's interesting you asked me that about my counseling qualifications. Why does that interest you?"* (This is a motives check.)

Emotional manipulators will impose a different strategy when one does not rock you, so be prepared for a barrage of manipulations. Manipulators are very controlling, and fear is at the root of their need to control. When they fear losing someone, they try to isolate that person. If they fear being "less than," they criticize others. They may have a fear of not being what or who they need to be, so they opt out.

Counselors need to be aware of this behavior and be prepared to confront it when observed.

A great resource for these situations is listed in the appendix: *Emotional Blackmail: When the People in Your Life Use Fear, Obligation, and Guilt to Manipulate You*, by Susan Forward.

Narcissism, Extreme Self-Centeredness

Narcissists lack empathy or any genuine concern for others. They rarely seek counseling because they do not see themselves as the problem—they are perfect. People involved with a narcissist will express tremendous frustration at the narcissist's behavior and thinking.

Once you educate them about their partner potentially having narcissism and they begin to see this as probable, ask them to read about it on the web. They usually agree that it is an accurate diagnosis and are relieved to learn about the disorder. Be aware, though, that narcissism is not curable, largely because the narcissist isn't motivated. However, we serve a God who can change anyone. Thus, if a client decides to stay in the relationship or has to because they are family, you can teach him or her strategies to respond and not react defensively. This will be a challenge for you and the client.

People Pleasing

This is when someone will do whatever others want or need him or her to do at the loss of his or her own identity, needs, and wants. In a counseling situation, people pleasers may not ever disagree with you, even when you are not correct in your observations, or they will not have the emotional strength to broach an issue they need to discuss because they fear disappointing you and derailing your agenda.

You will detect this behavior quickly and need to discuss it. Sometimes they will admit their propensity to please people, but other times, they do not see it. Sometimes they are very resentful of always doing for others and not getting any acknowledgment in return. Help clients see that an expectation is a premeditated disappointment. Help them establish boundaries, define their own likes and interests, and pursue them. Their growth is inspiring and affirming to watch.

(See chapter 24, "Codependency.")

Behavioral Surprises

You might spend several sessions or months with a client who has some issues (but certainly appears to be normal), when he suddenly discloses a behavior that is unsettling. Perhaps he gambles daily, late at night online or at a casino, and has done so for years. He has "only a drink or two" each time he gambles. Or, he decides he knows you well enough to discuss sex and reveals serious issues or perversions. Or, maybe a client discloses she is on medication for a serious mental health issue and has had it under control for months. Again, this client is probably appropriate for referral because she may have mood swings or medication issues that would make the case too complicated.

When surprises like these turn up, they help explain why a client may have been "stuck" in his progress or in making headway in his relationships. Take an inventory of your ability and your relationship with the client to see if you need to refer him elsewhere. If you decide to keep the client, tell him you will see if you can help, but if you cannot, you will need to refer him to a professional counselor.

Sometimes a client will focus on someone in his life who has understandably exhausted him. The client feels exasperated, frustrated, angry, and hurt at the other person's behavior and at his own response. As you listen to the antics of the other person in the client's life, you may suspect the other person has a mental disorder of some sort.

The client has tried to accommodate her partner's mood swings or unprovoked outbursts of anger, sometimes for years. She may say she feels like she is walking on eggshells or that the person loves her one minute and then hates her the next, but she will not leave. Ask if the partner has been previously diagnosed.

If so, consider the diagnosis and assess whether you need to refer your client to a professional to learn how to manage the relationship. If the partner has not been diagnosed, see if the partner will seek help. There are two books worth reading about borderline personality disorder, which is one of the most common problems presented at mental health clinics: *Stop Walking on Eggshells* and *I Hate You—Don't Leave Me*. (See "Suggested Reading" in the appendix.)

Helping the client respond appropriately and effectively, while releasing his or her codependency, are some of your goals.

If you ask clients if they think their partner has a mental disorder, they may become defensive. Other times, they may say it would be a relief to know because it would explain a lot. Your challenge is to help them manage a difficult situation and all the constant drama that comes with it. Realistically, it would be best to refer these clients to a professional.

Learn to ask clients early on about drinking and drug use as well as medications. Learn to suspect, anticipate potential surprises, and learn from all of them.

CHAPTER 8
Assessing the Presenting Problem: Family and Historical Factors

What is *your* assessment of the *real* issue?

A presenting problem is what the client (initially) identifies as the issue. As stated previously, this may or may not be the real problem. Many problems are rooted in childhood or teenage experiences or from an adult experience with previous relationships. Clients may or may not see the root of their problem or the connection to their current behavior. That is one challenge of counseling.

How long?
It is helpful to assess whether the problem is new or has been going on a long time. Also assess if it is related to their current relationship or circumstances.

Family history—assess this as a potential contributing factor
When you meet with clients initially, it is helpful to get a *brief* summary of their family history. Ask them to be brief for now, because there is often a great deal of (drama and) strong emotions associated with this part of their lives. As a result, it takes a lot of time to get a full family history, and the process may upset the client. If family issues appear to be the main issue, ask the client to talk about his or her family life in stages (for example, childhood and then teen years), so you can cover these age stages in separate sessions.

Assess the current family status

"How is your immediate family doing? Any concerns?" (Not historical or biological; that is next.)

"Is everyone emotionally and physically healthy?"

Get the historical or biological history

"Did anyone in your family history have any mental or emotional health issues?"

"Did anyone have alcohol or drug issues?"

> *"Did your husband's parents have a good marriage?"*
>
> *"Did he get along with both parents?"*
>
> *"Was faith or religion a part of his family life?"*

Some counseling centers have clients initially fill out an extensive history sheet as well as a list of their family members and/or past and current relationships. This can be overwhelming and upsetting for clients and may seem impersonal. Although the content is important, it may also be revealed in subsequent counseling sessions or through specific exercises. However, you may learn content from an inventory that reveals your need to refer the client to a professional. Thus, there are pros and cons to forms for getting a client's history.

It also seems more natural and comfortable to conversationally explore historical areas as they are mentioned. You might say,

> *"That is helpful for me to know about your dad. Would you want to tell me more about your thoughts about him, maybe as a father?"*
>
> *"You mentioned your first husband. Do you want to tell me more about that marriage, what worked and what didn't?"*
>
> *"You had a lot going on during your teen years. Would you want to tell me how the rest of the family felt about those events and how they treated you back then?"*

If you decide to wait to get a brief family history, start right out by asking,

> *"What brings you to counseling?"* or *"How can I help you?"*

(See chapter 13, "Getting Started and Setting Goals.")

CHAPTER 9
Assessing the Client's Experience with Counseling

Assess Their Previous Experience

In the initial interview, ask the client if he or she has ever worked with a counselor or therapist. If so, ask about that experience. Ask a few questions:

"Did you complete the work assigned?"

"How long did you attend?"

"Why did it end? Who ended it? What did you learn?"

The last question is asked to potentially help identify issues to work on.

If the client had a bad experience before, but you suspect that counseling would be helpful now, encourage the client to consider trying again, either with you or a professional. Remind the client that his or her expectations and the outcome might be two different things.

If the client has been in counseling, especially if it has been on and off over the years, ask,

"Why have you been ambivalent about counseling?"

You ask this because you do not want to work on issues that clients have previously addressed. However, when they say they have worked through an issue, but you can see that it is clearly not resolved, you can gently point this out to them and ask how they want to deal with it.

For some people, counseling becomes a way to stay unhealthy, and your job is to see what the payoff is for them (attention or sympathy as examples).

Misconceptions about Counseling

Some people have the misconception that counseling includes interrogation and that clients are forced to talk about subjects that are uncomfortable for them. It involves issues they do not want to discuss, or they are given assignments they do not want to do. This is not the case in counseling. Counselors honor boundaries and will not press on subjects clients do not want to discuss.

(See chapter 13, "Getting Started and Setting Goals" and chapter 14, "Counseling Strategies and Tools for Clients.")

Counseling Devotees

You might be wondering why some people participate in counseling on and off for years and why their problems have not resolved. These clients (sometimes even self-referred to as "therapy junkies") may have any number of things going on:

> They like the one-on-one attention of a counselor (perhaps rather than a group).
> They do not have other people in their lives who listen to them.
> They like to complain and feel they are paying you to listen.
> They are constantly upset because there is so much drama in their life.
> They have a lot of baggage and need much help.
> They got bored with their previous counselor and wanted someone new.
> They do not want to do the work but like to be in counseling.
> They cannot accept things about themselves and are never satisfied with who they are, how they are, or how they look.
> They cannot accept forgiveness from people or from God for something they have done.
> They are not comfortable in social situations, except for counseling.
> They resolve their problems, but more issues crop up for any number of reasons.

Barriers, Boundaries, and Expectations for Participating in Counseling

Barriers to counseling may exist—things like finances or transportation—so address these individually.

If a client needs to be referred to a professional counselor, let the client know that many use a sliding scale or accept insurance. Churches may or may not charge a fee for counseling services. Counselors in private practice will charge a fee.

Various resources might handle transportation issues. Some volunteer organizations offer a service that drives people to medical and other appointments.

Emotionally Fearful Clients

For people who fear counseling, encourage them by suggesting they go to a counselor one time to see if they and the counselor are a good match. It is their right to determine which topics they will or will not discuss. Helping clients set boundaries around what they will and will not discuss may help with most fears. In time, those boundaries typically evaporate as trust in the counselor grows.

Helping Clients Who Have Never Been in Counseling

Clients who have not been in counseling before may have erroneous assumptions. Correct their thinking and remind them of proper boundaries.

- Explain to new clients that a counseling relationship is confidential, even from their spouse.
- Clients are expected to honor appointment times, session time frames, and any commitments made, including homework or other growth exercises.
- Contacting the counselor after a session by phone or text should be limited to emergencies or a short update. For liability, keep your written and phone/spoken comments minimal, and let clients understand the liability issue.

(See chapter 13, "Getting Started and Setting Goals.")

Explain the Types of Counseling to Help Reduce Fears

Secular Counseling and Christian Counseling

Some people misunderstand Christian counseling. Explain how Christian counseling differs from secular (nonreligious) counseling.

Secular Counseling

- This counseling is based on psychology and psychiatry. Unless requested by a client, spiritual issues usually will not be addressed.
- Sessions are treated somewhat as a business relationship. For example, time frames are strictly adhered to, little if any personal information is shared by the therapist/counselor, and the client is rarely contacted outside of scheduled appointments.
- Secular psychology believes that changing clients' thinking and behavior is critical. Christian counseling agrees.
- Secular counseling does not emphasize spirituality—things like a relationship with God and the need to surrender your heart, thoughts, and behavior to God as the only *permanent* cure in recovery—as Christian counseling does.

Christian Counseling

- Christian counseling has a foundation and value system based primarily on truths of the Bible and may include secular psychology tools, as applicable. Clients with reservations about Christian counseling may think prayer is the major focus of the session, that they will be tested on their knowledge of the Bible and their faith or faith practices, and that they have to be holier than they are or will be judged as being out of God's will. This should never be the case.
- Christian counselors may or may not open or close in prayer at each session.

- Christian counselors should not judge but will gently confront actions that are out of God's will. The counselor may ask what the client thinks God or the Bible has to say about an action and if that matters to them. Sometimes Christians will admit they are out of God's will and justify their behavior, which may include such things as living with someone of the opposite sex, practicing homosexuality, or committing adultery.
- When the morals of a client collide with Christian values, it is important to understand where he or she derived the values that are steering his or her behavior. Often people are oblivious to the magnitude of the consequences of their behavior and how those behaviors affect the feelings of others, their finances, their children, society as a whole, and so forth. (See chapter 18, "A Perspective on Our Family of Origin's Influence.") Ask in a neutral way if their conscience bothers them about their behavior.
- As they talk, you can get a reading on their defenses and strategize how to proceed. If you push faith too hard, you may shame them, and they will feel judged. Learn about their faith first and its relationship to their value system. Tread gently and with great sensitivity.
- Ask,

"Have you considered changing your behavior to be in God's will?"

Their answer will tell you their fears (for themselves as well as their spiritual relationship) and help you begin your strategy to help them.

If they are adamant about not changing, respond by saying,

"From a biblical perspective, God doesn't see it the way you do. Help me understand how you came to have this value."

This lets them know you respect their feelings, even if you do not agree with them. You want to encourage a change of heart and attitude, not force that change. Again, this is why your presence serves as a godly example, your lifestyle as an inspiration, and your obvious contentment with yourself and life as a desirable image. Work with them wherever their values are morally. It is an opportunity to guide them to a healthier and a godlier morality.

An Example of a Technique Used in Both Secular and Christian Counseling

Secular and Christian counseling may use different wording for the same techniques. These techniques are the same package but with different wrapping.

As a Christian counselor, when you need to say something difficult to someone, use the "heart-head-heart" tool:

- Speak from your **heart** first, so the person knows you mean well and care about her.
- Then speak from your **head** and make your point.
- Then speak from your **heart**, reminding her of your good intentions.

Different versions of the Bible express Ephesians 4:15 in terms like "wrap the truth in love [and grace]" or "speak the truth in love."

A helpful tool exemplifying this is the "Oreo Cookie Strategy." (See the appendix.)

God Can Change Anyone
Another essential distinction of biblically based counseling is we believe that once you put your faith in Jesus and recognize Him as the Son of God, God *can transform anyone* and make him or her into a new creation.

> **"If anyone is in Christ, he is a new creature; the old things passed away; behold new things have come" (2 Corinthians 5:17).**

God will give them a new heart, and that will change their behavior. Only God can change a heart, and He can change anyone permanently.

(See chapter 27, "Encouragement" and chapter 30, "Spiritual Issues and Personal Growth for Counselors and Clients.")

CHAPTER 10
Understanding Clients' Coping Mechanisms and Boundaries

Coping mechanisms are the mental and emotional tools anyone may use to manage a situation that is threatening or disagreeable in some way. We cry as toddlers, and this coping mechanism gets us attention. Our defiant behavior as teenagers prompts our uninterested parents to become involved with us. A wife overeats to soothe the loneliness of an absent husband. Overwork compensates a father who perhaps does not feel competent as a dad.

Coping mechanisms can be healthy. For example, a person may act composed when he or she is nervous or take charge in a crisis if he or she feels powerless. Coping mechanisms can also be unhealthy. For example, a person may carry out self-destructive acts like cutting or isolating to dull emotional pain.

Be observant to clients' coping mechanisms and try to discover what they are hiding, attempting to fix, or trying to forget. They may admit readily why and how they use their coping mechanisms. Quite often, though, they understand only how they use a coping mechanism when it is pointed out to them in counseling. When they make the connection, it can be an aha moment for them. Healing will follow because they will decide to give up being imprisoned by their coping mechanism and learn to live freely.

Boundaries

Boundaries are verbal, behavioral, and emotional lines of protection we draw around our bodies, our values, our finances, our family, and our time—anything we value and want protected and acknowledged. Boundaries need to be honored and respected. When they are not, we feel violated and vulnerable. Examples of boundaries may be the physical privileges afforded in a relationship, language deemed acceptable or not acceptable, or the specific conditions under which money is loaned.

Boundaries are not quite the same as rules or values. Boundaries are drawn for psychological protection. They may not even be developed or stated until there is a need—for instance, when an inconsiderate teen suddenly takes things without asking, or when someone uses foul language in your presence, does not repay loans, or is abusive. These are examples of boundary violations regarding respect.

An example of a verbal boundary is when you tell your clients in the first session that any time they want to honor their own boundary about what they will and will not talk about, all they need to say is "I don't want to talk about it now/just yet/ever," and you will honor it. This is a helpful agreement because it fosters safety and trust and gives the client control.

It is helpful to remind clients that if they do not feel comfortable letting *you* know about their boundary lines even though you have clearly given them permission to tell you, then they may be vulnerable to letting *others* violate their boundary lines—for example, relatives who come to visit without asking, people who borrow items without first getting permission, or those who schedule activities that include them without asking. This is an issue they need to work on. We need to set up verbal (and sometimes written) lines that indicate what we will and will not tolerate and the consequences of violating these boundaries. "If you borrow money and don't return it by the agreed-upon date, I will no longer loan you money," or "It is not OK for you to use that language around me. Please stop, or I will not participate in this conversation," or "If you hit me even once, I will call the police and press charges."

Unfortunately, boundaries can be disregarded or manipulated by both the person who established them and the other party. Sometimes people are intimidated and can't enforce their will or boundaries. Other times, the consequences are so great that they are overwhelmed. They are not prepared emotionally and cannot follow through. Manipulation by another person is one of the most common reasons boundaries are reduced, changed, or ignored.

Clients need to be comfortable with the boundaries they set, and they need to be coached on how to enforce them using their own language. Brainstorming a potential dialogue helps clients think through and practice what to say.

Suggest they use "I" statements rather than "you" statements. For example, suggest they say,

> *"I feel disrespected when you talk to me like that. It's unacceptable."*

This is more effective than saying,

> "You stop talking to me like that!"

Sometimes a situation, such as being pressured to volunteer, is such that it is enough to say, without an explanation,

> *"I appreciate your problem* [validating]; *however, I'm sorry, I can't help you."*

You may need to repeat that phrase again if the other person is insistent or manipulative. Your response strategy is simply **letting your "*yes*" mean "*yes*" and your "*no*" mean "*no*,"** as written in Matthew 5:37, and not feeling obligated to say more.

Boundaries and Cultures

Boundaries include physical, emotional, and cultural space. It is essential that you are aware of these, so you do not offend or alienate others.

(For etiquette, language, and dress boundaries, see chapter 13, "Getting Started and Setting Goals.")

Cultures around the world have different boundaries, and being sensitive helps build healthy relationships. For example, in some cultures, eye contact for more than a second is considered inappropriate, disrespectful, and perhaps even flirtatious. In some cultures, men do not communicate with women, especially unmarried women.

Emotional Boundaries

These are the lines we draw regarding what we will express, as well as what we will relate to. How we express ourselves can be the right to cry, get angry, or shut down. Emotional boundaries protect us from feeling out of control, uncomfortable, or other emotions.

For example, if you were raised to think it is inappropriate for men to cry, you may stifle your tears and feel very uncomfortable when you are with someone who is crying. On the other hand, if you have been raised to believe anger is unacceptable, you may stifle your frustration and turn to silence. When someone is angry with you, you may experience an extreme reaction or not know what to do.

Emotional boundary issues are frequently the cause of miscommunication and tension in couples and families.

In counseling,

- It is important to understand how each person defines his or her boundaries and what triggers set him or her off.

For example, if someone was *not* raised around yelling or even loud voices, especially in nonanger situations, he may interpret the yelling or loudness as disrespectful or intimidating. The yeller, however, may see this as normal, because his family communicates this way.

(See the "What I Offer a Partner" worksheet in the appendix.)

- It is important for clients to understand the source prompting a person's response, reaction, or behavior and give each other grace as a compromise is worked out, which will resolve mutually frustrating behaviors.

Another example is language. Some people swear because it was common in their home. Others began to swear after they left home. Still others picked up swearing in prison. A person who is not used to swearing finds it offensive and not tolerable.

In relationships and therefore in counseling, it is helpful to understand how clients or acquaintances came to be who they are. Therefore, ask about their behaviors.

Crying Clients

You may want to hug a client who is crying. Do not. Let clients experience their pain and own their feelings. God gave us tears for a reason. When they settle down some, you can say something tender like,

"Your pain will be gradually healed through your tears."

Often clients will apologize for crying, at least until they know you welcome their tears, so you can say,

"Crying is a good thing. It is healing. It shows your tender heart. Jesus had a tender heart and cried. Your tears are welcome. We do a lot of crying here. Sometimes I will cry, too."

- Keep tissues where the client can see and reach them. The client knows where they are, so do not hand them one. Handing them one will interrupt their feelings and emotions, while not handing them one respects their choice to take one or not.

Financial Boundaries

Many couples have issues with financial boundaries and most have minimal or no training in managing their finances. Sometimes couples come to a marriage with expectations that are based on the way their parents managed finances. In some cases, one parent was responsible for all financial matters.

One option is to have the spouse who is gifted with financial matters manage the finances. The other spouse needs to review the finances to appreciate the true status of their situation. That spouse needs to respect the manager's financial suggestions. Without this sharing and acknowledgment, spending issues that are not discussed or financial boundaries that are ignored can cause dissension.

Some couples have three accounts—"yours," "mine," and "ours"—and this works for them. Others see this as divisive.

Bottom line: It is important to remember that everything belongs to God, and we are only temporary stewards. (Also, the Bible calls us to tithe or even give sacrificially, so that needs to be taken into account.)

The Financial Peace University, under Dave Ramsey, provides money management training that is Christian based and has proven to be very helpful in teaching others about saving, debt reduction, budgeting, and other financial issues.

(See www.daveramsey.com.)

Physical Boundaries

Touch can be helpful in counseling, but be on guard. If a client is negatively sensitive to touch, any touch can be offensive and threatening. A two-handed handshake (your hands clasped around the other person's hand) held a couple of seconds longer than usual is a nonthreatening gesture that makes a verbal greeting or closure seem very sincere and so promotes bonding.

More valuable than touch is your presence, and that is a much safer way to convey caring. Respect is another. As you get to know a client, you may know what is comforting to him or her. On rare occasions when someone is sobbing, I may move and sit next to him or her and put my hand on his or her shoulder. If a client makes a move to hug me, I hug her (women only; with men I just touch his arm or shoulder).

Different cultures and different generations expect certain boundaries concerning physical touch. Be aware.

Affection is normal in some cultures if it is between men, or women, or a man and a woman. In some cultures, a public show of affection is discouraged, while in others, it is romanticized, like when a couple kisses when greeting at an airport.

Hugging can be misinterpreted, so a safe hug is a side-to-side hug, especially between people of opposite genders. Some people are very affectionate and may want to hug you after the session. Be cautious, and know it is best to opt for a two-handed, enthusiastic handshake. If he or she seems insistent, ask first. Say,

"Would you like a hug?"

On another occasion where it seems natural, you may ask,

"May I give you a hug?"

But then, some may surprise you by saying, "No, thanks. I'm not a hugger."

Others will open their arms to you willingly. If so, give a side hug if you wish.

If you have a particularly rewarding session with a couple you have counseled for a while, hugs may be natural. After you hug the person of your same gender, ask him or her if it would be all right if you hug his or her partner (if the partner seems willing).

Some clients will have emotional confusion about any physical contact because it brings up tender or shameful memories. That said, any physical contact can be quickly and dangerously misinterpreted, so it is always prudent to not be physical.

It is important in counseling to tell the client you will respect all her boundaries, but there are times when she must tell you when that needs to happen.

Boundary Violations

When an emotional boundary is violated, it is essential to make it known with love and grace. Clients should not say to their partner, "There you go again," or "I told you not to do that!" It would be better for them to be in control when they respond *rather than react*.

Teach the clients that with total composure and the Lord's help, they can respond and not react. Ask for His help, and then gently, but very firmly, have them remind offending people that they are crossing their boundaries by saying,

> "I'm uncomfortable with that language / tone of voice / finger pointing, and I need you to respect me and stop it."

- If the offending person cannot shut it down immediately, have the client ask him or her to leave the room, calm down, and pray for composure.
- If the offender will not go, tell the client to say he or she is leaving until things calm down. (See chapter 21, "Managing Arguments.") As long as one person is composed and in control, issues should not escalate.
- When a physical boundary is violated, including hitting, slapping, in-your-face posturing, shoving, or any other threatening physical action such as showing a weapon or other intimidating object, then the situation is already out of control, and the client needs to calmly remove herself, if possible.
- If the abuser obstructs the way, the client needs to stay calm and show control rather than yelling back.

Hopefully, the client's calmness will defuse the offender's anger. When things de-escalate, he or she needs to speak to a counselor and perhaps the police and decide what his or her options are for safety and emotional well-being.

CHAPTER 11
Understanding Clients' Defenses

Be alert to clients' use of defenses as they tell you their fears and needs in regard to protecting themselves or others. Two descriptive names for defenses are emotional walls and behavioral strategies. We all use defenses to protect our emotions, values, personality, family, and traditions. They can be healthy—or not.

Defenses are coping mechanisms we begin to use early in life. For example, a young child might deny something he did to avoid punishment and then might carry that mechanism into adulthood, causing him to lie or be deceptive to avoid confrontation or blame. Sometimes those who employ these strategies are deemed annoying (like those who use sarcasm), frustrating (like perfectionists), or socially inappropriate (like incessant talkers).

Our defenses may have become so much a part of our personality that we do not realize how they impact others. Then, when confronted, *we* become defensive.

Counseling accomplishes the following:

- Gently points out our defenses and affirms the need for *healthy* defenses.
- Helps find the root cause of why we protect ourselves with the defense. For example, perhaps we talk too much because no one listened to us when we were growing up.
- Uncovers the fears our defense mechanism is able to hide. Perhaps no one takes the time or cares enough to listen.
- Helps people understand their behavior.
- Helps replace the behavior with a healthy alternative.

Clients may complain defensively that they are misunderstood socially, or they may become frustrated when they have to explain or defend themselves. After all, they were "only kidding."

To others, however, it was heard as sarcasm or an attempt to be funny. It was seen as teasing and was not kind. Clients may claim they talked a long time because "no one else was saying anything." (No one had a chance.) They may acknowledge that sometimes they alienate people. It is more likely, however, that they do not even pick up on social cues even though partners and friends have tried to tell them about their offensive habit.

Remind clients that

- it is not only about their intentions, but it's also about how those intentions are perceived by others; and
- it is also about what the hearer has been through. That is, the hearer may employ mental/emotional filters through which he or she hears and sees things.

Therefore, it is not only what the receiver hears or experiences, but also the receiver's history that interprets the situation. For example, a person who was always teased about being short may be highly sensitive to jokes about stature.

These factors influence communication tremendously. If someone reacts in a way that is surprising, it is helpful to ask what the reaction was about.

If a client has an unpredictable or unreasonable reaction, gently ask,

"I can see I have said something that you are reacting to and you seem upset." (You are validating. Do not ask *"Why?"* because it can make someone defensive.)

A remark may trigger an emotional reaction in someone. He or she may be overreacting because the remark reminds him or her of a highly sensitive hurt, or the person may have "had enough" of someone's insensitive behavior/words.

Examples of defenses follow. You will see these in counseling, and clients will complain about these behaviors in others.

Types of Defenses

There are numerous types of defenses. In this section, we will cover controlling behaviors, avoidance/procrastination, the silent treatment, retaliation, crying, sarcasm, lateness, detachment, and a wall of words.

Controlling Behaviors

Controlling people want to tell you what to do, say, or think based on their opinion. They are very threatened if you challenge them because they cannot be wrong and will not admit it if they are proven to be wrong. They tend to talk all the time, argue without ever conceding, and arouse feelings of stupidity (if you let them) for believing what you believe, do, or choose, so you don't challenge them and take it—until you blow up.

The art of developing patience with controllers is to realize that

- fear of being wrong and being "less than" is at the root of their controlling behavior, or
- they may have been in a frightening situation at one time where they didn't have control, or are in a situation now where they don't have control.

Somewhere along the line, most likely growing up with a domineering parent or sibling, controllers could never get anything right, were always criticized, or were made to feel "less than." They develop a wall of control so they are never challenged or made to feel that way again. So, much patience on the part of the counselor or partner is needed, along with recognition that a scared little child is inside the controlling person. He or she is terrified of being wrong, disappointing anyone, or being involuntarily controlled.

When a client feels controlled by someone in her life, she has to learn to confront the controller. It may take considerable work for her to have confidence in how to do it. Start by asking,

"Can you give me an example of when you felt controlled?"

"What were the feelings you were experiencing at that time?" (Get as many feeling words as possible.)

"How did you respond? What did you say? Was that a typical response for you?" (The client will probably express her frustration in not handling the situation.)

*"What would it have been like for you to tell this person that it feels **controlling** when he talks to you like that?"* (The client probably will give excuses of why that will not work.)

"What would you like to say to him?" (The response will probably be said with passion.)

"Would you want to work on responding to him in a way that might shift things?" (She may need to have her fears explored about the consequences of change.)

Help the client tell the offender the truth, but wrap it in grace and love. (See the "Oreo Cookie Strategy" in the appendix.)

Avoidance/Avoidants and Procrastination

Avoidants cannot deal with tasks because it may bring on anxiety, criticism, stress, arguments, confrontation, or change. They may avoid family, socializing, housework, or any number of responsibilities. They use as excuses things such as they have pets to take care of, they did not get enough sleep the previous night, they have too much to do, and so forth. They just ignore things, minimize them, or claim it is not a big deal to them when it really is.

These people

- don't feel competent to manage a contrary or challenging situation, so they don't deal with it;
- procrastinate to feel in control;
- avoid select responsibilities by being workaholics or super preoccupied with a project, and being perfectionist about certain achievements;
- put things off out of fear of failure, fear of criticism, or fear of what the next step is once they complete the task, such as not going on a diet because they might be asked out and would then experience anxiety; and

- may be passive-aggressive, which is an avoidant behavior. In this case, the person is doing something out of spite or intentionally wanting to be defiant.

The counseling dialogue for procrastination is much the same as with a controlling person. Ask,

"Please give me an example of your husband's procrastination."

"What feelings were you experiencing toward him at that time?" (Get as many feeling words as possible.)

"What did you say? How did you respond? Was that a typical response for you?" (She will probably express her frustration.)

"What would it have been like for you to tell him that it feels disrespectful when he won't take care of responsibilities?" (She probably will give excuses of why that will not work.)

"What would you like to say to him?" (The response will probably be said with passion.)

"Would you want to work on responding to him in a way that might shift things?"

She may need to have her fears explored about the consequences of change.

Help her tell the offender the truth, but wrap it in grace and love.

(See the "Oreo Cookie Strategy" tool in the appendix on how to do that.)

The Silent Treatment

Some people just walk away from tension and will not talk for hours, days, or weeks. That is *their weapon*, and it is a severe one. They feel unable to manage the situation or argument, so they refuse to participate. Sometimes they fear they will lose their temper or be abusive, or they know they will lose the argument because the other person is better at arguing or manipulation. (See the section on "Emotional Manipulation" in chapter 7, "Assessing the Problem: Understanding Clients' Feelings and Reactions.")

The other person may also enter the silent treatment, or he or she may give up and agree to any solution just to resume normalcy. This breeds resentment and does not solve the problem. Teaching couples how to discuss their differences or issues in a healthy way helps fix the use of this defense.

(See chapter 21, "Managing Arguments" and "Communication Tool: The Table Meeting" in the appendix.)

Retaliation

People who subscribe to the mentality of "do unto others" get back at others by doing to the offender what they did to them, like get drunk, have an affair, or buy an expensive item—or worse. They usually know what will hurt the other person. They may just say things that are hurtful or they may do hurtful things. Sometimes, this is an immediate reaction; other times, it is calculated and delayed. From a partner giving someone the silent treatment to a fired employee killing his or her boss, retaliation can be serious and is never helpful.

A "rebound" relationship, where someone enters into a relationship quickly after one is broken, is a retaliation reaction. These relationships frequently end disastrously as the person has not healed from the first relationship or learned what truly went wrong.

This is another case of a person who attempts to secure control (when he has been hurt) with a new relationship that is a rebound, so there is a large amount of unresolved feelings that need to be worked through.

You will also need to be aware of transference. The client may be dumping what the previous offending partner did to them onto their current partner. Help him or her see what they are doing and help the partner have patience and not respond defensively.

There will be much work to do. Help your clients

- separate history from the present—for example, clients should not compare the last partner to the current partner; and
- build trust if an affair was the reason for the last breakup and so forth.

Teach the client to patiently remind her partner that she will not hurt him or her like the previous partner, and remind him or her that building trust will take time and work.

Additionally, a client may choose a partner who is a cheater to replace his or her ex for the reasons previously cited: it is familiar, the client wants to fix what he/she could not in the previous relationship; the client wants to punish someone because he/she was hurt, and so on. In such a case, find out what the client's motives were in choosing his or her partner and what the expectations are for the new relationship.

Alternatively, a client may express his or her feeling of intense anger and admit it has been buried for years, even decades.

To begin, review chapter 21, "Managing Arguments."

Help the client express why he/she has chosen to not express his anger all this time.

Correct any wrong thinking ("Justice will never win," "You can't fight city hall," "They will threaten my family," and so on).

Crying
Crying can be a defense to

- stop the other person's behavior,

- bring on an anticipated response (perhaps an instant apology), or
- cause a shift/concession in the power struggle. ("OK, you win. Go buy the Mercedes.")

Sometimes people, especially women, can be very emotional and cry easily. That can make it an effective defense and a manipulation tool. Even though tissues may be within reach, they ignore them and wipe their face with their hands or sleeve. They may do this in your counseling session or elsewhere.

There are a couple of reasons people may do this. They appreciate having someone see how much they are hurting. The most likely reason is they want the attention, and they want to be in control even when they are crying. They have used this as a manipulation tool to get what they have wanted in the past (for example, sympathy, an object they wanted, or their own way). They are relieved to be free to express their emotions and are just very involved. This is also a likely reason, especially when as a crying child they may have been ignored.

As children, men—and sometimes women—may have been told not to express their feelings, especially tears, and to "be a big boy" or "man up." They quickly learned not to express their tender emotions and shut down an important part of their character and personality. They shut down as a way to cope because they would be punished or experience disapproval from their parents. Shutting down became a coping mechanism that was necessary as a child or young adult, but as an adult, it becomes a handicap. Partners/spouses will complain that the man is cold or unemotional, not understanding the root cause. Frequently, the man will not make the connection with his lack of emotion and his past until you help him connect the dots.

Sarcasm
This defense is veiled hostility. Perhaps the person was shamed years ago for showing a gentle side or was funny but was mocked for it (because of a dysfunctional family dynamic). Some potential explanations include that the person may not have the social skills to say what he really wants to say, or he thinks he has a higher level of humor than most and is therefore arrogant about it. Sarcastic people are usually quick witted, bright, and naturally funny. Help them to use those God-given gifts in conversation and not resort to sarcasm. Find out the reason they switched from using those gifts positively to sarcasm. Something happened. See if they realize that sarcasm is alienating them socially and can be hurtful. Ask why they choose that.

Lateness
This defense is veiled anger and control.

A sample dialogue:

> "What do you think when I tell you that lateness is veiled anger?" (He may deny it for a bit and then admit it.)

> "If I gave you a thousand dollars to be on time for something, could you do it?" (He will say, "Sure.")

"So being late is a choice. Can you admit that?" (He will.)

"Do you want to talk about what you're really mad about that your lateness is masking?"

If they will talk about it, ask why they keep doing it. (It is probably taking control of time when they do not have control over something else, either in the relationship or in their life.)

If they do not want to talk about why they do it, explore how long they have been choosing to be late and ask if they care about the frustration it causes others.

Explore what else is going on that causes them to use the behavior.

You can use other examples to demonstrate that their behavior is a choice.

"If you thought you were being followed, would you still stop at a porn store?" (Probably not.)

"If your partner could look at your phone or computer when you were not aware of it, would you have contacts and history always available to her?" (Probably not.)

This shows that their unhealthy or hurtful behavior may be premeditated and is intentionally covered up. Ask,

"If I could guarantee recovery, would you opt for it?" (Probably yes.)

"There is recovery potential in all of us, but it takes work, time, and perseverance. A commitment to surrendering our weaknesses to God is the most important change agent."

Detachment

This defense is when we shut down emotionally and just go through the motions as if we were absent. It is a mental and emotional coping mechanism where we choose not to confront or be involved in a situation that is so overwhelming, horrific, or incomprehensible that we cannot deal with it.

Examples could include detaching when being a victim of incest, when being abusively punished, after watching a catastrophe, or even after hearing about a catastrophe.

Another example is detaching when hearing of the death or horrific injury of someone close. The hearer or witness may function on "autopilot" just to get through the funeral and afterward have little recollection of what went on.

God gives us detachment to be used in a healthy way as a means of coping through a difficult time. However, it becomes dysfunctional when we put all of the painful memories in a mental/emotional vault and never address the emotions (grief, injustice, outrage, fear, and so on) connected with the memories.

The pain eventually will seep out anyway because we are wired to be healed. The pain shows up in anger, physical issues, and bitterness.

When you realize that a client has used or is using detachment, tread gently and be very careful when asking about the root of her emotion. Let her open up in small steps at her own pace. Ask when she first started using this defense.

Sometimes the client will already understand the concept of detachment. Help her realize that healing comes from talking about the incident and being helped to understand the reality of her role in the trauma (for example, in the case of incest, that it was not their fault). (See chapter 26, "Grief and Depression," for additional comments.)

A Wall of Words

Some people will talk continuously as a way to put up a wall, making it impossible for you to get in your turn to talk. These people are called monopolizers. They may smile the whole time as they look right at you and make you feel guilty (if you let them) for interrupting them. They may slide seamlessly from one subject to another.

In a group situation, it is especially frustrating when others do not get a turn to speak. People who monopolize the conversation are exhausting, and you will feel controlled by them. That is their intention. If they let you talk, they may learn something uncomfortable they do not want to face. It may also be that they do not want to give up the attention, or they are concerned you may judge them or find them unworthy to talk with.

One way anyone can take charge with an incessant talker is to raise one's hand.

The client-talker will ask, "What are you doing?" While smiling, the listener can respond with "Is it my turn to talk yet?"

The talker will probably apologize profusely but quickly resume taking over the conversation.

If a client does this,

- remind him whenever he does it. You are teaching him a behavior that corrects the social alienation problem.

If the wall of words is especially a complaint of his partner, remind the monopolizer

- that in a healthy conversation, each person gets to take his or her turn talking. That is, if there are four people gathered, you get a fourth; with two people, you get half the talk time.

Ask monopolizers to practice this and let you know if they are becoming more disciplined about it.

You can also challenge an arrogant client who is in denial about this to ask a couple of people he socializes with to tell him the truth about whether or not he talks too much. Often people will gladly tell him that he does.

Clients may use a wall of words in the session. They may talk nonstop, resulting in your frustration. It is awkward to interrupt with a question or an observation. They talk nonstop because

- they have a fear of what you might say and their inability to handle it, or
- they fear the conversation may go to a painful or uncomfortable situation, so they try to control it.

If so, you can say,

"I need to interrupt you. I'm wondering if you realize you're talking without giving me a chance to say anything." (They will probably apologize.)

"Talking continuously is a defense. What do you think would happen if you rested during a conversation?"

"Do you have any fears about what I might say regarding what you are talking about?"

"Do you do this with most people?"

"If so, let's talk about it. If not, what's going on here that compels you to talk incessantly?"

Remedies for Unhealthy Use of Defenses

Teaching clients not to go to their defenses takes time, practice, and trust between you and the client and other people in their world.

- A safe place has to be created to talk about the problem.
- A safe place is cultivated by keeping voices in a normal range, giving each person equal time to talk, looking directly at the person who is talking at the time (showing that you are *really* listening), and not interrupting, as well as by letting the other person know you heard her by giving feedback on what you thought you heard (mirroring) and what you think she may be feeling (validating).

People will not need to raise their voices to be heard if you are paying attention to them when they speak, and if they feel they have time to express their view without being interrupted or challenged.

(See "Communication Tool: The Table Meeting" in the appendix.) Use mirroring and validation. (See chapter 7, "Assessing the Problem: Understanding Clients' Feelings and Reactions.")

The following are some suggestions for *fishing*, which allows you to see the extent of the problem, as well as some resources. For example, for an alcohol issue where the client is using his defense of denial, you might say,

> *"I think there is more of an issue here than you are willing to admit. So if you are willing, go to a twelve-step group two or three times a week and do not drink for a month, and let's see what shows up."*

Someone who does not have a problem will not have an issue with following these guidelines, but someone who does will make excuses. Some may agree to stop drinking for a month but not go to a program.

- Work with whatever she will commit to, but have a plan for consequences. For example, if she does drink, she will go to a twelve-step program for at least a month.
- If she does agree to go to a twelve-step program for a month, you might ask her to listen hard and share with you what she learned at the program. Sometimes attending the meetings is a very helpful wake-up call, or sometimes clients come back saying they are not as bad as "those people."

Twelve-step programs root out one's defenses. The focus is on the individual and not his or her partner, child, or boss, which helps the person get a perspective on his or her own behavior. These programs have a proven track record of success. If you as a counselor have never been to a twelve-step program, it is very helpful to go to an open meeting to observe. (Open meetings are for anyone to attend, whereas closed meetings are only for people who have an admitted addiction.) Consider going to various meetings for different issues such as drugs, alcohol, overeating, and so on.

(See chapter 23, "Addiction and Other Issues" and chapter 25, "Twelve-Step Recovery Groups: An Overview.")

If a client has an unpredictable or unreasonable reaction, you need to gently ask,

> *"I can see you are upset and that I have said something that you are reacting to."* (You are validating.)
> *"What's going on?"* (Do not ask *"Why?"* because it can make someone more defensive.)

A remark may have triggered an emotional reaction in someone. He or she may be overreacting because you have touched on a highly sensitive hurt for him or her, or, in a group setting, the person may have "had enough" of someone's insensitive behavior/words.

You will see the above examples of defenses in counseling, and clients will complain about these behaviors in others.

SECTION IV
Preparation for the Meeting/Session

CHAPTER 12
Preparation

Be Prepared

- You will not always know the emotional or mental state of potential clients or what may upset them. It is prudent, if possible, to have your desk near the door and your exit unobstructed. Have a procedural emergency plan to get help from someone else in the area. Also, do not block a client's exit.

If a client loses control emotionally or physically—including yelling, throwing objects, or any kind of violence—at any time during your interview or session, call your supervisor immediately.

Make It a Safe Place

- Going to a counseling session, especially for the first time, provokes anxiety. Be intentional about making the client as comfortable as possible. First-time clients especially do not know what to expect, so the more you can respectfully direct them, the better. Let *your* presence say, "I will take care of you and treat you with respect. I will not talk down to you. I will make this a safe place."
- Show them the seating options and ask them to "please take a seat." (Good manners and starting clients off with a choice helps by giving them a semblance of control.)
- If you are working with a couple, have two chairs nearby so they can turn their chairs and face each other when talking.
- If you can, have bottled water available and ask if they would like some. For showing extra respect, when you hand it to them and they say, "Thank you," you can say, "My pleasure."

Listen

- Listening is one of the most important skills you can acquire and demonstrate. Often, just knowing someone has sincerely listened heals a person; just being heard sets the person free from all of his or her bottled-up emotions.
- Additionally, sometimes people come to find the answers to their situations by hearing themselves talk it through, so discerning questions can be very helpful.
- Verbal validation: use selective validation, which means you do not comment or nod constantly. Be selective so your nonverbal message is

"I'm a careful listener, but know I may not always agree with you. However, I am attentively listening."

Nod your head slightly, not vigorously. Say,

"I see."

Or validate what they appear to have been feeling by saying something like,

"That sounds so frustrating."

"I think anyone might feel like you did in that situation."

"You are right. From what you're saying, it sounds like the problem was how it was handled."

Body Language
Lean in, arms uncrossed, hands open, with constant eye contact. Nod when you can acknowledge the client's frustration. Be careful not to nod in agreement when you do not know something is true or when something is brought up that you can't deal with effectively. If you do, you are sending a false message.

Etiquette for Each Session: Show Respect

- Always be polite and respectful.
- Always model Christ-like behaviors.
- Always listen intently, with *constant* eye contact. (However, there are certain cultures where this is considered rude.)
- Be careful how you dress, especially women. Short skirts, revealed cleavage, and tight clothing are often regarded as disrespectful, and unlike Christian behavior. It can add a dynamic to the conversation—for example, presumed flirting, jealousy, or resentment—that interferes with progress.

When a Client Is in a Wheelchair
If the person is in a wheelchair, try not to stand up while holding any lengthy conversation with him or her. It puts the client in a "less-than" position. If necessary, squat at the client's side and converse until you get him or her situated.

When There May Be a Speaking Barrier
If there is a language or elocution (speaking) barrier, respectfully ask the person to speak slowly for you and ask for repeats as needed. The client is probably used to repeating, but you can ease his or her awkwardness by being extra patient and respectful.

"Please say that again for me, Mr. Ramos. Thank you."

Illiteracy

Nonreaders sometimes try to hide their illiteracy. If you sense that a client is illiterate, very gently ask if they would like some help with understanding or filling out the paperwork. Then, frequently ask if they are clear on what you have both done so far.

Language

Watch your language. Have the highest Christian standards. Never say, "Oh my God!" at some alarming thing they shared or use the Lord's name in vain. If clients say a curse word, it is OK to very gently say,

> *"Please watch your language. Thank you."*

They may be temporarily embarrassed, but if they were talking to our president, they would be able to watch their language. Therefore, it is a choice. They will probably apologize and try not to do it again, and you will be teaching them a life lesson about respect for others and themselves.

If they slip and do not apologize, gently say, *"Language, please,"* and they will get it.

If during sessions clients use cursing in expressing their anger at someone, sometimes it is OK to let it go and not interrupt their expression of intense feelings. They will often apologize afterward and acknowledge appreciation to you for letting them vent.

Introduction and Greeting

- Always greet the person with a smile and introduce yourself. If a family is involved, introduce yourself to the man first, then the woman, and then the children. This will help them to feel safe, and it shows respect for the parent(s).
- Ask them to "Please be seated" as you show them where to sit. (This is respectful and helps relieve their anxiety for what is expected of them.)

Creating Order and Comfort

If they begin to talk right away, politely ask if they could wait for a minute while you get things ready to help them (for example, forms may need to be filled out). This will set a boundary that shows you are in charge, displays your intent to help them in an organized manner, and shows that you are not caught up in their urgency. (Clients new to counseling may not be aware of what to do and when, so a gentle explanation along the way helps put them at ease.)

- Try your best to direct your questions to the person from whom you need the information. It is respectful to assume the person can answer, even if others try to answer for him. By showing your patience and honoring his effort to speak, you are being respectful. If the person starts to talk out of nervousness or not knowing the protocol, gently remind him,

"Please wait a bit before sharing until I take care of a couple of things."

- If the potential client does not have much to discuss, say, *"Thank you."* Then ask the person who accompanied the client if he or she wants to add any information.

Complete Forms

If it is applicable and appropriate, a basic informational form needs to be completed. Aside from people who are not in counseling and dealing on a personal level with their parents, adult children, and/or close friends, it would be advantageous for counselors to have the form completed.

- Once seated, let them know you have a simple form you would like them to please review and then ask them if they would please complete the contact information.
- Read their completed forms, ensure that all the information is completed and legible, and then thank them.

Your Credentials and the Option to Refer

- When done, sit back and say,

"I would like to share a couple of quick things before I give you the floor. The sheet you just signed indicated that I am not a professional counselor. If during our interview or other sessions, I believe I need to refer you elsewhere, I will do that to ensure you get the best help. If along the way you want to go elsewhere, please let me know. I will understand. You deserve the best care, and I want to ensure that. Are you OK with continuing? Good. Thank you."

Praying

- Next, ask if it would be all right with them if you prayed. You cannot assume they honor Jesus, but typically honoring "God" will be accepted and appropriate (because they understand that you provide Christian counseling).
- If they agree, and it is appropriate for your position, you can ask if you can pray in the name of Jesus. Christians will always say yes and may look questioningly. Tell them you do not know what faith they follow, and you want them to be comfortable because people of various faiths come to counseling. They will see this as respectful.
- Then (if you are Catholic, make and say the sign of the cross), pray a *simple* prayer for wisdom and knowledge as you minister and thank God in advance for all He will do. End (if they have agreed with acknowledging Jesus) with the sign of the cross or in the name of Jesus. Do not make your prayer long or intimidating because you want to model how to pray, especially when getting better at prayer may be one of their goals. Always model a godly humility in prayer, and speak of your dependence on God.

Explaining Counseling

Tell them that counseling is a unique partnership, and mutual boundaries are to be respected. This includes starting and ending on time, calling twenty-four hours in advance if they cannot make an appointment, not using inappropriate language, and other topics related in more detail below (for example, their right to not talk, and the confidentiality of what is mutually said).

Talking and Choices—Talking Is Their Choice

- An important rule to tell them is that if at *any* time they do not want to talk about a topic for *any* reason—they are tired of it, it is too painful, it is not the right time, they do not know or trust you—then they need to say they do not want to deal with that matter. Then, it is off the table. This empowers them and reduces their anxiety about issues they are not ready or willing to discuss. They will appreciate this rule.
- Also, let them know it is important for them to set this boundary because if they cannot set boundaries with you when you are giving them permission, they probably are letting others violate their boundaries.
- Always give choices. This gives the client a feeling of having some control.

(See chapter 15, "Types of Questions to Ask and a Strategy to Ask Them.")

- If the counselees are a man and a woman, speak to the man first out of respect. Do this even if the woman takes over. Gently say,

"One moment please, [name]. *That question was for your husband."*

Confidentiality

Tell them that all topics discussed are confidential, except for those on the sheet they signed (about reporting abuse). If they choose to share what is discussed in counseling with others, that is their option.

(See chapter 15, "Types of Questions to Ask and a Strategy to Ask Them.")

It's Not about You

Say to clients that you may, from time to time, share a little bit about yourself and your experiences if it is applicable to the conversation.

On occasion, you may share a line or two about your own similar experience, but be discerning. You might say,

"I have been through a similar trial and think I understand what you are saying."

It is not appropriate to say you "understand" because of anything but *your own* experience (not your relative's experience nor a friend's nor anyone else's). Sometimes a simple *"I understand"* is sufficient for some situations, except grieving (covered elsewhere in this book). Saying you understand can be a trigger for some clients who resent others thinking they know how they feel. Be careful and consider saying,

> *"I haven't been through what you have. Please know that I care and will help you feel safe as you share your experience."*

Note-Taking
Have a few sheets of paper and a pen within reach and encourage them to take notes. Suggest they bring a notepad to future sessions if they wish because it is helpful in remembering what is said.

Opening Sessions after the First Session
At the second session and at subsequent sessions, open by saying

> *"It is good to see you. In a word, how are you?"*

Ask this with sincerity while looking at them directly. Let them know you really care how they are. This opener will provide you with an ongoing measure of their moods and may require a shift in goals.

Ask what they thought about their first session, and ask them to be honest. Do not be defensive, and thank them for whatever they say. Then ask how their week went, if they did not dive in talking immediately.

Winding Up the Session
About five minutes before the end of the session say,

> *"I'm sorry to interrupt you, but we need to close our session for today, and I want to thank you for sharing."*

This is awkward because the client may be in the middle of a painful disclosure or may be sobbing. Sometimes you have some control over that, anticipating the tenderness of the situation, and you can say in advance,

> *"I want to hear about it, but please know that we have only fifteen minutes left in the session, and we may need to stop in the middle of your sharing."*

That is about all you can do. It is challenging, but you will get better at saying it gracefully.

Closing in Prayer
Then say,

> *"God wants to hear what help you want from Him, what you are asking for. Would you be comfortable closing our session in prayer?"*

This encourages them in what to pray for.

If they agree, good. Most likely, they will say they would rather not, that they have never prayed out loud, or some other explanation. Say,

> *"OK. In time, hopefully you will be more comfortable leading us in closing our session in prayer."*

Then you pray.

Sometimes, however, you will be pleasantly surprised at how well some people pray. Affirm their praying as good, or beautiful, or whatever word you like. Then thank them (especially if they asked God to bless you in their prayer).

Managing Talkers When the Session Has Ended
It is important to know that people will often bring up more issues as you are trying to wrap up and make the next appointment. Even though you remind them that the session needs to end, they may persist. They may do this for a variety of reasons. For example, they may enjoy talking with you and being listened to, they may want a measure of control, or they may realize they were not talking about the things they really wanted to talk about and now have the courage. Say,

> *"What you are sharing is important and deserves my full attention, and I can't give that to you now. Please save that for next time. Thank you."*

Unfortunately, they may do this often. You do not want them to feel dismissed, but you don't want them to manipulate you either, so be respectful but firm.

Another closure when they bring up new problems is

> *"I have confidence in your ability to handle things until I see you at our next session."*

This is more encouraging than "Call me if you need me" or "I'm here for you." Neither reflects your confidence in them and encourages codependency.

(See chapter 14, "Counseling Strategies and Tools for Clients" and applicable chapters in section III.)

Payments and Next Appointments (or Not)

- If you are owed payment, take care of that next, and then thank them and give them a receipt.
- Ask if they would like another appointment. If they say yes, ask when they would like to meet. Also, ask if they want a reminder card. Again, always give clients choices and control where you can.
- If they say they do not know their schedule or have to check their finances first, these may be excuses or they may be the truth. They may not want to return or they may need time to process all that happened in the session and get their strength back up. Say,

"I understand. I look forward to hearing from you when it works for you. I sincerely hope to see you soon."

Make sure they know they are welcome to return and are not disappointing you. That can be a trigger for some people who want to please others at any cost, so they may come back when they do not want to just to please you.

Ending Counseling

- Six is the average number of sessions a client will stay. There seems to be a pattern of those who stay the average number of times, those who stay one or two times, those who stay for three months, those who stay for a year or more, and those who come for a few months and pop back in from time to time for years.
- You can remind clients when they leave that they are always welcome to come back for a tune-up after they are done or have graduated or if they need to work more on issues. Leaving that door open for them is all you can do. Some will take advantage of your offer; others will not for multiple reasons.
- For those clients who reach their goal(s), it is mutually rewarding and a good time to affirm the hard work they have done and the milestones they have accomplished. These clients are "graduating," and they take great pride in telling that to others. It is inspirational for them and for others.

Managing Clients Who Get Stuck

Clients may be diligent about coming to counseling but may get overwhelmed by all that is happening in their lives and therefore need to take baby steps that result in less progress than you two originally envisioned.

Or when complications, interference, or a setback happens (for example, a family death, loss of a job, sickness, or financial issues), they may regress or need to spend time on those current emotional issues rather than their original goals.

- Sometimes you need to help clients reidentify the acceptable versus the ideal goals. Then adjust the time frames for counseling accordingly.
- However, when they are stuck and insist on continuing to rehash the same material and are not doing what has been suggested, or they have admitted what needs to be done but don't do it, you

need to give them the option of coming back when they have changed *one* thing. Fueling their inertia is enabling. Let these clients go. They will return if you assure them they are welcome back when they are ready to work more consistently.
- Assess if they are being emotionally manipulated into keeping things in their life the same. Sometimes a client does not want to change. Ask yourself what he is getting out of his present behavior. Sometimes other people in his life do not want any changes. They may work very hard at keeping things the way they are and even prevent change by not allowing the person to continue counseling, discrediting the counselor or the work being done, or perhaps upping their issues/drama—like escalating their drinking—to create so much chaos that nothing else gets attention. Warning clients in advance of potential family dynamics and reactions, and discussing how to handle them is a helpful course to explore.

Dropouts

Clients sometimes just disappear. Too often it's because of embarrassment or being overwhelmed and not being strong enough to face their issues. They just drop out and never give an explanation. Ask permission ahead of time to contact them if they change their typical attendance pattern.

You can send them a text, e-mail, or letter questioning if there is a problem, encouraging them to contact you to talk about options. Know that someone in the family may block your client's receipt of your correspondence.

It is awkward when clients disappear because you never know if you may have said something wrong, they were just tired and wanted to try someone else, or what the reason may be. One thought is that you are a reminder of a problem they had/have, and if they have not made their goals, they may not want to be reminded of it.

It is frustrating to realize that you have invested care, time, and skills into helping a person, only to have him or her disappear. It is a loss and it is upsetting. One wonders how someone can open up to a counselor, especially when it may have been very hard for that person to do, and then just walk away. Unfortunately, that is the nature of the occupation.

Pray for them. Know that God will honor the effort you have poured into others' lives.

CHAPTER 13
Getting Started and Setting Goals

Getting Started

- Remember, throughout the session, make constant eye contact to show you are paying full attention.
- Now it's time to say,

"OK, your turn. So what brings you to counseling?"

Clients may tell you their whole life story, while others may recite a blame list and not take personal responsibility. Still others may talk about an issue that clearly isn't the real issue. Whatever they say, just listen and silently assess.

Coercion
If it is revealed that a client is in counseling because someone is forcing him or her—a partner, the courts, or an employer—be hopeful. Even though the person is there under duress, you can still be a seed planter and open his or her eyes to the possibilities of change. God will be at work in you.

Ask if the client cares how others perceive her or how her behavior affects others. Ask how much she values her relationship with whomever to change.

A Relapse
The client may have returned to counseling because there was a relapse or outbreak of the issues he or she has been or is working on in previous counseling or twelve-step groups. Ask for details.

"Before you relapsed, did you try anything different?" (Did the client try self-talk, prayer, leaving the situation, and so on?)

"Did you observe anything different?" (Was the client intimidated, emotional, feeling pressured, and so on?)

Teaching clients to *respond* rather than *react* (an essential goal) forces them to be observant of what is going on. They start to see things from a fresh perspective. They may say they saw their triggers, didn't react, and for the first time felt encouraged. Affirm their insight.

Thank them for sharing, and ask them to recap their goals in a few words.

Setting Goals

The client needs to come up with the goals, or you may not get the commitment from him or her to do the work. Goals need to be realistic. If there are multiple goals, ask him or her to prioritize them. Ask if he or she realizes that change takes time, and there are no quick fixes.

As stated, six to ten sessions of counseling are unfortunately the average, depending on the problem. That is also the average length of stay for most people seeking help because they primarily want to just get out of the pain or get the situation fixed. Unless they have been in counseling before, they don't appreciate how much time it typically takes to undo wrong behaviors in themselves let alone try to manage a partner's behavior.

Ideal and Acceptable Goals

They may also have to consider goals/outcomes that are acceptable and not necessarily ideal. Discuss what each would look like. If they have many goals, ask them where they want to start. Say,

"What are your goals for counseling?"

Clients may say, "To make my relationship better so we can get married." Ask,

"What needs to get better?" (Clients may give a list.)

"Do you think the relationship is a good fit? This means does he want to get married, too? Will he do whatever it takes to make the relationship better, like come to counseling?"

Accomplishing Goals

Ask clients,

"How will you know when you have reached your goals?"

Sometimes it is easy to figure out. They might say, "Not drinking for six months" or they might say something vaguer, like "My marriage will be *better*."
Keep talking together until you figure out what accomplishing the goal will concretely look like.

Then remind them, praise them, and caution them at each session when they do things that do or do not contribute to their goals.

Faith Goals

As a Christian service/ministry, encouraging clients to have *spiritual goals* is essential. It is always OK to ask what their thoughts are about faith and God, even to ask if they have put their trust in Jesus. What is revealed will probably need to be included in a goal of growing their faith.

Often, people who call themselves spiritual or Christians have a minimal "walk," and there is little if any fruit in their lives. They may be openly disobedient in several areas. An obvious goal would be to stop any ungodly behavior.

Let God lead you in helping their faith journey because their spiritual issues may be complicated and may not be their primary goal, at least at this point. You will be able to infuse sacredness into the session by your godly example. Be patient, and you will learn how they feel about faith and God as they share.

(See chapter 30, "Spiritual Issues and Personal Growth for Counselors and Clients.")

What Is the Real Problem?

Typically, the problem that is described is not the real problem.

For various reasons, clients will not see or admit the real problem. For example, the husband may be an alcoholic, and the wife is an enabler. She really does not want him to stop because this gives her something to complain about and focus on, instead of her own issues. A husband may say his wife spends too much time with the grandchildren, when he is really saying he misses her company but is angry that she does not want to be around him. Thus, the vicious cycle keeps turning. Parents may talk about their kids, when it is really a marital problem. Listen between the lines.

- Bringing up what you believe is the true goal can be threatening to clients and you can lose them. Work with the information and goals clients give you until they trust you. Every other week, you might ask if they want to continue working on the original goal. Then say something like,

"Because I see that you seem to want to talk about your husband's anger more than his drinking, shall we make a goal related to that?"

- Clients have to define their goals, but be aware that what they bring up is not typically their true goal. After they trust you, they may tell you the real goal, or it may be revealed along the way. Then you can ask if that issue is something they want to now include as a goal.

God Reveals Issues in Time

They may or may not be aware of the source of their pain. It may be buried subconsciously. If so, let it reside there. God will reveal the things He wants us to know and work on in His perfect timing. If He made all our faults and pains known to us at once, we would not be able to handle them. So if a client does not know or want to deal with the source, let it go. When he or she learns to trust you and does various homework exercises, he or she may open up.

CHAPTER 14
Counseling Strategies and Tools for Clients

Communication Tools Both You and Your Clients Can Use

The "Jesus model" is one strategy that enables clients to set communication boundaries. Jesus had a convicting way of teaching that revealed people's hearts and motives. Although He was asked many questions, *He often responded with a question—one that made the inquirer look at both his motives for asking and his heart.* This shifted the inquirer's focus from being about his agenda, to seeing a need for another way of thinking, feeling, and behaving. Then Jesus offered Himself and His teaching to replace what the inquirer knew.

It is important to take the time and anticipate the questions you can ask that will reveal a person's motives and heart. It is also noteworthy to resist giving answers to questions; let the client struggle and speak on his own terms.

The following application of the Jesus model is an effective communication tool for counselors and clients to use. When a client—or anyone else—asks a personal question that makes you or the client uncomfortable or feel intimidated by the way the question was asked, think about what you will say. *However, neither you or the client have to answer.* You or the client can manage the conversation, just as Jesus did. One can say something like

> *"That's an interesting question. I'm wondering why you want to ask me that."*

> *"I hadn't thought about that. What do you think?"*

> *"What would you do?"*

You or the client can also answer indirectly by saying something like

> *"We all have problems. Thank you for asking about mine. But I want to know how you are doing."*

Another response might be

> *"Perhaps we can talk about that sometime, but I wonder why you asked me."*

If they persist, respond with

> *"I'm puzzled as to why you are so determined to talk about this now."*

"Maybe sometime we can talk about this, but not at this time. So how are you doing?"

You can see that the strategy is to shift the conversation by setting boundaries around what and when *you* or *your clients* choose to talk about with others.

Gentleness

Jesus was also gentle, and His comforting presence invited trust. Gentleness is evidenced by a soft voice, open gestures, eye contact, and enrolling others to one's point of view *through conviction, not force*. Jesus wanted people to accept His teachings as desirable—as a higher standard—without being forced to adopt them. Gentleness is especially important both in grief work and in building trust.

Another way Jesus used His gentleness was when He was confronted by anger. He responded with tenderness to defuse the person's anger or to model forgiveness.

> **"A gentle answer turns away wrath, but a harsh word stirs up anger" (Proverbs 15:1).**

For example, teach clients what to say when someone says something mean to them. Teach them rather than reacting, do the following:

- Assume a gentle, open position.
- Continuously look the person who hurt them in the eye and almost in a pleading-for-their-insight way, say their name and then say with tender emphasis,

"Richard, that wasn't kind; it was very hurtful."

- Keep looking *through* them with the heart and tenderness of Jesus.
- Ignore *anything* they may say that is defensive. Let it go. You did your part.

It takes *tremendous* self-discipline to respond this way. Be inspired by how Jesus took so much and still forgave. Remember, it is not that person, but Satan, who is being mean. Let the Jesus in you convict the person. Let God's love show through you. It is powerful. You may well see the speaker stop in his or her tracks, feel shame, and perhaps even apologize.

- Have them ask for an apology if desired.

Develop Discernment

Discernment is a careful screening of what you are observing, hearing, or reading to test the truthfulness or integrity of the content. It is being sensitive to another's motives, being cautious regarding suspected false information. Some of us are more discerning than others and can see when a person is attempting to use us, or if you are in a helping ministry, seeing the client attempt to use the system.

A careful discerner can reveal a person's heart and motives quickly and then make more informed decisions about how to help him or her or even if helping is the best option to take. Learning about emotional manipulation will make you more discerning. (See the section on "Emotional Manipulation" in chapter 7, "Assessing the Problem: Understanding Client's Feelings and Reactions.")

Read between the Lines

Teach clients to read between the lines when communicating with others. This is valuable for counselors as well. Watch for the message behind clients' words. **"I'll never talk to my brother again."** This really means "He has really hurt me." **"I hate my job"** may mean "I'm not valued." **"He never compliments me"** may mean "I need attention; I have poor self-esteem, and his compliments would help." **"We have communication issues"** means "We argue, we don't talk, we avoid each other, and we don't resolve conflicts."

As you read between the lines, note what clients are inferring. Three examples reflecting the above exclamations follow:

"I hear your comment about your brother. No doubt it is painful for you to say that." (You are validating.)

"I wonder if you would agree that pain usually underlies our anger."

"Do you want to talk about how he hurt you so much?"

"I hear that you hate your job. That's hard to deal with." (You are validating.)

"How do they treat you at work?"

"Do you feel respected and valued?"

"I can see it's hurtful when your husband doesn't compliment you." (You are validating.)

"Has he ever complimented you?"

"Is something else going on that prompted him to stop?"

"In what areas do you want a compliment?"

Considerations about the last example above can tell you about her self-image. Then

- find the root of any hurtful and impactive things ever said to her (probably in her childhood),
- see how she felt when she was hurt, and
- help her see how her response has influenced her behavior today.

Mirroring

Mirroring is a classic communication tool used in psychology. In this exercise, before responding with one's own thoughts, the receiver needs to repeat what she thinks the other person said and/or is feeling. The person can summarize or repeat back as much as she thinks is needed to show she was listening attentively. The speaker then tells if she was heard correctly or not. To promote success in this exercise, do the following:

- Ask both people to look at each other and concentrate on what the other is saying. At the same time, they are to notice cues that reveal the emotions behind the words.
- One person repeats what he thinks the other person said and/or is feeling. He can summarize or repeat as many points as are needed to show he was listening attentively.
- The speaker then tells if she was heard correctly or not.

If you use this exercise in a session, be sure to find opportunities to offer positive feedback to encourage the participants or note the need for a correction. Remind them that this exercise takes practice. You might say,

"Good eye contact" or "Good start."

"Did anything else that was said strike you?"

Validating

The purpose of this is to encourage attentiveness when conversing. Many couples will say they have nothing to say to each other or the other person does not listen. Validating helps people focus during a conversation and lets the talker know he or she is being heard. This is a very, very important communication tool that few people practice.

- Essentially, it expresses an acknowledgment of how you believe the person felt after he said something, and *before* you talk.

For example, he said he had a hard day at work.

She would say, "Your job can take its toll; I hear that." (She is validating or showing that she is listening to more than what he is saying; she is *hearing* him.)

Now, to encourage that person who had a hard day, she can also add, "I'm proud of what a good worker you are." (Encouragement)

Other responses might be:

"I respect that you value working hard."

"I respect that you give 100 percent at your job."

"Even if your company doesn't always show you appreciation, I am sure God sees it and will reward you."

Another example for your clients: If your partner complains how irritating her mother can be. You can suggest they say,

"I can hear your frustration; it sounds stressful sometimes talking to her." (Validating)

"Based on what you're telling me about the conversation, I'd be frustrated, too." (Validating)

"Sounds like you were at your wits end!" (Validating)

To add encouragement, he or she could also say,

"You are a good daughter for making sure you call her weekly even when you need God's help to do it." (Encouragement)

Validating often combines "mirroring" with "encouraging."

Performer and Performance—the Double Shot

Another spin on this is to acknowledge the "performer" and "the performance." This tool helps with learning how to compliment and can build self-esteem for the receiver. This exercise is particularly helpful for children and teens who long for validation and need to build self-esteem. Men like this tool as they typically have a hard time coming up with compliments, so this double shot of validating the performance and the performer is seen as doubly helpful.

An example for your clients: Your wife made a great chicken dinner.

He can say,

"That chicken was great." (Complimenting or validating the performance)

Then also add a validation for the performer: "You are a great cook."

Here are some other examples:

"Thank you for the pretty card." (Performance)

"You are such a thoughtful person." (Performer)

"Your call to me the other day was nice." (Performance)

"I like your being so considerate when you know I worry about you." (Performer)

"You take good care of the yard." (Performance)

"I appreciate the fact you are a conscientious person." (Performer)

"Thanks for taking out the garbage." (Performance)

"You are a helpful person. I appreciate that." (Performer)

"I'm grateful you are a helpful person." (Performer)

"Thanks for cleaning your room." (Performance)

"You are a person who has pride in your home and respect rules. I like that." (Performer)

Journaling

Encouraging clients to journal is usually fruitful, but few sustain a commitment. Journaling does not have to be lengthy and can be written or recorded. Suggest to clients that they do the following:

- Date each entry to track progress with issues they are working on or activities and efforts that are significant.
- Just write a phrase about what happened. For example, "Went to counseling today."
- Describe a feeling about the activity or effort. For example,

"It was stressful, but I got through it."

"Had an argument with my mother again. Frustrated that I was intimidated by her and didn't use the counseling tool I was taught."

"Was ignored by my husband when I asked him about a chore he said he would do. I felt dismissed, invisible."

- Ask clients not to use the same *feeling words* more than once. They can get a list on the web if they search for "feeling words." This will encourage them to acknowledge and articulate their feelings, which helps to encourage their recognition of the spectrum of feelings. This may be a new experience for many clients who have detached (disconnected emotionally) or minimized their feelings.

As an incentive, ask if they will

- journal for just one week, and
- bring in their work and read it to you.

This says to clients that you care about their feelings, which may be a new experience for them. It also helps them realize they have a limited pool of feelings from which they have drawn, and that they need to honor all of their feelings while responding appropriately.

Journaling can also reveal the influence of medications a client is taking and adjustments that might be needed to help stabilize their moods.

Be an example

As a counselor and a person of faith, you need to be an example constantly.
Be able to

- share your *relevant* experiences *very briefly*, but
- focus on the recovery/restoration piece, and
- always give God the glory.

If you have never genuinely experienced repentance, you will not be able to see and sense it in others or lead them to it.

Assess regularly how you live out the fruit of the Spirit.

Your presence is everything. Remember, one reason people followed Jesus was because of His charismatic *presence*.

Model Praying (this is for counselors and clients)

Pray with sincerity, depth, and humility. Clients will learn from you. Wait a few seconds before you begin to pray for the Holy Spirit to guide your words. If you catch yourself being more concerned with what you are saying, it has become about you and not God. Refocus!

Have a Testimony (this is for counselors and clients)

Write down your testimony. Update it yearly. You will be surprised to see what you have learned. Encourage clients to do the same. Consider presenting your testimony to Celebrate Recovery for the benefit of clients in your counseling session or your Bible study or life group when they have testimonies. Remember the focus:

- Who I was, who I am, and who I hope to be as Christ works *through* me.

Discipline, a Godly Virtue

Learning how to be disciplined is essential to building self-esteem and godly character. You have to model it to be able to give meaningful examples. Ensure your lifestyle, exercise regimen, diet, health, faith practices, and so forth are worth respecting. If you have any undisciplined areas in your life, you will not be able to use examples from your own life to teach and model. You have to be disciplined.

Discipline is godly and is mentioned often in scripture. Discipline leads to the rewards of God's peace that passes all understanding as it builds dependence on God and leads to victories. It is also a great tool to develop self-esteem and to help manage addictions. For example, when you say to yourself, "I passed on dessert yesterday and that felt great; I can do it again today," or "God, you gave me the strength to ignore the drug dealer's calls yesterday. Thank You for rescuing me. With Your help, I made it through another day of abstinence, so I can do it again today."

These baby steps of discipline are building blocks to self-esteem and relying on God. It will not happen overnight, and we need lots of encouragement and accountability.

Build a support team and an accountability team you can call whenever you need strength. It will be especially helpful if they will pray for you and remind you of God's strength and how He is victorious.

(See chapter 30, "Spiritual Issues and Personal Growth for Counselors and Clients.")

Helping Clients Gain Insight

Let clients figure things out for themselves by talking while you listen attentively. Some clients gain insight from hearing themselves talk through an issue. That is a very helpful exercise for them. In addition, when they self-discover, there is more buy-in from them to acknowledge a situation and find a potential solution.

Letting clients do the majority of the talking is essential. Whether they talk out of nervousness or are trying to make sense of something, let them talk through it. (If they detour, remind them to get back on track.) It is rewarding to hear clients say, "Now that I hear myself talk, it sounds like I'm having a pity party," or "In telling you about this, I can see how emotional I am about it. I guess we need to do some work on it."

Modeling

When you speak to a person a client has come in with because of a mutual problem (parent and child, husband and wife, or cohabiting partners), you are always modeling a number of behaviors:

- body language
- voice tone
- vocabulary
- eye contact
- respect for both clients to observe and ideally replicate

Consider saying,

"Did you notice how I spoke to your daughter? How I validated her sharing?"

"Did you notice how you interrupted your wife?"

"Did you notice how you seem to start many of your comments about your husband with 'you' instead of using 'I' messages?"

"Your way is one way of looking at what was said. Another way is…" (give a suggestion).

"What do you think about that interpretation?"

"I hear your perspective on that. What do you think your husband would say?"

The Truth Will Set You Free

Tell the truth, and encourage clients to do the same. Not only is this biblical, but it also honors reality and your feelings. Additionally, it sets the stage for clarity. Understanding one's feelings is the beginning of freedom. Relief comes after a truthful admission. The truth will always set you free.

You will be surprised how often lies come up in the session. Clients will not tell the truth to you or someone else for various reasons—because of fear, because it is easier, because the truth is embarrassing, and so forth. On the other hand, a client may exaggerate blatantly. Call it for what it is when you hear it. The following shows how to pursue the truth with a client about her feelings.

The client says, "I ignored my mother's hurtful comment; that is just who she is."

Say,

"It's hard when anyone says hurtful things, especially your mom." (You are validating.)

"What would it be like for you to talk about that with her?"

(Response) "She would get mad and say I was rude for criticizing her."

> *"Let me offer you a way to handle this. When she says something hurtful, you can interrupt her and say, 'Excuse me, Mom, I know you love me and would never intentionally hurt me [validating]. Please know that what you just said was hurtful, so please do not say that again. Thank you.'"*

> *"Your mom may apologize or say something defensive. Let it go. You did your part. If it happens again, you know what to say. Your mom will learn that you have a boundary around what you will listen to."*

Teaching clients to honor their true feelings is important; otherwise, they will get resentful. Jesus said, **"You will know the truth, and the truth will set you free" (John 8:32 niv).**

Face the truth in every area. When you discern the slightest exaggeration or outright lie, say,

> *"Is that the whole truth?"* or *"I suspect that part of what you're saying is not the truth. What is that about?"*

Another example involves two people who are going through a hard time. One does something malicious, and the other does something back.

Ask why they retaliated. They will probably say,

"The other person shouldn't get off; he or she deserves to be punished."

You can say,

> *"God says that revenge is Mine. But I want to go to the emotion that prompted your action. What was it?"*

The client may not say he was hurt. Your goal is for him to admit the truth. Say,

> *"Jesus says the truth will set you free. What is the truth about your feelings?"*

Clients may not always answer, but by your asking, they will think about what was said.

Wrapping truth in love and grace is critical. It is better for the client if they learn to say to someone,

> *"You know I value our friendship* [validating with love], *so I need to tell you that I am worried about your drinking* [truth]. *I am here to help. Can we talk about it* [grace]*?"*

Another way is to remember that wrapping the truth in love and grace is a tool called the "Oreo Cookie Strategy." (See the appendix for this tool.)

Finally, as the counselor, during the session, **listen** 90 percent of the time, talk 10 percent, and pray constantly—period.

CHAPTER 15
Types of Questions to Ask and a Strategy to Ask Them

The following are ethical, practical, and godly considerations to take into account when you ask questions:

Be sure not to ask out of curiosity—always have a purpose.

Do not ask for details when you get the point. Time is limited.

Do not push when you sense clients have had enough, cannot process any more, or are wrestling with the pain of new revelations. Let them process their feelings and be respectfully silent. Do not rescue.

Silence is an effective counseling tool. Sometimes in the silence, the client, out of nervousness, will open up or explain additional thoughts.

Use the silence to pray silently and ask the Holy Spirit to guide you.

Do not fill in others' words for them. Honor their right to choose their own words, however long it takes. It also shows you are listening and not directing.

By asking carefully timed questions, you can move clients in and out of emotions, enabling them to tolerate as much as they wish.

Move between questions that engage their emotions and questions that engage their mind.

Encourage the client to reflect out loud on their behaviors. This balance keeps the session *safe* and is not overwhelming for the client.

Sometimes a client will sense you are giving him or her a rest emotionally and will say, "It's OK; I'm able to talk more about that."

Timing
Another important consideration is timing. You ideally want the client to leave a session feeling positive or at least encouraged. However, sometimes he or she will leave with dissonance, and this is OK too. Talk

about it next time. Gauge your interaction so you have enough time at the end of the session to allow the client to calm down and leave emotionally rested. If you are unable to achieve a place of encouragement at the close or during the session, you can pray at the end and express confidence in God's control over the situation.

An hour is typical, but you can do one and a half hours if you have the mental and emotional energy. Sometimes it is practical to do one and a half hours if there are time-availability issues that prevent clients from coming weekly for an hour, or if they are in crisis and need more time.

Last Call

Sometimes clients will bring up critical subjects near the end of the session. They may do this as a means of control, because they want more of your time, or because they appreciate your help. Be gentle but direct, and say,

> *"I'm sorry to interrupt you; however, what you're sharing is important and needs my full attention. I need more time than we have now. I would appreciate it if you'd hold that until our next session. Thank you."*

You show you are honoring them, not dismissing them, which is an emotional trigger for many clients.

Thinking, Feeling, and Action Questions

Each kind of question you ask provides helpful information about your client. We operate in three realms: thinking, feeling, and doing. Posing questions in each area gives a broader picture of the situation and of the people involved. Be careful not to sound judgmental with your questions or make comments like, "You didn't put up with that, did you?"; "I hope you aren't blaming yourself for that"; or "You poor kid. That was horrible." Such responses will shame the person and shut him or her down.

- When you are not asking a question, you most likely should be validating by nodding in understanding and/or encouraging the client to keep talking, and listening attentively.
- Start with the least threatening realm—the **thinking realm**—or try to determine factually what happened. The client will feel safer if you begin with a "head" question.
- Try to keep the client in the realm you are attempting to cover, knowing he or she will detour back to the head or thinking realm. This realm is the least threatening emotionally.
- Be careful not to drill down with your questions.
- Be comfortable and silent with long pauses, and make comments to validate correct thinking, feeling, and actions.
- Try to normalize their feelings if they are being truthful. For example,

"Anyone would be frightened by what you went through."

"It would be normal to feel confused in that situation."

Ask, *"What were you thinking when…"*

- Move to the **feeling realm**:

"Would you tell me what you were feeling when that was happening?"

They may struggle to find words to express what they were feeling because they may have suppressed their thoughts and feelings about the matter. They may have shut down their feelings and learned to only admit to themselves a few generalized feelings, like "sad," "OK," "not that bad," and "confused."

- Encourage them to think of other descriptive words to help grow their personal vocabulary about feelings.

To drill deeper, ask,

"Please give me another feeling word for what you were experiencing."

Validate by saying, *"Good/yes, and another word?"*

- Don't suggest. Let them do the work. They may give you action or doing words or phrases, so gently correct them and persist in getting at least a couple of feeling words.

Then ask (note that this is now the *doing* or *action realm*),

"What did you do then?"

Their tone or answer may reveal their shame.

- Be careful that your expression or response does not judge them in any way.

The Past

Subjects in the here and now may be harder to talk about than those that are historical. Sometimes, the past will come up along the way; other times, you need to go directly there.

"I appreciate what you're telling me about your marriage, and it leads me to wonder about your parents' marriage. Can we talk about that a bit?"

Moving in and out of the present and past can also give emotional relief. When dealing with the past, discern how it affects them in the present.

Expressions to Encourage Continued Talking

"I'm getting to know you."

This can be said in order to thank a client for sharing, especially something personal. It is an encouragement.

Sometimes clients will say they resent someone presuming to know them when they really do not. I see this as an indirect warning to counselors. The client is cautious and appropriately controlling about what he shares and when he wants to share. He wants to do this in his own time, not because the counselor is trying to pull information out of him.

> *"Help me understand."*

This can be said when the client is not being clear. It is a more gracious way of asking for clarification than asking, "What do you mean?" It also gives some power to the client in a counselor-client dynamic where the counselor is typically seen as having the upper hand.

Remember to lean forward when the client is sharing something difficult or very personal to show that you are really listening. Do not stay in that position too long, though, as it implies "tell me more" and he or she may be in overload. When you sit back in your chair, you are sending the client a subtle message that it is OK to rest a bit from that tough subject, if needed.

Sample Questions for Use in Various Situations

Mischievous Smiling

Sometimes a client will smile and seem to gloat as she recollects something she did, such as getting high, getting into some mischief, or engaging in sexual activity. This reveals she is still attached to the emotion that the act provided. Call her on it. Say,

> *"What does your smiling about that mean to you?"*

Her answer will reveal much. If she is smiling out of fond memories, this reveals she is not fully claiming the wrongness of her actions. Granted, sometimes our childish pranks are laughable, but if what she is talking about has had serious and hurtful consequences to her or others, her reaction is inappropriate. You can say,

> *"The fact that you are smiling telling me about this incident seems to reveal that you consider it a fond memory. That concerns me. Do you know why it concerns me?"* (Then see if she has any idea.)

If she is smiling out of embarrassment, she may switch expressions quickly and say, "It's embarrassing to admit that my action was stupid." You can thank her for her willingness to talk about it. You can say,

> *"I'm getting to know you and beginning to understand you; thank you for helping me do that by being honest."* (You are validating.)

Painful Memory
When clients share something that was said to them that was no doubt a painful memory, ask,

"What was that like for you to hear/experience that?"

If they have buried their feelings, this question may help them begin to work through them.

- Be patient and wait for the response.
- As discussed elsewhere, consider drilling down with feeling words so the client can name as many feelings as possible. Pursue the expressed feelings where applicable.
- Encourage and affirm along the way.

Opening Their Eyes
A question to help clients realize that it is not just about them is

"How is your behavior impacting others?"

The Impact on Kids
A question to help them realize how their kids are being impacted is

"What are you teaching your kids about marriage and relationships when they witness you arguing and yelling?"

No Motivation
When clients do not seem motivated or do not like their options, ask,

"What are you willing to change?"

Payoffs or Rewards
There is always a payoff for everything we do, and sometimes clients know this and admit it, and sometimes they don't. An example is clients who act out promiscuously after they have been molested. They are acting out how they feel about themselves: damaged. Ask,

"What is the payoff for your behavior?"

Go to the Here and Now
When there isn't time or motivation to explore the past, ask,

"How does the past affect you now? Sometimes it doesn't matter how you got where you are; let's work on the here and now," or *"Let's work on where you want to go from here."*

Another question would be,

"OK, here we are (for example, you have an admitted addiction); where do you want to go from here?"

Feelings
A good question to help clients claim their feelings and have freedom to voice them is

"What was that like for you?"

Alienating Others
When a client admits he alienates people but really does not understand why, you can ask,

"I have some thoughts about it, but it may be hard to hear. Do you want to hear them?"

Then be silent and see what the client says. If he says, "Talk," thank him for being open enough to hear what you have to say. This is a good opportunity to practice the "Oreo Cookie Strategy." (See the appendix.)

The Christian Perspective
Because most clients will claim to be Christians, feel free to say,

"As a Christian, would you like to know what the Bible has to say about that?" (You can ask this of non-Christians, too; who knows where this might lead?)

If the client says they want to know, then look up the topic and passage right there.

Get the Impact
To learn more than the facts, ask,

"How did that impact you?"

The Past
Put the past in perspective. It is difficult to help clients see the past as just that—the past. Ask,

"How do the things of the past affect you today?"

Help clients see that

- we can't change the past;
- the issue is not with the past—*it's their present perception of the past*;
- in counseling, they can get another perspective on the past and learn to accept it while not condoning it; and
- if they can learn to think and feel differently (that is called assigning new meaning to something), a client can change his or her behavior or attitude.

Visualize Forward

To help them visualize forward and not get stuck in recent pain, you can ask,

"What do you want your life to look like from now on?"

SECTION V
Foundational Information and Strategies for Managing Common Issues

CHAPTER 16

Sexual, Physical, and Emotional Abuse, and Anxiety

Suspected Sexual Abuse

The following material is primarily for sexual abuse but may apply to physical abuse as well.

This may be a painful subject and must be handled very delicately. If clients have addressed these issues with previous counselors and say they don't need to talk about it at this time, honor that.

Some clients will talk about their current problematic marriage or intimate relationships and spontaneously say, "I have had some abuse." Or they may say, "Something that happened to me when I was younger may be part of the problem." It is good they are opening up, so proceed gently.

Some clients will not label abuse (especially sexual abuse) as that. It is too horrifying for them. One way to pursue this area, if the timing is right and you feel you have a trusting relationship with a client, bypass the word *abuse* by substituting "being touched in an inappropriate way." Sometimes a client will readily admit to this but not to abuse.

After you have established rapport and have some sense of the client's openness, and when it is relevant to the conversation, gently ask,

"Has anyone ever touched you or physically hurt you in a way that made you uncomfortable or angry?"

"Was this as a child or later in life?"

(This is a safe way to broach the subject without labeling what may have happened as abuse, which is hard for some clients to admit. It is also hard for them to realize that someone they know or love has abused them. Later on in counseling, it can be valuable to call it what it was—abuse.)

"Would you want to tell me a little more about that?"

"Did you tell anyone? If so, what was that person's reaction?"

Family Denial

Because of dysfunctional family dynamics, family members will often deny abuse. This is true of mothers, especially if the abuser was the husband or boyfriend. She will often shut down and totally deny even the thought of it because it is too painful and embarrassing, because it may cause legal and financial problems, and because she feels guilty that she did not protect the child or catch what was going on, and so on.

Family Secrets

The mother may accuse the victim and then punish her severely for lying or telling, and demand that it is never brought up again. These are called family secrets, and sometimes they do not become known until the children are adults and decide to share what happened. Even then, the mother may still deny it, minimize the facts, minimize the victim's feelings once again, and dismiss it as history.

This parental response of "don't talk, don't tell" is confusing to the victim, who then questions her mother (or older sister if that is the case) as a protector, as well as her own sense of right and wrong. The victim becomes angry at being dismissed and frightened because she knows the abuse will continue. She may keep those emotions buried deep inside for years.

A Case Example

A young woman was raped multiple times by her father. The girl stuffed her emotions and grew into a vibrant, loving wife and socialite. Fifty years later, something triggered those memories, and she instantly suffered posttraumatic stress and became catatonic (nontalking, robot-like, terrified, and childlike). She had to be institutionalized and remained in that condition without successful intervention. Counselors, as well as relatives and friends, need to guard their questions and comments on delicate subjects such as sexual abuse and trauma, as it is possible to retraumatize a victim.

Shifting the Anger

It is significant to note that a victim's anger may be shifted to the mother, as opposed to the abuser, who typically is someone known, like the father, stepfather, brother, uncle, or babysitter. This is because the mother is an accessible target for anger, whereas abusers hold their threats over the victim, and that fear is very real. Later in life when coping mechanisms are revealed to the victim, she sees her displaced anger, and that is when work needs to take place so that her feelings for the abuser also can be healed.

Scapegoat

Siblings, who may or may not have been victimized also, in their effort to not deal with their own pain and anger, may select one person to be the scapegoat. This is the person who is chosen to bear the blame for all the family problems, whether they are at fault or not. Families do this to distract from their own issues. Your client may have experienced being the sibling or family scapegoat, and this will be revealed as he or she talks about that role in the family. (See the section on "Family Roles" in chapter 18, "A Perspective on Our Family of Origin's Influence.")

Fear

"If you didn't tell anyone about the abuse, was there a reason why?"

The abuser usually threatens harm to the victim, a family member, or pet if he or she tells. Sometimes victims carry so much fear, shame, and blame that they cannot verbalize it.

Opening up and talking about this is huge for clients who have not previously taken care of the issue successfully. So go slowly and let them set the pace. Be sure to follow up in the next session. Make a note to ask how they felt after the previous week's session.

Self-Blame

Victims may try to make sense of what happened to them by blaming themselves. This is wrong thinking.

Gently correct their thoughts, leaving brief pauses between your phrases so the client can absorb them.

"You were a child, he was an adult, and you did not understand what was going on. He was wrong and took advantage of your age and fears. No one deserves to be taken advantage of, especially children—especially by someone you should be able to trust. Can you see that it was not your fault?"

Be still and let them digest this. It may be good news to them. However, they may still not trust what you are saying, so you may need to repeat it.

"Let me say that again, because it is important, and I want you to take it in."

Then repeat it slowly. You can also ask the client to tell you what he or she thought you just said. They may still have doubts.

Mixed Emotions

One possible reason victims have mixed-emotions may be that the abuse felt pleasurable. Some fondling may feel good to a child, whereas most other sexual abuse acts do not. (Of course, if the abuse was rape or repeated outrageous violations, even as a teen or young adult, this is another story, and the client should be referred to a professional.) Be careful not to minimize. Any inappropriate touching may be traumatizing.

"One reason this may be so conflicting emotionally for you is that you recall some pleasure with the emotional confusion you were feeling. This is normal." (Then explain the above statements.)

Refer victims who were used by parents or caretakers for prostitution, voyeurism, or pornography to a professional.

The statistics on sexual assault/abuse are staggering—one in three women is suspected to be a victim.

Using Joyce Meyer as an inspiration is helpful. When she was a young girl, her father abused her sexually for years. She went on to share her grief and God's miraculous healing to the world and create a worldwide Christian ministry. She healed her relationship with her father before he died. Remarkable! Her book, *Beauty for Ashes*, is a must-read for counselors and clients who were abused.

The book *Mending the Soul*, by Steven Tracy, and Tracy's associated support groups are also excellent recovery tools; the book in particular is another great read for counselors and clients. There are many excellent resources to help with this issue. Go online.

In a testimony I once heard, a survivor of sexual abuse said her abuse was like a train running alongside her life. Even though it was always terrifyingly present, she was detached from it. She worked hard to free herself from the toxic shame she felt. While she waited for that deliverance, she worked the Twelve Steps of Celebrate Recovery and received counseling. She advised other survivors to "take the sins you have done as well as the sins that have been done against you—take them all to the Cross. Claim back all that was stolen from you."

> **Be encouraged by the Lord's words "I will restore to you the years that the swarming locust has eaten" (Joel 2:25 nkjv).**

Physical Abuse

Physical abuse is intentional bodily injury that is anything from a hard slap to pulling, punching, shoving, twisting, banging, cutting, scalding, or burning. Injuries are often covered with clothing. Victims make excuses, such as "I fell," "A door closed on me," or "A pot fell off the stove." This cover-up is done out of fear of the resulting consequences to themselves or their loved ones if the injury is reported to the authorities.

This is serious and could even be a life-or-death situation at some point, so this is a case that is best referred to a professional or applicable resources. You are required to report child/minor abuse to Child Protective Services (CPS). Elder abuse is reportable to the proper authorities as well. If in doubt, ask a professional or call the CPS hotline. The consent form that a client signs when he or she is first introduced to counseling alerts him or her that you are required to report any serious abuse.

If you are in a position where the client did not sign a form (for example, during a more casual conversation or where information was revealed about the abuse of someone else), you still need to report it. Advise the client as soon as the conversation starts revealing the abuse that what he or she says may require reporting to CPS. Will this reporting threaten your relationship with the person or client? Probably, but it is the law. You can encourage clients by letting them know that getting help will be to their advantage if CPS indeed finds a cause to investigate.

For those who need to, but will not see a professional, consider exploring the following comments to open their eyes and assess the situation.

Witnessing abuse can be traumatic and prompts emotional insecurity in children and adolescents. It is obviously bad role modeling. It can cause physical and emotional reactions in others, such as bedwetting, poor grades, isolation, and tantrums in children.

Victims of physical abuse try to hide the effects and make excuses for the injuries. They do this out of embarrassment and fear of retaliation by the abuser if he or she is accused. The abuser may be repeating what his or her parent(s) did to him or her and out of anger repeat the abuse. Some abusers have stuffed their own pain so deep that they have rationalized that abusive behavior is no big deal and treat their loved ones with repeated beatings, whippings, and slaps, sometimes daily for years. Hearing such horror stories is not unusual, so be prepared.

The damage done in these situations is tremendous, and the victim carries battered emotions into adulthood. The damage hinders healthy development of their relationships.

Emotional Abuse

Emotional abuse occurs when the victim is intentionally verbally abused, battered, belittled, insulted, cursed at, or threatened with physical harm. The abuser is in control of the relationship and lords it over the other person.

The abuser criticizes the victim so much that he or she begins to believe that the abuser's words are true. The abuser typically is a controlling person who does not want the other person to discuss what is going on, thinking that the influence of others will prompt the victim to leave.

The abuser criticizes the other person's family and friends because he or she is threatened by the relationships. This is an attempt to prevent the person from associating with others. He or she does this by making demands, scheduling other essential activities when the victim wants to see friends or family, taking the car keys, or taking the only car and not divulging the destination or time of return. The abuser may start an argument so the victim is too upset to leave. Isolation from others is a key strategy that is used. (See the section on "Emotional Manipulation" in chapter 7, "Assessing the Problem: Understanding Clients' Feelings and Reactions.")

Emotional Issues—A Quick Assessment

Emotional issues can be overwhelming or annoying, depending on the person experiencing them. Assess the depth of the problem and then refer to a professional if needed.

For emotional abusers:

> *"Do your emotions get out of control?"*

> *"Do your emotions rule you?"*

> *"What are your triggers?"*

"What feelings do the triggers arouse?"

"What do you typically say and do?" (Drink, eat, take drugs, sleep, or pray?)

"Can you handle your emotions better with some people than with others?"

"Can you handle your emotions better under some circumstances than others?

"What are some examples?"

"Do you see your response as a choice?"

Search for Emotions Anonymous (a twelve-step program) on the web to gain more information about serious emotional issues. Their resources can help you gain an understanding of people with mental health issues or disabling anxiety.

Read about all of these issues addressed more thoroughly elsewhere in this book, as well as online. It is inevitable that more issues than those presented initially will come up. Be prepared.

For Generalized Emotional or Anxiety Issues

"When did you begin to experience these feelings?"

"What specifically happens when you get anxious?"

"What kinds of situations are you in?"

"How long does it last?"

"What do you do?"

Seeking the cause of anxiety:

"Can you cite a possible cause?"

"What have you done to address it?" (Legal and illegal medications, doctors, counseling, and so on.)

"Did you follow the advice given to you? Did it change anything?"

"How has your anxiety impacted your daily life?" (Does not leave the house, reduced social activities, cannot work, and so on.)

Managing anxiety includes distracting one's mind from the obsessive thoughts. Selecting one issue to focus on managing in one's mind. Assess the catastrophic thinking and counter it with realistic thoughts. Add only positive thoughts. Only allow 10 minutes of being preoccupied with the issue, then distract yourself by doing something soothing and healthy (pray, call someone and don't talk about yourself, exercise, dance, etc.) After you have managed that one issue, you probably won't need to continue to be distracted at that time. If you are still anxious, start on another source of your anxiety and repeat the process. Remember that your mind dictates your feelings so what you think about will temper your emotions. You do have more control than you think or believe.

CHAPTER 17
Why People Stay in or Return to Abusive Relationships

There are several potential reasons why people stay in or return to obviously unhealthy relationships. One or more of the following reasons may apply to your client's situation.

- **Fear** that the abuser will hunt her down and hurt her, her children, pets, family, or property
- **Denial**
- **No transportation** to get away
- **No financial resources** or not enough funds to survive elsewhere
- **No housing options** because the social service housing resources may be at capacity, are not safe for small children, or are not accessible
- **Ineligible for assistance** because she has exhausted her allowable opportunities for help
- **Using drugs or alcohol** chronically, so she can't function
- **No one** to take care of the children, pets, and so on.
- **Addiction to the relationship** and all that comes with it. This is a common explanation and occurs for a number of reasons. The abuser has so exhausted the emotional strength of the partner that she cannot function clearly. The abuser has emotionally manipulated her to the point that she feels trapped and without options. The abuser has convinced the partner that no one else would put up with or even want her.

(See the sections on "Addictive Relationships" and "Emotional Manipulation" in chapter 19, "Marital and Relational Issues.")

- **The couple thrives on the drama** of breaking up and getting back together. This adds distraction and excitement to an otherwise depressing situation. The abuser apologizes and convinces the partner that he or she is sorry and will not do it again—they will get help. Unfortunately, the abuse typically continues and escalates, and the abuser usually will not get help or stay in counseling if he goes.

(See the section on "Love and Relationship Addictions" in chapter 19, "Marital and Relational Issues.")

Your strategy is to find out the following from the client:

- The amount of time the relationship has had serious problems
- What has been tried to change the situation (counseling, rehab, groups, and so on.)
- What worked, what didn't, and why

- The extent of the physical, verbal, and emotional abuse
- What his/her expectations are for the relationship (leave, stay, get help, try one more time, and so on.)
- What he or she will consider doing if counseling doesn't change things

Explain relationship addiction and ask if he or she sees that as an accurate description of the relationship. This will tell you the level of denial and help you and your client set realistic goals. (Obviously, if either person has physical addictions, these need to be addressed first.) Often the person will not see the relationship as addictive, as he or she will have conflicting emotions about the person (love and hate/frustration, loyalty but also wanting to leave).

Explain that he or she is emotionally conflicted and that is why it is so difficult to make a decisive move regarding the relationship. There may be other circumstances (religious commitments, family pressures, and so on) that add extra pressure to remain. Assess all of these.

Case reflection: Another counselor referred a woman who was codependent to me. Tina was more than just codependent; she was obsessed with the relational connection with her abuser. They had been on and off for two decades, with drama galore in the exits and reunifications. He was clearly emotionally manipulative and had demeaned her to the point where she felt beyond worthless and was certainly not able to make a healthy life on her own.

One minute she could admit the damage he had done; the next, she claimed she deserved it because when they fought, she was hostile and deserved to be treated badly. She frequently called for an emergency appointment in addition to her weekly appointment. I usually was able to talk with her briefly and postpone a crisis appointment. She revealed that she had been diagnosed with borderline personality disorder earlier in her life, which explained much of her behaviors. I had given her some of the paperwork off the Co-Dependents Anonymous (CoDA) website to complete in order to assess the extent of her codependency. She was off the charts on most scores. She rarely listened to any coaching as she thrived on the drama of the relationship. Her mantra was, "I know it is an unhealthy relationship, but I love him and can't live without him."

She was an extremely draining client to work with. Although she was bright, pretty, and had a good personality, she did not see any of these assets or her potential capability to move on. After about six sessions in counseling, I suggested to her that she change one thing to move forward or I would need to refer her elsewhere. She tried unsuccessfully and then dropped out. She did call me a few months after her last session (in crisis) and wanted to come back. I did not resume counseling with her, and told her she needed a psychotherapist.

The lessons I learned: I should have had the client sign a release of information in the first session so I could talk to the referring therapist. I probably would not have taken the case had I had more information, as I am sure the therapist knew she had borderline personality disorder.

If you think you would benefit from another professional's insight into a client's life, secure consent to contact him or her early on as you may realize the case is out of your league or that there is an unlikely chance that the client will change. You need to decide how best to use your precious time. Remember, you do not have to rescue the world.

I also should have asked the client earlier on if she had ever been diagnosed. To my error, I got somewhat caught up in her drama and was preoccupied by getting her calmed down rather than getting a thorough medical/mental history. This was early in my counseling practice, and now I am wiser. It is easy to be overinvolved, distracted from an appropriate agenda, and caught up in the drama. Clients in these addictive and abusive relationships thrive on drama. It is their emotional connection when a genuine and healthy emotional connection does not exist. So be on guard.

I currently have another client with borderline personality disorder who is also bipolar. She lapses into drama frequently, but it is short lived, and when she calms down, she is well aware of the seduction of her moods and her yielding to drama. She, too, is in a blatantly emotionally abusive relationship but chooses to have fantasies about it turning out like the American dream. She makes progress, although it is only in inches, and she is very conscientious about keeping appointments. I set very clear boundaries about her behavior with me (she can be very time consuming), and she honors those boundaries. Although she is trying to leave the relationship, she admits that if he wants her, she runs to him. It is a painfully slow process of rebuilding her self-esteem and convincing her to rely on God for strength to honor her own boundaries.

CHAPTER 18

A Perspective on Our Family of Origin's Influence

The Role of Our Families in Shaping Who We Are Today

Our family experience may be the source of our unresolved behavioral issues, but that is no excuse for not being accountable for our behavior and choices today.

Our Parents

Studies show that our families, particularly our parents, have a tremendous impact on our lives—more than any other influence. When a parent is absent emotionally or physically, significant emotional consequences occur. We may become excessively independent of them or too emotionally dependent on others as a defense. We all look to our same-sex parent to provide role modeling in a number of areas, and to both parents to show us how to manage social and marital relationships. Each parent becomes a role model, whether it is healthy or not.

We are born with an innate desire to please our parents and to feel valued by them. When they are not responsive, for whatever reason, we question our worth and may try to earn acceptance by achieving success in school, sports, or our careers. Some turn to gangs, cults, the drug world, or the bar scene to feel a sense of belonging, even though it comes at a high moral price.

Sometimes a parent figure, a relative, or a family friend, may provide some of the missing parental influence, and that is helpful. Studies have shown that children raised in dysfunctional families, even those who have been in multiple foster homes, have done well if they have even just one person in their life who is stable, who is invested in them, and who is trustworthy. Grandparents or other close relatives, especially today with so many single-parent families, usually have a positive impact on family dynamics and can fill that longing for stability and love.

In most families, a child—for example, a son—may take on a role that serves a purpose, either to cope with a personal situation or to help fuse the family. Sometimes, if there is tension or extreme dysfunction, especially between the parents, the children will attempt to divert their parents' attention from arguing and direct it elsewhere, even to themselves.

Children may or may not keep these roles or show a strong semblance of them as adults. If, as adults, they become aware of the roles they played as children and then see how they continued to play the roles as adults, they have the opportunity to change or modify the roles. These adaptive roles are defenses or coping mechanisms. However, the roles that may have worked when they were children may not be appropriate or healthy when they are adults. Usually, clients can see the "there and then" connection and are inspired to change their role to what is appropriate for the here and now.

Some of these family and childhood roles are as follows:

The Martyr

The mother typically plays the martyr. She claims to be unselfish and giving, but underneath she is resentful and tries to make others feel guilty by wrapping her sacrificial choices in dramatic self-denial. For example, she might say, "No, you take the last piece of meat; I don't really need to eat any meat today." "No, I don't mind being alone on Thanksgiving while all my neighbors are spending the day with their families." A martyr tries to make others feel sorry for her and guilty so they will do what she wants.

(See chapter 24, "Codependency"; chapter 10, "Understanding Clients' Coping Mechanisms and Boundaries"; and the section on "Emotional Manipulation" in chapter 7, "Assessing the Problem: Understanding Clients' Feelings and Reactions.")

The Ruler

The father typically plays this role, but the mother can also play it overtly (openly) or covertly (hidden). The ruler finds security in ordering rules to be followed because this gives a sense of control. However, it prevents any input from others, even if the rules are unreasonable. The rules may be known or never articulated. For example, one unspoken rule might be, "Don't argue with Dad because he will blow up" or "Don't complain about anything or Mom will start crying."

(See section III, "Foundational Material to Know before You Begin.")

The Lost Child

This person is ignored because of the drama that goes on with either the parents or other siblings. The lost child retreats into his or her room or some other quiet place and may read or play alone, trying to not be a bother, add to the commotion, or get involved in the drama.

(See chapter 24, "Codependency.")

The Superstar

This child tries to excel in academics or sports to get longed-for recognition. The time invested in these activities becomes a legitimate way to avoid the drama at home. These people frequently keep this role and become super successful in their careers.

The Scapegoat

This person is blamed for everything whether or not it is true. He or she becomes the source of all the problems and a distraction for people not to focus on their own problems. Sometimes the scapegoat will facilitate or encourage this role to protect others, like a brother with a disability, an abused mother, or younger helpless siblings.

(See chapter 24, "Codependency.")

The Drama Queen/King

This person likes attention and makes a drama out of everything, good or bad, causing everyone else to help her/him resolve the "crisis" or give her/him attention.

(See the section on "Emotional Manipulation" in chapter 7, "Assessing the Problem: Understanding Clients' Feelings and Reactions" and chapter 10, "Understanding Clients' Coping Mechanisms and Boundaries.")

Dysfunctional Families

Dysfunctional family structures and behaviors have been cited as one potential cause for homosexuality, addictions, poor school performance, and other behaviors.

A dysfunctional family has weak or unhealthy parental modeling, boundary violations, inconsistency, frequent crises, and often an underlying message of "don't talk, don't feel, don't trust, and don't tell." Children especially are self-taught to cope in a way that helps them manage the situation. Sometimes the degree of dysfunction is not realized until the children, later as grown adults, begin to compare how they were raised with other households. For example, they may know something is not right about incest but are not sure, and so they do not tell. Others may think every household has yelling and cursing or is physically abusive.

It is alarming to listen to clients tell what it was like to grow up or how their parents interacted. So often, the adult client replicates those behaviors and is not sure what is really wrong or if it is fixable. Help them gain a perspective and hope.

Are many families dysfunctional? Yes, many. Do those in the family see it as such? No, not often. Does anyone want to change? Not unless it causes a problem, like a potential divorce or a runaway child. Can a dysfunctional family be changed? Yes. If even one person changes, the whole family dynamic shifts. Is there pressure on the person who is trying to change to not rock the family boat? Yes. There is tremendous pressure, guilt, and anxiety, but with support, helpful tools consistently applied, and faith, they can break the cycle.

The Role of Each Parent/Gender

The following generalizations are just that. They are meant to show the contrasts between men and women and how God made them to complement each other, rather than to be in conflict or competition. They were made to balance each other. Are there reverses in these generalizations sometimes, and is that OK? Yes. Is this list complete? No. Are these characteristics the standard? No, but they are often a cultural model. It is important that children be *exposed to healthy and affirming role models in both sexes* and that they identify with the person of their own sex to help build their personal identity and emotional autonomy.

Men (and fathers) represent masculinity, protection, decisiveness, strength, emotional maturity, and steadfastness. They are the ones who take care of things, the providers. Men are typically "doers" and especially bond with other men through activities or sports and afterward may discuss some emotional issues. Women (and wives) represent femininity and nurturing and are more open to change than being decisive. They are emotionally sensitive and flexible but determined, and they are typically caretakers.

Fathers who demand an interest in sports, despite a child's preference to be artistic, can cause shame and mutual frustration. A father who shows little emotional expression toward a son can prompt the boy to seek it from his mother. That can keep him from being comfortable with men. Male peers and the activities boys engage in provide opportunities to build playfulness and teasing, and help boys become comfortable with the way men and boys interact.

Men view their bodies in terms of *how they function*, so sports become relevant to their gauge. Success is more often measured in position and salary than other factors. Hence, men may have a different frame of reference for their emotions, interests, and measures of success than women do.

Women typically relate more by connecting emotionally than by doing something together. They are generally more comfortable with their emotions and do not need to spend a lot of time *doing* something together to be able to share comfortably.

Women see their bodies based on appearance. Hence, as an example, the dramatically higher incidence of eating disorders in females than males. Women measure their acceptability with more emphasis on appearance than function, their success on how people relate to them, and how they manage their household, regardless of their economic status.

Children gravitate toward mom for the first year, and by the second year begin to identify with the parent of the same sex. If a parent is absent physically or emotionally, there may be an overreliance on the available parent and that parent's characteristics may be more nurturing than those of the same-sex parent. Sometimes this prompts role confusion early on. The characteristics of the same-sex parent need to be affirmed in the child and encouraged, or the child will gravitate to where he or she gets affirmation. Without that affirmation, he or she may not be comfortable with his or her gender identity.

Childhood friends are critical to bonding, especially for boys, so they learn competitiveness, physical competency, playfulness, strength, sharing, teasing, and so on.

The increase of fathers as single parents or stay-at-home dads is noteworthy. How this shift affects the health and dynamics of the family model is to be seen. It would appear to be favorable; however, the ideal is still a two-parent (a man and a woman) parental model as it is biblical and functionally optimal.

The Influence of Our Parents' Marriage

We tend to repeat the roles we played in our families later in life unless we acquire an abundance of insight through reading, prayer, or counseling. Our parents' marriage influences the way we manage our marriage. We typically choose to marry someone who is like our opposite-sex parent, but sometimes like the same-sex parent. We do this whether the parent was good or bad.

We may repeat this, perhaps because

- it is familiar;
- it is desirable on some level even though it was dysfunctional;
- we have no clue how to change things;
- we fear making a change;
- we want to fix the relational dynamics now that we as adults have some power, because we didn't as kids; or
- we want to punish our parents through our partner because we couldn't react at the time.

Outsiders sometimes observe, "You're just like your father/mother." You may say, "Gosh, I'm acting just like my mother!" or "When my husband yells, it reminds me of my father, and I freak out." Clients gain insight when they see the potential reasons they partnered with someone who is like one of their parents. Ask if they think any of the above bulleted reasons may be true for them.

It is very helpful to learn about the marriage of a parent or the parent figure who played that role for them. You might say,

"I would like to understand about how you grew up. Would you tell me about your parents' marriage?"

"Are they still married?"

"Do you think they had a happy marriage? Why?"

"Were they affectionate?"

"Did they argue?"

"What was that like?"

"Was there yelling?"

"Who was the boss in that marriage?"

Ask if your client

- would be willing to describe each parent, and
- would share what he or she knows about how each one grew up.

You will typically see a pattern because the client will be much like his parent. Because the behavior is passed down through generations, it is rarely questioned. "That's how my father treated me, and that's how you are being treated."

Helping clients see the good and the bad in the way they were raised and its influence on them, without sounding condemning or judgmental, is helpful for them. You can be direct if it seems appropriate. For example:

"From what you are telling me, it sounds like abuse. What do you think?"

His or her response will let you know how defensive he or she is. Or,

"You were emotionally abused, and that sounded horrific."

"What is running through your mind as you tell me about it?"

This response leaves clients with the choice to "take what they like (from your observations) and leave the rest," as they say in Alcoholics Anonymous (AA). They may or may not want to talk more about it.

Values

We acquire our values mostly from our parents and the way we were raised. Other adult influences can be teachers, relatives, clergy, camp staff, and so forth. Those values may be good or bad and may have served us well or they may have been problematic.

For example, a parental value might be "all work and no play" or "we go to church three times a week—period." This rigidity can bring resentment because of its inflexibility, and sometimes children will be defiant and turn the other way completely when they get older.

- Learn about the family's values from a client and what the client thinks of them today.
- It is important to understand a client's value system without judging it.

Even when a value may be clearly dysfunctional to you, the client may not choose to acknowledge it for various reasons that he or she may or may not verbalize. For example, he or she may be thinking, "This would make my parents wrong. Then I couldn't trust their judgment, and I would feel insecure," or "Even if it is not a good value, it's what the family practices, and I don't want to be different," or "There will be sanctions if I disagree."

Asking a person about his or her values as you go along or on an inventory sheet yields a lot of helpful information.

(In premarital counseling, sharing and understanding values is critical because it reveals how each person grew up. See the sections on "Parent and In-Law Issues" and "Premarital Counseling" in chapter 19, "Marital and Relational Issues.")

- Remind clients that God enlightens our wrong thinking in stages. He opens our eyes to another way of looking at life at a pace that will help us—a pace we can handle. If God were to allow all of our warped thinking to be exposed all at once, we would be overwhelmed and probably want to give up.

So do not be impatient with clients when they do not see things as you do. Realize that the way they (or you) see things is not necessarily accurate. Keep trying to understand the way they think. They will realize you care and eventually may be willing to change.

CHAPTER 19

Marital and Relational Issues

(See also chapter 13, "Getting Started and Setting Goals," chapter 21, "Managing Arguments," and "Communication Tool: The Table Meeting" in the appendix.)

The Call for Help

Typically, a person calls in desperation to say her partner will leave if they do not get help. Another caller may say the marriage needs help, but her partner refuses to come in because he says, "Counseling is a bunch of baloney," "It's not anyone else's business," or "You're the problem, not me." The caller may be convinced her partner will not come in, citing stubbornness as a prime example of what she is dealing with.

The Strategy

When you see the caller alone and hear her side of the story, you can give her a tip on a strategy that is 99 percent successful in getting the other person to come in. Ask her to tell him, "The counselor wants to hear *your* side of the story," or "The counselor wants to hear from the man of the house." This is the truth, as there are two sides to every story, and you need both. Ask her to tell him to call for an appointment and let him know the session is free because he is coming by invitation. That brings him in because he does want to tell his side of the story. It could also be that he wants relief, but he does not want to ask for help.

(Personally, I choose not to charge under these circumstances because he is coming at my request. Not charging the person also eliminates another potential excuse. Whatever it takes to get him in is worth it in the end, but this is a counselor's personal choice.)

This strategy usually works, but wait until you see the caller in a session. Do not relate this strategy over the phone. One reason for this is that the other person will wonder what his partner/spouse is telling you in counseling and does not want a one-sided case presented. He will probably make an appointment to come in.

Hearing the other side of the story:

- When you see that person alone—let us say it is a man—immediately and genuinely thank him for coming. (This shows respect when he may think you already have formed a negative opinion about him.) Then ask if it would be OK with him if you pray. (See chapter 13, "Getting Started and Setting Goals.") By asking, you will also show respect.

- If the person asks what his partner told you, say it is confidential. That gives you credibility and encourages him in that what he says will also be confidential (and you will explain that to him in your opening comments).
- Ask him about his take on the issues, and then let him talk.
- Do not interrupt *at all*. Just rest and pray silently in any silences.
- Nod as applicable (per chapter 13, "Getting Started and Setting Goals").

You will be amazed how freely he will talk. You probably will not need to ask questions initially. When he is done, he may well tell you that he appreciated being listened to, that his wife constantly interrupts him when he tries to talk, and he hates how she makes him feel so disrespected.

At least three problems were just revealed:

- He does not feel he has a voice.
- She interrupts him.
- He does not feel she respects him.

If you can mirror what he said back to him, he will know you really listened. So say it back:

"I appreciate how open you were in discussing your side of the story. Thank you."

"To be sure I am getting it right [you are showing respect to him], *let me recap three of the points I heard. Your wife does not listen to you, she interrupts you, and you feel disrespected in the relationship. Am I hearing you right?"*

He will no doubt say, "You got it right."

You can say,

"OK, thank you. Well, those are significant concerns." (You are validating.)

"Would you feel more comfortable coming in alone or with your wife next time?"

He probably will ask for another appointment alone, and then he will come in with his wife. God provides. (And don't ever be afraid to say that to your clients.) Amazing!

- Be patient:
  Sometimes if the tell-them-your-side-of-the-story strategy fails to get someone in, the nonattending/resistant partner will be encouraged when he sees changes in his partner. That may be the turning point, and then he, too, will come in.
- Be neutral:
  Ideally, though, if agreeable to both, see both partners together for the first time. When you give your opening remarks, be sure to do the following:

- Say that you will not take sides. (However, if there is abuse in the relationship, and the abuser is not invested in counseling despite every possible recruitment effort, you would need to work with the victim toward his/her goals of safety, and that most likely will mean separation, for a time at least.)
- Say that in every relationship each person is wrong half of the time because more than likely his/her *response* has not been helpful.
- Say that you are promarriage and that divorce is never an initial goal.
- Say you would like to see them invest 100 percent in the work done in counseling for at least a couple of months. Bad habits take a while to shake, and emotional hurts take time to heal as well.
- Look at each person, addressing questions and comments equally so you are not showing any bias. If the woman made the appointment and dragged her husband there, he will already think you are on her side. So be sure you let them know in your introductory comments to them both that you do not take sides.

It is interesting that often when one partner comes and finds that she *also* has much work to do, she may drop out while the man continues. He appreciates having someone listen to him, and he really wants the drama to end.

Observe the Dynamics

Observe how they communicate. (Do they look at each other, interrupt each other or you, defer to the other person? Watch their body language, eye contact, and facial expressions.) Couples will later say they were amazed at how different their partner presented himself or herself in counseling than at home. They may also say they never talk to each other at home as they do in counseling. Actually, that is a good thing because it shows that behavior is a choice, and they each have the potential to be appropriate. Share that with them.

When you begin with the questions below, just put them out there and see who answers first. It will show who is dominant in the relationship. Look back and forth at both of them, waiting. They may defer to the other person and say, "Go ahead; you're the one with the concerns" or "You can talk, sweetheart." (She looks at him and then at you curiously because she will say he *never* calls her that.)

Managing Complaints

Usually the person with the most complaints begins and, although he or she will try to be tactful, will quickly be direct and begin using unhelpful words like "He always…" and "He never…" If the other person attempts to interrupt or defend himself or herself, gently ask that person to please wait until his or her turn. Do not make any comments at all if possible on what he or she says. Wait to speak until you have heard both sides of the story.

After the second person takes his turn, thank them both for sharing their sides and validate how frustrating it must be for them to go through this trial. Tell them that some of their concerns are common (if this is true, and it probably will be), and there *are* helpful strategies to resolve them. It will take time, patience, practice, and prayer.

Help Them Create Respect and Truth in the Relationship
Right off the bat, you can say something like this:

"Using 'always' and 'never' is not helpful and probably isn't the whole truth about your behaviors. It is especially frustrating when one person works sincerely on the problem and the partner still uses those terms. It shuts down his or her efforts."

They will see your advice as a meaningful correction, and you have set the stage to correct when either one of them uses those words. The couple may learn to gently correct each other in session and at home.

Make Correcting Each Other Nonthreatening

- Encourage them to be each other's accountability partner and to do it with love, grace, and playfulness.

Their first task is to correct each other whenever the other person says those words. This will be a new experience for them, and you will have to prompt them. For example, Nancy is talking negatively about Ed and uses the word *always* regarding his behavior. You interrupt and say,

"Excuse me, Nancy. Ed, it is your turn to correct your wife on using the word always *now before she continues. You need to say something like, 'Nancy, please don't use* always*,' and she needs to say, 'Thank you' or 'You're right' and correct her wording to say,* most *or* some of the time.*"*

- Then, they need to do that.
- Thank them for practicing and showing respect for each other and themselves. Even if they do not get it quite right, (they may put their own spin on it as a demonstration of control), if it addresses the issue, just say, "Good work. Thank you both." You do not want to discourage them because everyone feels awkward doing these exercises.
- Also, encourage partners to distinguish between the person and his/her behavior. For example, it is not the *person* who is messy (the problem); the problem is how he takes care of his side of the bedroom. "The way you take care of your side of the bedroom is a problem," not "You are so messy."

Bring Back the Lovey-Dovey

- Another goal is to have the couple renew being tender and loving with each other.
- Ask them if they have a special affectionate name for each other, like, "sweetheart," "honey/hon," or "babe." They probably have stopped using them because of the relational tension.
- Ask them if they had such names when they were courting, and they will probably look at each other and smile or blush. It is good for them to recall those loving ties. They may say they just use their real names, and he may say how it drives him crazy when she calls him by his full first name like his mother used to do.

- Ask them to think about a name they want to be called and then tell the other person to use it as much as possible during the day so it becomes second nature, especially if they are asking for something. "Sweetheart, could you take out the garbage, please?" obviously is better than "Do you have Alzheimer's? You said you were going to take out the garbage" (sigh).
- Ask them to help each other when they forget and gently say with a questioning look, "Sweetheart?" That should prompt the other person's memory about using the affectionate name.
- Couples will do this for a while and then forget, so remind them to keep practicing it, especially in session.
- Couples will use you as the reason for doing or asking for something sometimes when they do not have the confidence themselves. She will say, "The counselor said we need to use our lovey-dovey names" instead of "I like it when you call me sweetheart." Sometimes it is too much to admit. That is OK. Be patient with them.

Focus, Focus, Focus

The next instruction is to do the following:

- Ask them to look directly at each other *whenever* they speak to the other person at home as well as in session. You will have to correct this often when in session.
- Remind the receiver of a comment to maintain constant eye contact as well. This will be challenging and awkward because they have lived with tension for so long. You will probably have to remind them gently multiple times because they are not used to doing this.
- Ask them to turn their bodies or chairs so they face their partner when they speak in session. Not only does this show respect and create intimacy, but it also helps with telling the truth. It is harder to exaggerate or lie when the other person is looking at you. They will often want to look at you, so you will need to say,

"Please face your husband when you're talking about him," or *"Please tell your husband what you are saying, not me."*

Say "I" Not "You"

It would be too much for the first session, but another common communication problem is making **"you need to"** statements instead of **"I want you to"** statements. Use the same strategy with them as above for corrections in session, and have them do corrections at home as well.

(See chapter 21, "Managing Arguments.")

Always Model for Them

When you work with couples, remember you are always modeling appropriate behavior. When applicable:

- Point out your response to them and what you are doing.

"Did you see how I validated her point before I gave my thought?"

"I need to interrupt you because this is a good opportunity to remember to practice something we (not 'you') *have learned. Both of you need to look at each other whenever the other person is talking."*

(They will do that obediently).

"Thanks. OK, continue your dialogue."

Here is a sample of how a typical initial session goes for most relationship issues. Ask,

"What is the problem from your perspective?" (Get examples.)

"What is the solution?"

(If the partner is not there): *"What would your partner say is the problem?"* (Get examples.)

"The solution?"

"How long has it been going on?"

"What have each of you done about it?" (Counseling? Books? Marriage retreats? Recovery groups?)

"Did you both follow the advice given to you?"

"For how long?" (If they have not followed the advice, ask *"Why not?"*)

"What kind of family/friend support do you have to encourage you?"

(She may have talked to more people than he has, which is typical, although not necessarily right.) Family and friends typically side with their family member or friend, so their advice is skewed. Goals become apparent: (1) others may know way too much of the couple's business, so boundary work is needed, as well as (2) healing and (3) making amends.

"What is your family and friends' position regarding your relationship?"

"Are the people Christians or people of biblical faith who are giving you that advice?"

(Note that many people without a strong faith will not encourage staying in a problematic marriage. You may well be the client's only source of encouragement.)

(See "Ways to Improve Communication" in the appendix for a relational tool.)

Premarital Counseling

Couples who come for premarital counseling too often come when the wedding is only weeks away. They sometimes have come under pressure by parents or perhaps one member of the couple or both have realized they have some issues that need to be addressed.

Occasionally, you will see a couple who has a strong Christian or faith background and are young but mature and seem to have all the right answers. Even with one session, you get the impression they will do fine and are willing to get help if they get into trouble.

Most couples, however, admit some issues and wonder if they can be fixed before the wedding. That depends. If they are open and not defensive and will practice the new behaviors, they can master their issues. Encourage them to return to counseling if you cannot settle everything before the wedding. They do tend to return after a few months of marriage.

They may or may not be "equally yoked" not only on spiritual issues, but also socially, in level of education, culturally, in financial management styles, and so forth. This can be an obstacle. As far as faith goes, God may not endorse it when Christians marry nonbelievers; for Catholics, marrying Christians or Catholic Christians is endorsed.

- Ask about each aforementioned area and let their answers open their eyes.
- Ask how they met and what they have in common.
- Ask how they settle disputes. This will typically reveal immature behaviors and minimal knowledge of how to communicate and argue respectfully. They can be taught how to do this. Patterns set in the beginning of a relationship set the tone for the rest of their lives.
- Ask about finances and their plans for handling money. This will probably reveal that one person is better at finances, so they have decided that person will assume that responsibility. That may be OK as long as the other person is well aware of the budgeting needs and their respective responsibilities. Both need to be well aware of the finances so there is not ignorant spending that causes problems. Refer them to Financial Peace University under Dave Ramsey (www.daveramsey.com).
- Ask about future in-laws and how that is going.
- Ask both about their own relationships with their parents and siblings.
- Ask about expectations regarding holidays and time with relatives, and whether there are expectations about regular contacts (for example, Sunday with the relatives), time on the phone, and so on.
- Ask them about their parents' marriages and what they like about them (and want to have in their marriage) and what they do not like.
- Ask about their current faith practices and what it was like for each of them growing up. Ask about their faith goals.
- Ask if they have given their lives to the Lord, and if they are willing to talk about when that happened and what changed about them after that.

You may be able to cover all of this in the first session, or it may take a few.

Premarital Relational Inventories

There are inventory sheets available online under Premarital Relational Inventories for eliciting couples' values and opinions about a wide range of topics from courting to sex, roles, money, friends, chores, and so forth. These kinds of inventories are useful because many couples have never thought about some of the more complicated life issues they may face, and it helps them to get to know each other better as they talk through their responses. You can go over the inventory with them or have them take it home where each should complete it and discuss their answers between themselves.

Helping Couples Understand Each Other's Backgrounds

Before you go over an inventory's questions and their responses with them (or not, if they do this at home), it is important to remind them not to judge each other's responses but to *respectfully* request, "Help me understand why you think or believe that," even if it is outrageous. They each will realize if they are just repeating their parents', church's, or peers' values, or they may realize they do not have their own personal values in some areas. This exercise can be a maturing lesson for them as they struggle to find values that are their own and that are compatible with where they are in life, and ideally, what the Bible has to say about these things.

- In areas where they differ from what the Bible says, ask them to explain how they came to their thoughts about the topic. Often, they will have immature ideas, and you do not want to shame them but give them new ways of considering the topic, knowing that the choice is up to them in the end. You can say,

"What do you think about this way of looking at that issue? It happens to be in the Bible."

- Ask them about the man being the "spiritual head of the household" as the Bible says, and what they think about that concept. You probably will need to describe what that looks like on a day-to-day basis. (Be sure your own routine is worth using as a model.)
- Encourage them to read or listen to CDs or attend retreats yearly for newlyweds and for couples.
- Encourage them to find an older Christian couple who is happily married to meet with monthly for support.
- Encourage them to return to counseling as needed, saying that this is good insurance that can lead to a great relationship.
- Consider scheduling a counseling appointment once a year, as it can be a good tune-up.

Letting Go of the Past

A frequent problem in relationships and marriages is either person not being able to forget the "sins" or relationships of the past, whether it was before they got together or after. If the past is being brought up, it may be because of the following:

- It is a weapon to hurt.

- There are still questions about whether the "sin" will occur again (perhaps an affair or resorting to drugs or drinking).
- Her own poor self-image needs such an inordinate amount of validation that she chooses to keep feeling as if *she* was responsible for the "sin" because she was not good enough (if there was an affair or pornography, for example).

Bringing up the past is a common complaint. When arguments happen, those sins are brought up, any progress made is doused, and the "sinner" feels condemned (again or still), frustrated, and defeated. Thus, any healing is lost.

This is also a way for the "victim" to have some control over the sinner. The victim might have been involved in a situation where she *did not* have any control, so she is taking it now. It is very unhealthy and not God-like.

(See chapter 29, "Forgiveness" and chapter 23, "Addiction and Other Issues.")

Newlyweds

- Ask them individually what they see as the problems (finances, chores, time spent away from the home, relatives, sex, and so on) to first see if they are on the same page. (These may not be the *real* problems, but this will be revealed as they talk.)
- Often the core issues are a lack of respect from the man's standpoint and lack of feeling loved from the woman's standpoint.

(See the book *Love and Respect*, by Emerson Eggerichs. Encourage clients to read it together, talk about it as a homework exercise, and have them talk about the result in session with you.) Examples: When he leaves the wet towels on the floor, she sees it as not caring about her role as the homemaker, and she feels unloved and may not want sex. When she complains about not having enough money, he feels disrespected as the provider and wants to push the issue of sex or hide out with Internet games to vent his feeling of not being respected.

Remind the couple that relationships go in cycles.

- There is an initial "high" during the first year (which is equivalent to a drug high from the release of endorphins). That release drops dramatically after a year, causing some emotional confusion and questions about the changes each person feels. They each may wonder if they made the right choice. Remind them that the changes are nature's way of normalizing the sexual emotions especially so the other responsibilities of life can also be attended to.
- During the courting time, we can be blind to our partner's weaknesses and come to an abrupt awakening as we live with someone and witness all sides of his/her personality and character.
- Some people fear that with the loss of that initial high, they must have made a wrong decision or they have just fallen out of love. Remind them that this probably is not the case. It is part of the

natural pattern of relationships. There are people who thrive on the high of the initial stages of a relationship, and they are the people who change partners frequently.

- "The honeymoon's over" may be a complaint of newlyweds when they are bombarded with the adjustments of living together. Assure them that this is natural; it is a relational shift, not the end.
- Each of them may compare their marriage to their parents' marriage and roles.
- There is a shift in the way they treat each other now that they have secured their partner with marriage.
- There are unrealized expectations about money, time spent together, sexual frequency, and so forth.
- After the first year (or before), couples begin to see the weaknesses in each other, and those godly character traits of patience and long suffering need to be developed. Remind them that the marriage union is the most intimate relationship they will have, and it is the forum to practice being more Christ-like with someone they love and trust, who will encourage them as they each work on their own weaknesses.
- If they can make pointing out each other's weaknesses playful and not accusatory, they will be more likely to work on them and not feel ashamed. For example, instead of saying, "Stop saying curse words," one could gently say, "That language doesn't become you," or "We agreed that whoever cursed would put a dollar in the savings jar. Your turn, kiddo."

(See chapter 21, "Managing Arguments.")

Babies

Babies come in the next cycle, and with them come shifts in attention, energy, time, sex, finances, and more. Husbands may be somewhat jealous losing the wife's full attention. Both parents will have little energy to do the things they used to enjoy, and sex may drop a lot in frequency for physical and hormonal reasons as well as exhaustion. Help clients realize what is normal and work on helping them manage and accept their new awareness.

Children

Having and raising children adds another dimension to a marriage that brings out new expectations and issues. Sexual interest shifts for many women because they are exhausted, and men and women sometimes settle for "hurry-up sex" or just going through the motions, if that is all that is offered.

As you can see, the progression for potential sexual problems increases. You may need to have separate conversations about this very delicate topic.

Mutual Vulnerability Increases

- Dissatisfactions sometimes are buried.
- Resentments build.
- Barbs fly and each person emotionally retreats.
- The couple begins to grow apart.
- The vulnerability for an affair or an addictive behavior is set up.

Hence, it is critical to help them *communicate their needs honestly* and respond *sacrificially*.

(See the section on "Sex" in this chapter.)

Adjusting to Responsibilities

For couples with young children, especially if stepchildren are included, there are many adjustments to be made. The difference between how they spent their time previously and now that they have children can be a source of frustration. If both parents choose to work, there has to be a renegotiation of responsibilities; otherwise, resentments will arise.

- Rotating responsibilities helps.
- With cooking, try rotating: one person has Tuesday, Thursday, and Saturday, and the other Monday, Wednesday, and Friday. Sunday is a free day when they both decide what to do.
- The person who cooks may not be the person who cleans up. That is negotiable.
- There are rules when you rotate cooking responsibilities: the spouse must eat whatever is made and does not complain, each spouse does his or her best in the kitchen, and there is to be no criticizing the other person's cooking. If an unbalance continues, they should talk about it. Probably something else is going on, and one person is or both people are using being uncooperative as an outlet.

Dates with the Kids

Planned weekly dates with each one of the kids separately (breakfast or ice cream out, a ride in the car to a special place, fishing, and so on), reserved on the kitchen calendar, will give kids something to look forward to. A parent should not threaten that time when he or she disciplines. The time is for having fun and/or talking through any issues.

Couples' Date Night

Planned date nights—even if it is at home—help. Couples should build quality time with each other, even if they cannot afford to go out. A couple can consider trading babysitting responsibilities with another couple. Encourage couples to be creative in their free time:

- Have a picnic on the living room floor after the kids are asleep.
- Enjoy a date-in night where they both dress up a bit and have a romantic dinner, even if it is just fast food.
- Learn a game together.
- Review pictures and memorabilia especially on anniversaries and at the holidays because it will help them remember the good times.
- Schedule time together in advance and write it on the calendar, especially romantic nights, so both can be "geared up" emotionally.
- When apart, text romantic notes or call just to say something loving, not to ask for an errand.

Sex

At any stage in the marriage, sometimes the following happens:

- The wife uses sex as a reward card.
- The husband expects sex even if she is not invested.
- Sex can become a tool they each use to vent their frustration in the relationship, and this can happen throughout the decades of marriage. (Yes, many older people still have sex/intimacy.) Obviously, if this is happening in the relationship, you need to help them talk about what is in the way relationally.

Remind them that sexuality is more than the physical act of the union of bodies.

- For women especially, their desire is first fueled with verbal attention and physical affection. Women complain that men cannot be "just sweetly affectionate" during the day and "always" have to be too physical/sexual.
- Men say that they do not know how to do that or that they become pumped up so quickly with gentle affection that they get out of control. They see their sexual desire is a compliment, while women sometimes see it as lust and having nothing to do with love.

Teaching couples how to tease and be affectionately playful (something they can appropriately do in front of the children) is healthy modeling and adds fun for them.

Even with intimacy, women frequently complain that men are too self-centered, and the man's defense is that he cannot stop once he gets started. That is a myth. Actually, frequently repeating a "start-and-stop technique" will prolong the mutual lovemaking and foster his ability to manage his body better. When he gets older, this start-and-stop method will sustain his performance longer and help prevent frustration around not being able to perform.

- In between the starts and stops, remind the man to focus on pleasuring the woman, because women, as they age, generally need more time to reach climax.
- Also, remind them that both of them need not have an orgasm every time or in harmony, as that is a personal preference.
- Remind them to not make assumptions and to ask what their partner prefers.
- Couples say they have a hard time sharing what each wants intimately, as the other partner sometimes becomes defensive.

This is definitely a delicate subject, but if one's needs are shared gently, one's input will have a better chance of being received instead of being denied. "I told you not to be so rough," or "Can you at least pretend that you're enjoying this?" kills a romantic mood quickly, and "Get it over with" begins to be expressed. Such remarks are deadly to intimacy.

If as a counselor, you are comfortable having a practical conversation with the client of the same sex, then help. You probably want to have someone of the same sex speak to the other partner or perhaps refer this whole subject to a professional counselor.

Remind them of the following:

- When one of you wants to be intimate and the other does not, ask God to help right then with your desire. Sometimes when you get involved primarily to please your partner, your act of unselfishness will be blessed.
- It is not OK to make a remark that implies you are simply tolerating it. That makes the situation worse and is not godly. It is disrespectful and will hurt your intimacy. If you truly are too tired, consider the option like a promise for intimacy the next morning or evening, and then keep your promise.

If an issue is cleanliness, gently suggest a quick shower or shower together, and that will wake you both up enough to have meaningful sex.

If the person is drunk or high and pushing for sex, it is mocking the sacredness of the act that God created, so refraining is understandable.

Some men, especially today because of the accessibility of pornography, learned about sex from watching porn. What they saw was not tender, romantic, intimate lovemaking, which is what most women crave. Many men need to be taught how to make love, not just have sex. Is it OK sometimes to "just have sex" with your married partner? Perhaps, but there always needs to be godly respect and mutual fulfillment, unless one person is sincerely OK with only pleasuring the other at that time.

She may ask what to do when her partner asks her to wear what he considers to be a sexy outfit or when he asks her to participate in something she doesn't want to do. Say to her,

> *"If you are not comfortable, it isn't going to have the desired effect anyway, so don't do it, and don't let yourself be intimidated into doing something you don't want to do. This includes watching pornography, photographing, or filming or texting personal pictures of yourself or yourselves. It is not godly behavior."*

The intentional or accidental release of such films to others or having children find them has happened with horrific consequences.

Counselors will be amazed at the perversions couples participate in and that some partners expect their spouse to enjoy. Be prepared.

Love Is a Choice

Remind them that sometimes you have to make a choice to love. Is that hard? Yes, but it is a reality, and there will be rewards for your obedience.

- A marriage moves forward on commitment, not feelings.
- You can choose to love or not.
- Know that because God commands you to love, when you try He will help with returning your feelings of love. Remember that God *is* love.

Ask your clients:

> *"If you are holding back, are you afraid of being in love or loving again?"*

They may fear being hurt (again) or of a disappointment. Help them with forgiveness.

(See chapter 29, "Forgiveness.")

> *"What are you putting into the marriage relationship?"*

Remind them that if one of them is not done with the marriage, then it isn't over. Keep at it.

Empty Nesters

Empty nesters may find this time joyful and a long time coming. Many, however, are at a loss about how to rebuild their relationship and create a new life. The shift to just the two of them can be alarming, especially if one member of the couple is also retiring.

- One or both of the parents may need to do some grief work. The children are leaving, and a life they have known has ended. It is a loss.

(See chapter 26, "Grief and Depression.")

Know that each parent may see this new era differently, with one eager to travel, play golf, do ministry work, and so forth, while the other may be lost and have no interest or may already have a routine that is satisfying that he or she does not want to change.

Some couples lead entirely separate lives and lose their intimate connection. They have nothing in common anymore and so come to counseling.

Couples not making the shift to their new circumstances

- feel alienated and lost,
- resent each other's choices,
- feel little warmth in the relationship, and
- reveal that sex may have been nonexistent for years or was/is just "hurry-up sex."

It is alarming how many couples say they have not had a sex life for years, sometimes decades, and even affection is absent or an afterthought. When you meet with the couple to get a better understanding of what is going on, you will hear blaming and keeping score. For example, she will not have sex, so he has cocktails or plays a lot of golf, saying, "At least I'm not having an affair." She says he just wants sex and is impatient or self-centered sexually and shows no affection or genuine warmth.

Separation

This is rarely helpful to marital restoration. Sometimes one or both partners will date others, which just increases the frustration, and the comparison of a new interest just adds fuel to the fire.

Separation stretches finances, adding to the tension. It increases e-communication that so frequently opens the door to miscommunication and misunderstandings. It is particularly stressful on small children because they do not understand the change in schedule and being shuffled between places. Grandparents may be called on to babysit more frequently, and the children may resent not having the attention of their parents.

More often than not, separation is chosen to ease the pain and stop the fighting; however, the couple *can* stay together and begin to heal with honest communication and intensive counseling. Couples who stay in the house having a "cold war" and sleeping in separate bedrooms is also common but not helpful. Couples will say they are too mad or hurt to be in the same house, let alone the same bed.

The level of anger and hurt is very real but can be treated. Increase sessions to twice a week per person if possible to help him/her manage being in the fire. If they insist on separating, ask them to work out rules for the separation such as no dating other people, keeping the planned visitation schedules with the kids, not taking money out of the joint account without discussing it mutually, being respectful, not criticizing the other parent in front of the kids, and having a date night weekly. (Perhaps include sex in order to reduce the temptation to go elsewhere, but if tensions are too high for that level of intimacy, at least try to be affectionate and progress to intimacy. However, there is also value in having to live as if they were divorced and get a taste of what that would be like. Let the couple draft the separation contract, and if willing, discuss it with you in session.)

If there is abuse, then other options need to be considered at least for a time. Sometimes a temporary separation is a wake-up call for the abuser, but regrettably, often the abusive pattern continues.

The abuser minimally needs to be in treatment and a support group, and the partner needs to be in a support group and get counseling.

God can heal even this most difficult situation. Help them both surrender this trial and increase their dependence on the Lord in prayer, self-examination, confession, repentance, and accountability.

Divorce

Most couples have not really thought through the consequences of divorce. They just want the pain and drama to go away.

- First, address the pain issues by getting them on the table. If there is a person who did "wrong," he or she needs to be repentant. The "wronged" person has to work through his/her feelings and forgive. (See chapter 29, "Forgiveness.")
- Help them realize that it will take at least a few months of hard work before they will start seeing changes, so they need to be patient. There is more to lose than to gain. Encourage them to work

100 percent for those few months and then assess if there have been enough positive changes to be hopeful. If they both feel after a few months that they have worked 100 percent and the marriage is still in trouble, separation may be the next step.

The Impact on Children If a Couple is Even Considering Divorce

The following material is not meant to guilt-trip parents but to give them a wake-up call. Ask these questions gently but seriously. Suggest that they do not have to respond to each one but just hear the entire list and then talk with you about each one. They may not have thought about all of these issues, and it can be heart changing.

"Do you accept the fact that if you both remarry that someone else will be raising your kids half of the time?"

"Are you OK with the kids shuffling between two houses, plus each set of parents and grandparents for holidays?"

"Do you realize that the kids will be subjected to two sets of rules from two separate households and parents?"

"Do you think that will be frustrating for them and make enforcing your rules easy?"

"Do you think being Disneyland parents will help one or both of you to deal with your feelings?"

"Do you think the kids will resent the other parent not spoiling them as well?"

"What if one parent wants to move or has a job option far away? In general, the custodial parent may not move out of state without the other parent's permission. Typically, that means summers and holidays with one parent and the rest of the year with the other. Although that arrangement has pluses because it allows the kids to have a stable school year, the parent with the kids during the school year winds up being the disciplinarian and the other parent the vacation-time parent."

"Do you believe the statistics that say kids from divorced homes have a much higher rate of divorce when they become adults?"

"Do you think the kids will suffer emotional consequences due to your divorce?"

"Do you know that most kids blame themselves regardless of what they are told? They think parents are divorcing because the child was not good enough, smart enough, athletic enough, lovable, or some other thing was wrong with them. They may think their parents may leave them as they left each other and live in that fear."

"Do you think that your past behavior, if you argued and you were disrespectful in front of the kids, has made an impression on your children about what marriage and relationships look like? Many kids from divorced homes say they will never marry. Wouldn't you want to teach them what a healthy relationship looks like for them and for you?"

Rebound Relationships

"The rebound rate and the probability of a second marriage ending in a divorce are both very high. If you do not get serious help, you will make the same mistakes again and again and again. I encourage you both to work on getting your marriage fixed and be a godly example."

Financial Impact

"What about finances? What would your lifestyle look like if your finances are cut in half until the kids are eighteen—or longer if they go to college?"

If Couples Will Not Resolve Their Problems:

Divorce Care is a great resource for mending the damage of a divorce. It is a group teaching and support experience. Go online and read about it.

Start Over

One remedy for any marriage in trouble is for them to start over from this day forward. This is not a fantasy solution. It is a solution that offers hope—a clean slate, a new beginning. This is a great tool that gives encouragement, and it is realistic. Couples are so tired of their drama that they welcome starting over and leaving the past behind. Incidentally, you can do this with a birthday or anniversary or any occasion that turned out disappointing. Do a redo; start over. It is your occasion; celebrate it until you get it right. Have couples design what a new relationship needs to look like.

- Create a totally new relationship and marriage.
- Completely forget any of the past that was painful.
- Encourage them to carve out a new marriage with new rules and new rewards, individually and as a couple.
- Let them each say or write down as homework what a perfect marriage for them would look like and then help them create it.
- Encourage them to invest in each other's interests. Even if they do not want to do the activity, encourage them to talk about how the game went or how their writing group went. This may be awkward at first because sometimes when asked, a one-word grunt or "OK" is the reply. That is not helpful.
- Learn to communicate. Often, couples will be talkative when out with others but not when together. They will explain that the other people seem interested in hearing what they had to say. Partners should listen sincerely. Looking at the other person and validating what they are hearing helps.

(See "Ways to Improve Communication" in the appendix.)

This strategy gives hope, and couples buy in frequently because deep in their hearts they want it to work but are at a loss as to how to get back on track. When they complain about their partner, remind them of the following:

- They are creating a *new* marriage, so be expectant that annoying behaviors will be changing.
- They are responsible for how they respond to issues and problems.
- They have one-half of the responsibility for stepping up and making the changes.

Retirement

Retirement is another stage of a marriage and can come with many issues. If it is planned and there are sufficient financial resources, that certainly helps. However, this is not typical. Usually, there is a downsizing of housing and/or relocation, which often necessitates moving and the loss of family, friends, church, and so forth. (See chapter 26, "Grief and Depression.") The status, friends, and value of working are losses. Being together more of the time is another adjustment. Health issues begin to arise with time spent on doctors' appointments and caring for each other. For retirees, the adjustment may be huge as they not only have lost their job, status, and friendships, but most importantly, they have lost feeling valued.

Potential Remedies

Have clients do grief work in counseling to heal from the hurt they are experiencing.

(See chapter 26, "Grief and Depression.")

Remind them of the following:

- They should fill their lives with something that has eternal value, like doing some kind of ministry work or volunteer work, preferably with their spouse.
- Take any of their job skills that might be transferable and use them in a volunteer position.
- Go to school or go online and take courses in either something they always wanted to learn or enter a completely new field of work (volunteer or otherwise). Volunteermatch.com is a good resource for matching people with opportunities, as is RSVP (Retired Senior Volunteer Program).
- Take up a new hobby. They may be surprised at a hidden ability that would give them great pleasure.

Complaints

Couples in this stage may come to counseling complaining of being frustrated because of being depended upon so much. They may have to shift what was once a lifestyle they loved to now taking care of an ill spouse or parents, babysitting or raising grandkids, and so on. Boundaries need to be set.

Personality shifts are common, with irritability and stubbornness replacing the once-tender disposition of a partner.

- Pursue what the root of the change may be.
- Remember to do a health assessment.
- Ask about differences between before the change and now. (Fewer friends? Less money to do the things the spouse loved? Missing the kids? No longer able to drive? Tired of being sick? Bored? Sexual issues? Embarrassment over incontinence or memory loss or other physical and mental issues?)

Build Closeness and Invest in Each Other

- Couples should cultivate things they like to do together (new games, ministry work, day trips on a tour bus, and so on).
- Learn about what the other person is already interested in.
- Remind them to ask questions, encourage each other, and celebrate as they complete their project or craft goals with a shared treat like breakfast out.
- Help with their spouse's project if that is appropriate (for example, carrying stuff for a sale or display, or just publicly commenting how proud he or she is of what the spouse is up to and being specific).
- Remind them that they may find themselves adopting their partner's interests, and that is common with activities like golf, shuffleboard, swimming, pool, and so on.
- Remind them not to compare with others—not their partner, their finances, lifestyle, or relationship.
- If nothing is what was once envisioned, adjust to reality.
- Get help if they need an attitude adjustment from the sin of coveting what they think life and their spouse should be like, and remind them to switch their attitude to gratitude.

Don't Be Selfish

Selfishness is the root of many marital issues. Avoidance is another. He plays too much golf; she spends too much time with the grandkids or on the Internet. She is off at church all the time; he sits in front of the TV doing nothing. She still wants to work; he wants to do things with her, but she is too tired after work.

In conclusion, as you do your assessment, you will see there are many factors that need to be looked into in trying to figure out what is really going on but is not being said. You will also feel the pressure knowing that people stay only six sessions on average and want everything fixed.

(See also chapter 21, "Managing Arguments.")

CHAPTER 20
Parent and In-Law Issues (and Part of the Marital Assessment)

The questions below will usually yield a wealth of information regarding problematic issues concerning roles, resentments, and baggage with each person's own parents, boundaries, loyalty conflicts, and so forth.

Caught in the Middle
It is very hard to be caught in the middle of stressful situations between one's parents and one's spouse, and most people want to avoid it. There is a loyalty conflict between the husband or wife and the parents or in-laws. The adult children may not ever have challenged their parents, even respectfully, so it can be very stressful. Typically, the whole situation is avoided to the infuriation of the one partner, while the other partner harbors resentment at his own impotency.

Expectations
How each partner was raised and the emotional health of that family will greatly influence his/her expectations about how family relationships should be. Someone from a fractured family may long for a close family and welcome family involvement. On the other hand, it may be threatening, and he may choose to isolate and complain about her being *too attached* when this may or may not be the case.

She may think her best friend relationship with her mother is ideal and cannot see how she appears to be turning to her mom for emotional support rather than learning how to trust emotionally and build a more intimate relationship with her husband. He may not have had a father figure who was emotionally available, so he has a hard time relating to parental closeness. Therefore, they both may have issues with how to get closer emotionally as well as mastering confidence in their role as husband or wife, separate from their parents' expectations. There is much teaching needed on expectations.

Sometimes a parent will come in for counseling with the adult child to work things out, but that is rare. With adult children, you typically will be trying to

- help mend fences,
- build confidence,

- redefine roles,
- remove fears,
- set boundaries, and so forth.

Boundaries

The boundary issue is huge. Helping couples set boundaries and then respectfully asking that they be honored is a challenge, but it can help their marriage tremendously.

Any change will likely produce mutual emotional confusion. That is an inevitable part of creating new roles as adult children who want to have their own relationships and identity.

Get Some History

You will need to get an understanding of all the relationships involved along with some history so you can see what expectations and needs each person has. Maybe incidents have occurred that need healing or attitudes exist that need correcting. Separating ties that are too close with parents or developing confidence in how to set and honor boundaries may be needed. Look through the contents of this manual and read the applicable sections (for example, Forgiveness, Boundaries).

Confrontation

Sometimes an adult child is hesitant to confront his parents and yields to them instead—to the infuriation of the wife.

- Help him understand *why* setting boundaries is needed.
- Teach him how to set boundaries with love and respect.

(See the "Oreo Cookie Strategy" in the appendix.)

Stepping Up

Stepping up will establish their identity as an independent couple and not as a parents' child. It reinforces the husband's (or wife's) ability to defend his own marriage and role and shows he will not cave in to either set of parents. Wives often lack respect for their husbands when their husbands will not defend them or their marriage. The same is true when husbands do not assert their role as head of the household.

Expectations

Couples often have the unrealistic expectation that their partner's relationship with their parents is just like theirs. Sometimes women tend to be more attached to their mothers and may be too emotionally involved, sharing personal and confidential information about their marriage with their mother and spending too much time together.

This may or may not be a distancing effort prompted by fear of not knowing how to relate to her husband or making the necessary transfer of dependence from her mother to her husband. Her relationship with her mom leaves him feeling ignored and disrespected. Out of frustration or resentment, he engages in his own distancing activities, like spending time away or with the guys. Thus, the distancing cycle continues.

Men may have the vision of traditional male/female roles based on their parents' marriage and have high expectations for what the woman's responsibilities are.

- Inquire about couples' parents' marriage and how much of that they each expect in their own marriage.

Some starting questions:

"What do you think about your relationship with your in-laws?"

"What would your partner say about it?"

"What would your partner say about his relationship with your folks?"

"What do you think?"

"Are there any issues with the stepchildren? Your grandchildren?"

"Is there a problem with how issues with your parents or in-laws are handled?"

"Do your parents and in-laws respect your role as the wife/husband?" (There may well be boundary issues concerning timing or length of visits, time spent together, treatment of the grandkids, and so on.)

"Are there any control issues?"

"Are there any boundary violations?" (that is, rules you have set that are ignored, like how to treat the kids or coming over without calling)

"What have you done about it?"

"What does your husband/wife say and do about it?"

"What would you want him/her to do about it?"

"Do your in-laws treat you differently than other wives/husbands? Why might this be?"

"Do you show your gratitude for any way that they help you? How?"

"How much time do you spend with your spouse and in-laws as a family? Would they say that is enough?"

"What would your spouse say?"

"What were and are your relationships like with your own family?" (Ask both people.)

CHAPTER 21

Managing Arguments (and Part of the Marital Assessment)

Clients often say they argue a lot with their partner/spouse or children. Help them to understand that it is sometimes OK to argue as long as it is done *respectfully and both partners work toward a resolution*. When a hot issue comes up, each person needs to have the opportunity to express his/her opinion and be listened to. That means

- giving the other person your full attention,
- maintaining constant eye contact,
- not groaning or making other gestures or comments that reveal your dislike or impatience of what is being said, and
- not creating drama when it is your time to respond. (Teaching teens this practice will help temper their tendency to dramatize everything and manage their part of a discussion more maturely.)

The Table Meeting

The Table Meeting is a very effective tool to manage arguments and discussions, whether it is concerning an upsetting problem or planning a vacation. It is helpful with most clients/families who have communication issues, and can also be used as homework.

(See the "Communication Tool: The Table Meeting" in the appendix.)

Ask clients to have at least two table meetings before the next session. Tell them that the first one may feel awkward, but they will still see its value. The second one usually goes well and becomes an easy tool to use. (Read over the instructions and conduct a Table Meeting in your own home or with colleagues before you continue with this section so you can appreciate its value.)

Why Yell or Argue?

Help the client to understand why people yell or argue:

- People usually raise their voices because they think they will not be heard or acknowledged unless they do. Therefore, giving someone your full attention helps to stop the raising of voices.
- To get attention because sometimes arguing is the only time their spouse pays attention to them.

- They miss having emotional depth in the relationship, so they think that if they are fighting passionately, some emotion is being expressed. Sometimes they are diverting and/or trapping the other person into bad behaviors or using arguing as an excuse for acting out.
- When people are adept at arguing, they may feel that this is a situation where they can feel in control, while there may be another part of their relationship that is not in control (for example, their sex life or financial affairs).
- Some people just like to stir the pot to create drama because that is what they are used to or grew up with.

Many of these behaviors are rooted in how arguments were handled while growing up. We think that the way our parents argued is normal. There *are* other ways that are healthier in resolving differences.

- Ask your clients what they observed and felt about arguing growing up.
- Help clients see they probably have a limited perspective.

Some of us grew up in households where we never witnessed our parents arguing or even raising their voices. The parents probably had a rule about never arguing in front of the children. While the thought is to protect the children, it doesn't give the children the opportunity to witness and learn respectful arguing and resolution of differences. However, it is obviously never appropriate to argue about the children in front of the children.

Sometimes the parents who never argue may have the kind of disposition that is sweet and very gentle, so arguing is not in their nature. This can be healthy and is inspirational as long as differences are discussed and resolved and not swept under the rug at any cost.

The Table Meeting exercise previously noted is a great tool to show kids that instead of watching their parents fight, they can observe them talking over an issue respectfully. The exercise offers good role modeling, relief, and hope when properly conducted.

Some clients spark arguments to get emotional attention.

- Get to the root cause to find out what is missing from the relationship.

For clients who like to stir the pot, you have to do the following:

- Dig to see why they are more focused on upsetting others than on growing themselves and being a blessing. Their behavior may be overt (open) or covert (hidden), and could be labeled passive-aggressive, which means it may seem OK outwardly, but there is an edge to what is said or done that makes you feel slighted or question what they really meant. Sometimes people have been passive-aggressive so long that they do not even see it as a personality and behavioral flaw.

Some reminders for clients:

Use "I" statements instead of "You" statements. Say to your clients,

"Instead of saying, 'You are always so rude to me,' say, 'I feel disrespected when you talk to me like that. I would appreciate an apology.'"

"Instead of 'Take out the garbage,' say, 'I would appreciate it if you would take out the garbage.'"

Whenever a sentence starts with "You," it is probably a criticism or a command. So eliminate starting any sentence with "You" by reminding them to catch themselves and use an "I" statement. (Of course when praising, "you" is OK to use.)

Opt Out of Arguing

One way to not participate in an argument is for a spouse say to the other person,

"I love you too much to fight with you. Please, let's drop it and talk about it later."

"I love you too much to listen to you talk to me that way. I'm not answering you, and I'm going into another room for a while."

Validating their love to their partner is key here. Obviously, couples must agree ahead of time that each will go into another room if needed. Then remind clients to ignore whatever is said because sometimes the rebuked person will come at them with more words that could set them off. Let the words pass by. Ignore them. The spouse should hold her ground, be still, and pray while the rebuked person calms down.

Stop Following Her

If a spouse needs to leave the room, and the other tries to follow, he or she is acting out of fear. He or she fears

- losing control of the situation,
- the spouse's rejection, and
- that the argument will not be resolved.

The spouse should turn around and gently (yes, gently) affirm her love, because that is at the root of his fear, by saying,

- *"I love you* [the spouse is validating]. *I need a few minutes by myself to calm down. I'll be back in the room very shortly. I commit to resolving this. Thank you for honoring my request."*

This exchange takes *immense self-control*. Remind the couple that

- they can do this with practice and prayer;
- it will help if they agree in advance that following someone when he or she wants to be alone or needs to cool down is not OK;
- they discuss in advance how it will be handled.

For friendship situations, say, "I care about you/our friendship/our relationship too much to argue with you. Let's talk about it after we both think about the issues."

One Issue per Argument

A rule for managing arguments is one issue per argument/discussion. When people believe they are losing an argument, they will bring out their other guns to help them feel in control. They often will bring up the past. "And fifteen years ago when you were dating so and so…" or "And besides that, even your friends agree with me…" or "You sound just like your mother."

Bringing up the past, or being critical of or comparing how their spouses family manages their affairs is not appropriate and not anyone else's business. Ever. Anyone else's business is not relevant and is only used to inflame the situation. Mind you own business and take the log out of your own eye. Period. If its brought up in an argument say to the offending person, "That's none of our business. I'm going to ignore that comment."

Let clients know they should stay calm and ignore the barbs or the argument will become a defenses match. Teach them to *calmly* say, "One issue per argument. I'm going to ignore your comments. Let's get back to the issue." That expression of control will rock the other person, so he or she may escalate the irrelevant comments or calm down.

Remember to tell clients the following:

- When one of you is in control, the argument is in control.
- As with yelling, if one of you takes control and refuses to yell back, the argument will usually downsize to a discussion. Stay strong.

The Silent Treatment

Another unhealthy controlling tactic is the silent treatment. The person who feels he is losing the argument will walk away in a huff and stay silent for hours or even days. Silence is a weapon. It is a very hurtful, negatively effective tool. The other person may also play the silent game for a while, but probably the relationship dynamic is that she will acquiesce, compromise, give in entirely, or say, "Let's forget about it" (none of which are helpful). She may lure him out of his silent mode with sex or any other enticement.

The Remedy

What really needs to happen with arguments is a leveling of the playing field so both parties are heard, respected, and have their opinion considered. The Table Meeting exercise works great at this because equal time is given to all who are involved. Even if one person is a better speaker or arguer, the other person can have his or her say without being interrupted or challenged, and that builds his or her confidence because he/she gets to present his/her side of the argument.

Words That Heal

Sometimes the very words that can heal lifelong hurts or arguments are the hardest to say. People cannot say them because of

- resentment;
- not knowing how, what, or when to say them;
- embarrassment and feeling uncomfortable saying words they have never said and have only heard sometimes;
- fear that the words will not be appreciated; and
- fear their words or requests for tenderness will not be returned.

Remind clients of the following:

- We can get past our fears by trusting God and asking Him to open our hearts and that of the person we need to talk with.
- They can find the courage to speak.
- Practicing with someone or writing what he or she wants to say and reading it to someone is also helpful and healing. Sometimes just saying the words in practice gives such a relief that it removes much of the anxiety of speaking to the person.

If the other person is deceased, there still can be healing. (See chapter 26, "Grief and Depression.")

A few of the things we all long to hear and often need to say to others:

- I love you.
- I forgive you.
- Will you please forgive me?
- What can I do to make this (or our past) right for you?
- Thank you.

(See the book *The Four Things That Matter Most*, by Ira Byock, for details.)

Some clients' thoughts on the words "I love you":

"I told her the day we got married that I loved her; isn't that enough?"

"I tell her I love her when I change the oil in her car."

"I tell him I love him by having sex with him."

"I tell him I love him by not hassling him about his weight/drinking/spending."

These are, regrettably, real responses, real beliefs that you will hear. We are all wired to be relational, and that means talking to and hearing others. Is *doing* important? Yes, but it is not a substitute for saying or hearing tender words. You will hear how some people never heard loving, affirming words growing up, and even when the parent is on his or her deathbed, they have refused (even when asked) to say, "I love you" to their child. Incredible.

Some people say "love ya" so much that it loses its meaning for the receiver, and she longs to hear the "real deal" of "I love you" said tenderly, eye to eye, and with sincere emotion.

Sometimes he needs to hear it when he knows he has failed at something or disappointed her. He longs to hear those unconditional words of "I love you"—*period*. Nothing else needs to be said.

The Five Love Languages by Gary Chapman is a classic book on what each partner needs. Chapman thoroughly shares how each partner can fulfill the other's needs with examples and inspiration. He addresses the love behind the oil change for your wife, and why she wants a long conversation instead of roses. Read it yourself. Also, suggest that clients buy it, read it together, and share with you what they learned about their personal love language.

Apologizing

Apologizing needs to happen as soon as possible before more hurtful words are said and before the spouse says more things he will regret and can't take back. Practice submission. Practice surrendering. It is God's way.

In Ephesians 4:26, the Bible says, "Be angry, and yet do not sin; do not let the sun go down on our anger." Is it OK to be angry? Yes, it is OK to honor your emotions but not in a way that will hurt oneself or others. This is good wisdom, and couples won't have any real peace until they clear their conscience anyway.

"Sorry" doesn't cut it when you have hurt someone, nor does "*If* I have hurt you…"

A truly repentant heart is a humble heart. Couples need to make that apology believable by saying, "I'm sorry [and name the thing that has caused the hurt]. I was wrong. Will you forgive me?" And, ideally, "What do I have to do or say to make it right?"

As part of the apology one can ask "what do I need to do to make it right?" and then do or say whatever is requested. If the response is defeating, just let it go, again, you did your part.

Naming what the spouse has done acknowledges it and means he or she is owning it. It is a confession. Asking for forgiveness is even more humbling and requires the spouse surrendering control to the other person. It is also freeing. The other person can grant forgiveness or not, but the spouse asking forgiveness has done his part and can let it go without guilt. The other person may be so hurt or flabbergasted by the apology and request that she may say that she needs time. That is OK. Again, he has done his part and should just say, "I understand."

I recently apologized to a friend who was mad at me. I asked her out to breakfast, and she grudgingly accepted. When she got in the car, I immediately said, "Sue [using her name is personal], I know that I have hurt you, and I am sorry. Will you forgive me?"

She replied, "You did hurt me. What you did was wrong. I didn't think that was right." I just said, "I understand. Will you forgive me?" She said, "Yes," and the tension drifted away. It was more important to me to restore the relationship than for me to be right or justify my actions. Spouses should do whatever it takes and know that they are doing the right thing in God's eyes. That is all that really matters.

Forgiving and Forgetting

Forgiving and forgetting are often hard. Some people can let things go easily. Others hang on and may hold a grudge for decades, bringing up the incident whenever it is opportune, so the transgressor is never able to pay off her dues or finish her penance.

Find out what the unforgiving person's motivation is for himself or herself for not yielding.

Sometimes unforgivers/unforgetters dump their junk on others or you and use it to feel in control. If they were hurt and did not have control at one point in their life, they may be taking it out on others.

Whether that is the case or not, we are still responsible for our actions today in the here and now. Apologizing, forgiving, and forgetting reflect values we all need to embrace without excuse.

Our model of forgiveness is Christ, who forgave as He was being persecuted:

- He also forgave us while we were still sinners (Romans 5:8).
- In Psalm 103:12, the Bible tells us that God forgets our sins as far as the east is from the west.
- Ephesians 4:32 reminds us to be "forgiving to each other, just as God in Christ also has forgiven you."

That is the standard. It is a hard one, but it is a godly one.

(See also "Ways to Improve Communication" in the appendix.)

CHAPTER 22
Anger Management

Various groups deal with anger management. However, as the name implies, it is for *managing* anger, not necessarily getting to the root of why anger, rather than a godly response, dominates one's reaction.

Counseling helps get to the root, and then healing can begin. One's temper becomes manageable or, ideally, eliminated. The once-angry person comfortably and successfully draws on other appropriate responses rather than reactions.

- Know that people use their anger to get what they want because they have not had success with other options.
- They feel uncomfortable expressing their feelings, including anger, so it is sometimes expressed in an uncontrolled way.

They need to be taught how to manage their responses and confidently handle anything that is thrown at them. Their aggressive reaction is a survival mechanism from

- fear,
- hurt,
- pain,
- disrespect, and
- any number of emotions connected with memories of having no power, as in when they were victimized, bullied, and/or ignored.

Angry people need to realize that there are other options for getting through an argument or ways to deal with infuriating or hurtful situations.

Often when they were growing up, anger was not tolerated or, if it was, only a parent was allowed to express it. Sometimes a withdrawn parent will uncharacteristically show pent-up anger, prompting everyone to back off and walk on eggshells.

Children may not have been able to show their own anger or frustration at the parent's verbal or physical onslaught and may have (fearfully) concluded that

- their anger/feelings were not worthy of expression, or
- anger directed at them was rejection.

These lessons boil down to the thinking by the child/adolescent that he cannot give or take anger, that he is powerless, which arouses feelings of fear.

This is a conflicting family concern. The angry parent may need to have his own feelings respected, but because of the family dynamics or other situations (perhaps a domineering wife or being undervalued at work, for example), the father may be transferring his own frustrated feelings to his son, even the very feelings of victimization he experienced when he was growing up. The son feels assaulted/rejected because of the father's lack of ability to control his feelings. Distrust of others, particularly men, if it was a father, may begin here and carry over to later years when triggers may cause the hurtful scenes with the father to replay.

If the father's expression of anger left the son feeling helpless and rejected, this may be one root of the angry feelings exhibited today. In addition, fathers who are emotionally absent especially create longings in their sons, and fathers who are angry prompt alienation, distrust, and anger.

You can approach the issue like this:

"What are the triggers for your anger?"

"What feelings do the triggers arouse?" (Infuriation, frustration, defensiveness, rage, hurt, fear, or helplessness?)

Ask him to name as many as possible. It will reveal where his vulnerability is.

"What do you typically say and do?" (Curse, yell, hit the wall, kick things, threaten others?)

You are trying to see the level of anger/violence.

"Can you handle your anger better with some people or circumstances than with others?"

This shows it can be a choice, as he will cite examples where he can control his anger.

"Can you give examples?"

Now that he has revealed that he does have some control over it, *ask him if he sees that he has some control over his anger, and that it depends on the situation.* His recognizing that he has a choice is a good thing and fosters hope.

"So would you say that it is a conscious choice that you manage your anger sometimes and sometimes not?"

"So it is a choice you make when you react rather than respond?"

If he admits it, fine; if not, let it go for now. Remember *he* needs to have the insight.

"Have you ever had a restraining order against you? What were the circumstances?"

"Have you ever been arrested for an anger-related situation?"

"How old were you when you first started feeling your anger was troublesome?"

"Can you give me an example or two?"

"What were the consequences of you anger?"

"Were you disciplined by your parents for your anger?"

"Were there others in your household who also had an anger problem?"

"What did it look like?"

"How did everyone react to it?"

"Was this typical for the person?"

"Was there verbal and physical abuse?"

"To whom was it directed?"

(Any sexual abuse that may be at the root of the client's anger will probably not be shared this early in the session[s]. Refer to chapter 16, "Sexual, Physical, and Emotional Abuse, and Anxiety" for guidelines to pursue and manage such a discussion. Victims of sexual abuse, especially men, may have anger [and control] issues from feeling powerless.)

"How did you handle it?"

This will tell you if he held back his emotions, perhaps tolerated it to prove his manhood, began taking drugs to blot it out, and so on. See if there is a connection between how he handled the abuse back then and how he handles his emotions now.

"Did you ever take on the role of protecting others from the anger in your childhood household?"

"What did that look like?"

Go slowly because he may have painful memories and perhaps guilt about what he observed and did or did not do. If applicable, ask about his relationships with those siblings he may have protected or abandoned. Ask if those siblings are doing OK today.

"When your parents or siblings saw that you got angry over something, how was it handled?"

"Was it dismissed, so that you learned to suppress it?"

"Did your parents defend you when there were times when you had a legitimate reason for being angry, like being bullied or physically assaulted?"

How we resolve a crisis is a reflection of our character. *Ask clients if they think this is true.*

People do not lose their temper; they give it away. It is a choice. They make a decision—to hit her or not, to fight or not. *See if the client agrees.*

The bottom line is, try to do the following:

- Get to the root of the anger and correct any distorted thinking.
- Glean some history about the parents and how anger was expressed and received by the children, and see what thoughts he has about his anger and its expression today.
- Help him find new ways to be comfortable expressing his anger so he will be heard respectfully and understood emotionally and mentally.

Work with the partner to encourage the angry person's expression of feelings and to correct any inappropriate behaviors or words patiently. Both people need to have a mutual understanding of this process so they can feel safe to practice and be held accountable if they slip.

Ask them to search for "anger management treatment options" or "managing anger" on the web and share with you what they learned.

The Christian twelve-step recovery group Celebrate Recovery can help with anger issues as well, especially in the area of accountability, although counseling is typically also needed.

CHAPTER 23

Addiction and Other Issues

(Addictions that are an exception and are not dealt with here are medication use that is necessary to manage chronic pain, and medications used for treating a symptom of pain in hospice patients. Additionally, the physical withdrawal symptoms for legal and illegal drug or alcohol-dependent persons are not addressed.)

Cycles

Addictions to alcohol, drugs, gambling, spending, Internet games, and so forth generally have a predictable cycle. It is important for you to discern where clients are in the cycle and educate them about their inevitable progression if they do not get serious about help.

Teach Clients What Happens to Our Bodies with Addictions

Here is a very simplistic explanation that may add to their understanding of the chemical as well as the emotional and psychological impact of addiction.

Let us use appetite as an example. The hypothalamus is that part of the brain that manages signals around appetite. When it detects a drop in blood sugar, we get hungry. By eating healthy food, like fresh fruit, our blood sugar spikes, a surge of insulin follows, and then comes a drop in our blood sugar and a return to normal levels. If we eat processed sugar, however, the spike is inordinate, the return to balance takes longer, and we are still not satisfied. Hence, our hunger remains after eating processed sugar.

We also have gut hormones that go up and down as we eat and digest, and provide our systems with a much-needed rest between meals. A lack of sleep and too much sugar are two culprits that can stimulate our appetites and get our systems off track. Our systems do not get a chance to rest and return to their natural, healthy balance known as homeostasis.

Our God-designed bodies have very refined systems that work to maintain balance. They preserve body fat for the body's physical protection instead of eliminating it, explaining why it is harder to lose weight than put it on.

Pleasure Prompts
We have a system in our brain called the hedonic system (you may have heard of hedonism or the word *hedonistic* to describe someone who is very self-indulgent) or limbic system. When parts of the hedonistic or pleasure system are stimulated, we feel a high and a desire for whatever produced that high. Anything that stimulates your limbic system can lead to dependency and potential addiction.

One of the chemicals released during pleasure is dopamine. This chemical is released when we do pleasurable things from flirting to eating chocolate. Dopamine is there to guide us to eat/indulge and encourage arousal primarily for procreation. Dopamine hooks onto brain cells and builds a permanent memory trace to the source of that pleasure source. It keeps *everything* that is pleasurable (images, acts, sounds, and so on) active in our minds so we can experience them repeatedly. The more intense the experience, the more we want to repeat the behavior.

Repeat, Repeat, Repeat
Recreational drugs give that pleasurable high and amp up the dopamine supply. Drugs stimulate the brain's pleasure spot and trigger an unnaturally exaggerated dopamine response. Therefore, the high makes us want to repeat the behavior repeatedly.

Our Bodies Lose It
With continuous bombardment of our system from dopamine, our dopamine receptors gradually fade out. We wind up with a decreased sensitivity to our body's natural response to regulate sources of pleasure like sex, art, music, socialization, and so on.

Sugar-laden and fat-rich foods affect the dopamine system similarly to drugs—that is, they increase our cravings.

Is Addiction Genetic?
We do not know if drug abuse and overeating, for example, and the resultant de-sensitivity of the dopamine reward system is genetic or learned. However, the members in a family where drug use or overeating are the norm appear to have an increased susceptibility to addiction.

Rewiring the Brain—The Good News
Thus, drugs, processed foods, and sugars as examples can foil our natural reward chemistry. The good news is that the brain can be rewired when these culprits are reduced or eliminated. When we substitute healthy choices for bad ones, our brain and chemicals will rewire to normal, and we can renew our desire and satisfaction with healthy pleasures.

Recovery
The following material can apply to the emotional, mental, and spiritual recovery process for persons in addictions of almost any sort from drugs to online affairs.

Psychological/Emotional Issue
Besides the chemical response of the body, also realize that addiction involves unresolved heart, emotional, and fear issues. (See section III, "Foundational Material to Know before You Begin.")
As you explore this area with a client, know that the emotional unrest due to a painful situation or traumatic experience may not be acknowledged psychologically or verbally. For example, a veteran who had horrific experiences might say, "Nothing happened" or "I don't remember," but his angry outbursts, restlessness, and violent nightmares reveal the true impact.

Finding the source of the fear and pain. Drugs, alcohol, spending, gaming, and so on, are all attempts to distract the mind and heart from painful situations, memories, or fears. The journey to discover the source of the pain and fear is the purpose of counseling. However, if you realize that the client has specifically suffered a trauma, he or she should be referred to a professional.

(See the section on "Who Should Be Referred Elsewhere" in chapter 5, "Who Seeks Help and Whom to Accept.")

When a heart or fear issue is the root of the problem, it can be attributed to many things:

- Those things that the client was personally involved in (like using a drug)
- Those that were witnessed (an accident where people were burning alive)
- Those that were threatened ("If you don't do this, your legs will get broken")
- One very hurtful remark such as "If you say anything, I will kill your mother"; "You are trash and always will be"; "You are ugly, and no one will ever want you"; "Why can't you be like your brother?"; "You were a mistake"; "I never wanted kids"; "I'm sorry I married you"; "You're the reason we have all our problems"; "You don't fit in with this family"; "No wonder you don't have any friends"; and so on.
- Ongoing remarks or incidents

How We Deal with Hurtful Remarks, Situations, or Incidents
Perhaps you can think of some wounding words that were said to you or someone you love. How were they handled? Not everyone is crushed by such words. Some people are launched into an obsession to prove the remark was not true. This may include some overachievers and people obsessed with being desirable and looking attractive.

Others remember well the historical remark or incident. They have "managed it," although they may continue to hold some resentment. This will be revealed in counseling.

Other people may have come to terms with the remark and have truly let it go.

Those people emotionally crushed by the remark or incident may deal with it by experimenting with ways to distract their mind and heart from it. It is just too painful to deal with, and they want the pain to go away. The distracting actions they think may not be dangerous may well take them down the slippery slope to an addiction.

Some drugs (methamphetamines and cocaine) are addicting after one try for many people, or their system cannot tolerate the drug or the amount and they overdose. Certainly, overdoses and getting drunk are not always intentional, but often people do not realize how much of the drug they are taking because they are already incapacitated.

Certain card games and Internet activities (games, social media, online gambling) can be addictive because they are so engrossing, and that relieves their emotional pain. It becomes an addiction based on the amount of time (and sometimes money) spent to the neglect or exclusion of other responsibilities (job, school, home care, relationships) and interests (exercising, social time, education, and so on).

The Addiction Journey Begins to Ease the Pain

The Experimentation Phase

The experimentation phase is dangerous. These people may be struggling with their conscience but try it with the intention of doing it just this once. That one time can change their life. Porn addicts remember well the first pornographic image they saw. Alcoholics recall their first drink (sometimes offered by a parent) or the first time they got drunk. Spenders recall the first time they bought something and because of circumstances had to hide it. The corruption of one's values begins, and compromises (lying, hiding, excuse making, and so on) happen regularly after that, thus producing shame.

The Anticipation Phase

The next stage is anticipation and excitement as the routine or drama of the indulgence progresses. The addict may experience the following:

- *Danger* in wondering if you will get caught.
- *Intentional defiance* to do what you want to do even if it is harmful.
- *Curiosity* about what the other options are for your drug of choice. For spenders, this may be from buying at stores, to online sales, to in-person or online auctions, and so on; for porn users, the variety of types of porn—such as child, homosexual, specific ethnic types, group sex, and so on—is plentiful; for drug users, it is about chasing the high with stronger doses, mixing different drugs, trying needles, and so on).
- *The addition of new behaviors*—for example, a porn user trying voyeurism or exposing oneself. The options are limitless.
- *More than one addiction*, which is fairly common. Addicts also switch addictions.

The Routine
The person develops a routine around his or her addiction that is absorbing and distracts from his or her pain. The routine becomes comforting and obsessive. The thrill of the routine can be as satisfying as the act itself. The routine becomes addicting.

Corruption
With this progression comes a corruption in one's values. The lying, manipulation, and denial escalate. Addicts may sincerely believe the lies they tell, much to the exasperation of their partners. The emotional manipulation may have the partner thinking they themselves are going crazy. (See the section on "Emotional Manipulation" in chapter 7, "Assessing the Problem: Understanding Clients' Feelings and Reactions.")

This progression can lead to arrests, jail, job loss, relationship issues, financial loss, and other calamities.

Help Them Face the Corruption
For any addiction or near-addiction issues, you are trying to get the person to see the corruption of his or her morals and the negative changes in his or her lifestyle, social life, faith practices, and so on as he or she progressively indulges in the addiction. This will help those on the verge of becoming addicts see the progression and the severity of what is going on. Getting them to see what is happening is far more effective than you telling them. Watch for denial, minimization, and emotional manipulation. When it happens, call them on it and pursue a line of questioning that will reveal the reality. Some questions to ask:

> *"I hear you saying that all your friends do it. Do you think there has been any negative impact on their lives?"*

> *"Do you think your friends have a problem? Do you think they would admit they have a problem?"*

> *"What's changed in your lifestyle since you began [whatever his/her addiction is]?"*

This could be a long explanation or not. Maybe there was not a specific incident that can be recalled. Maybe it was a shift in the family dynamic, such as the birth of a new baby. The loss of attention may have prompted someone to become withdrawn and preoccupied with solitary activities like games. The addiction may have arisen out of that preoccupation.

Perhaps the birth of children so changed the marital relationship and the wife's attention and her sex drive that the husband rationalized he needed attention and did whatever fed that—had an affair, established an online relationship, or frequented strip clubs.

Various questions to ask:

> *"When would you say you began to spend more time on (whatever his/her addiction is)?"*

"Was there an incident that happened to you or to someone you care about or know that started all this?"

Fish for the trigger with suggestions—for example, a divorce, a friend moving away, a friend overdosing, not making the team, a broken relationship—only if he does not have a response.

"Would you give me some more details about the incident?"

(You are seeking head, heart, and situational impactors.)

- If the person has social fears and/or likes to have fantasy relationships, hiding on the Internet can be his main connection to people. He can assume various identities and personalities. The intrigue of "Who will I be?" or "Who will I seduce?" plays into the person's feelings of control when something in his life or history led him to feel he had no control. On the other hand, maybe the person is socially insecure when face-to-face versus online.

Therefore, you are looking to identify the following:

- The initial trigger (for example, verbal abuse, humiliation, being unwanted). (Remember to validate their pain)
- The resultant feelings (for example, shame, self-consciousness, unworthiness)
- The wrong self-talk ("I guess I am no good") and if they corrected it
- What changed in their lifestyle and/or values (for example, they began hanging out with the wrong crowd) that fueled experimentation (for example, with drugs, porn, online affairs)
- The impact/changes of their choices (relationship troubles, job loss, and so on)
- How they have already tried to fix the problem (programs, self-abstinence, counseling, and so on)
- The result

This will not happen in one session. Be patient and remember the following:

- *They* need to see the progression.
- *They* need to own it.
- *They* need to be sincerely repentant in order for a life and heart change to happen.

Carefully thought-out questions to help the addict see the depth of danger, the consequences, and the corruption will all help bring him to reality. It is not about shaming; it is about bringing him to a willingness to make a confession and be repentant.

Additional Considerations

An Intervention

An *intervention* is a tool used to convince the addict that there is a very serious problem. It is a planned meeting of significant people who have been affected by the addict's behavior and who are prepared to tell the addict directly what has been done to them because of the addiction. The addict is usually resistant to help when this surprise meeting is forced on him.

Many feelings may potentially arise at the onset—for example, outrage that he has been victimized, embarrassment or intense anger at not being in control, and so on. If he stays (sometimes only by force), each person takes a turn talking. Ideally, their comments will be wrapped in love and grace. The addict often breaks down, weeps, and commits to getting help (usually inpatient). To tap his vulnerability, he is usually taken immediately to a rehab facility.

A professional usually runs this type of intervention, but sometimes a family will conduct a session on their own. Sometimes the aftereffects of the comments spoken to the addict cause more pain and family disruption than good. Read about interventions before getting involved or trying to convince a family this is needed.

Typically, the addict's partner or parents have enabled the addiction in some fashion. They may buy the alcoholic beer, drink with him to keep the peace, or resist confronting him because of his temper. Parents may not confront a teen who is a computer game junkie because they have their own unhealthy preoccupations. Perhaps they do not know how to relate to their children, or they justify that the kid is just an introvert and it's harmless.

Enabling

First, ask the partner or parents if they know what *enabling* means. If not, educate them and ask if they think this may be an issue, in their household or elsewhere (for example, the other set of parents, indulgent grandparents, or peers).

You do not want to shame them, so be careful as you ask. Remember that enabling is often a codependent issue.

(See chapter 24, "Codependency.")

You can say,

> *"Please know that many people enable addicts, thinking it is the best option at the time. They do not mean any harm but do not know what else to do. After hearing this explanation, do you think you or anyone else may unintentionally be an enabler?"*

They may admit it; perhaps even say it was intentional to prevent physical abuse to themselves or to avoid having the threats made toward them come true.

Recovery Plan for the Enabler

Now you have the agenda for recovery for the enabler, which is essentially the following:

- Hands off. Let the bottom fall out.
- Let go and let God take over.

This is terrifying for many enablers because it threatens a role they have played and are comfortable managing, even though the outcome is not helping. The enablers

- need to work on switching to a healthier way of feeling valued for themselves, and
- need to not fear the verbal onslaught by the addict.

(See chapter 21, "Managing Arguments.")

Adjusting to the new person the addict will become and how that may change many relationships can be threatening. Enablers need the following:

- Support of a twelve-step group like Al-Anon or Celebrate Recovery
- Codependency education and meetings
- Counseling, if possible

Chasing That Initial High

Alcohol dependency and the chemical dependence on drugs (especially the latter) are very real. The initial high and subsequent reactions by the body from the drug compete with the natural chemicals that are released during very fearful or exciting circumstances. These are the rush of protective chemicals that help us manage these situations.

As an addict's disease progresses, the body's chemistry shifts and can no longer compete with the intruding drugs. The body may slow down its natural supply of coping drugs. The victim becomes dull and zoned out, which necessitates more or newer drugs to capture that elusive high. That physical desperation is the drive that shuts down interest in everything else. It is truly a medical phenomenon that is serious and difficult to defeat. Expert medical assistance is needed to transition the body through detoxification and back to a natural homeostasis (balance). The psychological, emotional, and spiritual recovery probably will not work until the addict is detoxified.

Alcohol

Here are some questions you can ask to assess the problem:

"Is your tolerance higher than others?"

"Can you always control your drinking?"

"Do you stop for one drink and wind up there all night?"

"Have you ever tried to stop for any length of time?"

"What made you continue after you stopped?"

Assess if they seem protective of their drinking and alcohol and their right to drink because they worked hard or because it helps them unwind. They may say it is no big deal if they have a drink or two every night.

"What are the triggers that make you want to drink?" (for example, social situations where they feel uncomfortable when not drinking, peer pressure, tired/needing to relax, any type of pressure, anger, or wanting to be more sexual)

"What feelings does the trigger arouse for you?" (for example, uneasiness or anger)

"Have you used any other options besides drinking to manage your feelings when they are triggered?" (for example, drugs, walking away, calling a sponsor, yelling, or prayer)

"What do you typically say and do?"

"Can you handle your triggers better with some people or circumstances than with others?" (This can reveal that he makes a choice about how he reacts or responds.)

"Can you give examples?"

"What is your family history with drinking?"

"Do you think anyone in your family had a problem with it?"

"Did he or she/they do anything about it?"

"What was the impact on the rest of the family?"

Recovery Resources:
AA (Alcoholics Anonymous): twelve-step recovery group for alcoholics

Al-Anon: for friends and loved ones of alcoholics

Alateen: for teens who have friends or parents who are alcoholics

Celebrate Recovery

For Drug, Alcohol, or Gambling Issues

"How would you describe the issue?" (Leaving it open ended is more conducive than an accusatory question.)

"How long has it been going on?"

"Who and what has been affected? How?" (Relationships, finances, jobs. Explore each of these areas from the perspective of the addict and the partner.)

"Have there been any efforts at abstinence or sobriety?" (For example, periods of not using or attending twelve-step meetings. If they criticize twelve-step meetings, be sure their criticism comes from their own experience and not hearsay. Assess if their criticism is a defense.)

"What happened?"

"Do you understand what enabling is?" (Covering up for the user, providing drugs or alcohol to keep them from acting out, buying the substance, joining the abuser in the behavior to keep peace or to not feel alone, and so on. These enabling behaviors protect the addict from the consequences of his or her choices.)

"Do you think you have done any of these things?"

"Is there a history of drug or alcohol abuse or gambling in your family?"

"Did anyone get help? What was the result?"

Eating Disorders (anorexia, bulimia, or overeating)

Clients with anorexia or bulimia are to be referred to a professional. Some clients with anorexia and/or bulimia *are* overeaters, but it would be prudent if the client claims to have been or is anorexic or bulimic to refer elsewhere because the healing and recovery work is complicated.

For overeating issues, you can assess if you could be a support, but the client needs to go to a program, just like for any other addiction. Overeaters Anonymous has great permanent success rates. Most people with eating issues have swung on and off various regimens. The root of the problem is a heart issue, as discussed previously. (See chapter 6, "Assessing the Problem: Potential Contributing Causes of Problems [Health, Heart, and Fear Issues].")

Assess *why*, *when*, *what*, and *how much* they eat.

"Please tell me about your experience with overeating. When did you first believe you may have a problem?" (Usually there is teenage or younger onset.)

"What was going in your family life at the time?" (Divorce, fighting, unsettling situations, and so on.)

"Was there anything going on at school?" (Poor grades, bullying, learning issues, poor attendance, and so on.)

"How about with peers?" (Did they have friends? Do things socially? Feel comfortable with peers?)

"Were you ever teased?"

"Do you recall anything ever happening to you where you felt a loss of control?" (Victims of abuse feel this. She may not be prepared to talk about this, so if needed, switch to a "head" question.)

"When you did overeat back then, what types of things did you eat and how much?"

"Did you eat alone?"

"Were any other family members struggling with weight issues?"

"What was your perception of how they handled their weight issue?" (Attempting to see if the family culture was not to criticize eating or eaters.)

"In your family, was food a reward, a sign of love?" (Trying to find out if rejecting food would hurt someone's feelings. If so, that was/is a codependency issue. Refer them to a codependency group along with counseling.)

(See chapter 24, "Codependency.")

Pornography

(Know that women also watch pornography and are as prone to becoming addicted. Some women choose porn as it is "safer" than having an in-person affair.)

"When was the first time you were exposed to it?" (They will likely remember this well.)

"How were you exposed to it? By whom?"

"How old were you?"

"What was your reaction?"

"What type of porn was it initially?"

"Did anyone else in your household or peer group view it?" (Father, brothers, or friends?)

"What type of porn is viewed now? How often? Where?" (Internet, printed material, or porn shops?)

"Has there been a change in the type of porn viewed?" (Typically, it changes as boredom sets in. Then it escalates in hardness, vulgarity, or perversion. This is evidence of the progression of the addiction.

Note that porn addicts sometimes enlarge their addiction to include affairs, homosexual experiences, and so on.)

"Are you surprised at the type of porn you have viewed over the years?" (See if there is any remorse or if their heart has already been hardened.)

"Did your viewing porn influence the sexual relationship with your wife/partner/husband?"

"What is your attitude toward your wife and her body?" (Sometimes they have higher expectations in appearance after comparing their wife to some of the models or players, and/or they expect the wife to engage in some of the acts shown, some of which are beyond inappropriate.)

"Do you watch porn together? What type? R-rated movies? X-rated movies?"

"Whose idea was it? What is your partner's reaction?" (Sadly, even some Christians admit to filming themselves and/or watching porn. Later, after you get an assessment of the extent of the problem, address these actions against their values and godly behavior.)

"Has there been a change in your viewing other types of nudity?" (for example, strip clubs, voyeurism)

"Have you thought about experiencing any other type of sexual activities?" (for example, voyeurism, homosexuality, multiple partners, prostitution)

"Have you experienced any of these? How often?"

"Has there been a change in your way of thinking about these types of activities?"

"Do you think you are minimizing their effect on you and your values?"

"Do you think you are minimizing their effect on your relationships?"

"Does that help convince you that this is a progressive addiction?"

"Have you considered installing blocks on your computer? If not, why not?"

"Would you go to a men's purity group or twelve-step group for this issue? If not, why not?"

An excellent, classic book for both pornography and sexual addiction is *Out of the Shadows: Understanding Sexual Addiction* (3rd ed.) by Patrick Carnes. Anyone (partner or addict) reading it will have a reality check on the severity of this disorder, and hopefully the addict will be motivated to get serious about his/her recovery.

One tool for combating the objectification of women is for the observer to give the woman a name, recognize that she is someone's daughter or sister. Pray on the spot for her to become a new, cleansed woman through a relationship with Jesus Christ.

For an Affair/Sexual Addiction
(Much of the same line of questioning used here can be applied to pornography. Follow what is applicable. Of course, women also have affairs.)

When the wife comes to counseling alone for the first time:

"What happened?" (Get her side of the story, which may be quite different when you see her with her partner.)

"How long has it been going on?"

"Were there other affairs?"

"How did you find out? Were you suspicious?"

"How did you respond?"

Sometimes wives try to compete with the other woman by engaging in what the husband tells her he was drawn to, or she may go on a radical weight-loss regimen or change her looks drastically.

For the husband (when seen alone):

"What happened?" (How did they meet, how many times did they get together, and how often was it sexual?)

"How did it progress to an affair?" (Flirting, meeting after work for drinks, texting)

"How did you hide it?" (Disguising names on one's contact list, erasing calls and texts, destroying receipts, and so on.)

"How long has it been going on?"

"Were there other affairs?"

"Do you use prostitutes?"

"How often? How much do you typically spend?"

"Do you watch porn?" (If so, select applicable questions from the porn section of this chapter.)

Don't Tell

No good will come from the wife knowing the details of an affair. She will press to get information about the other woman's looks, how she was in bed, and so on. This information will only fuel her imagination and resentments. Even if she knows the woman, encourage the husband not to give any details.

The ruminating or racing thoughts the wife will experience will preoccupy her mind and prevent her from healing. She is trying to make sense of an experience that does not fit with her vision of what is normal or expected. Her defenses are kicking in to try to fit it in her brain and experiential history, but her mind is resisting. She has to accept the facts, and then she will have peace and eventually acceptance—and hopefully forgiveness.

If the wife presses, the husband can say (if the following is true):

> *"I have confessed to God, and I have accepted His forgiveness. I will not cause you any more pain by feeding your mind hurtful information. There is no good in it. It was my fault, and it is not because of you."*

Can they both learn valuable things about what may have been going on in the relationship (or job, or finances, or any other pressures) that they can work on? Absolutely. It can be a wake-up call for the marriage and for both of their roles in it.

Sample Dialogue of a Session

Background

Client profile: "Jack," an unmarried man, has been living with "Jill," the mother of their two beautiful small children, for eight years. He has had two affairs while in the relationship. He works steady, is physically fit and attractive, and is quiet with a nice personality. He admits to "somewhat of a porn habit" and is slowly considering that he probably has a sexual addiction.

Sometimes he exhibits flirtatious behavior or picks up on it when it is directed at him. He then texts the girl, and it is reciprocated. That may be enough for a while, but sometimes there are in-person meetings and eventually sex, usually on multiple occasions. He says he is committed to his girlfriend and family and wants to marry her. He did not think he had a serious problem but was convicted to come to counseling to figure out what is going on and to move his relationship with Jill forward. He seems very sincere about that.

The girlfriend is invested but has reservations about his ability to stay faithful. She was raised in the Christian faith, wandered off, and is only now beginning to grow her faith and faith practices (most likely because of the children and needing a port in the storm when there are relational issues).

He believes in God but is not interested in church and has read parts of the Bible in the past. He does not have a personal relationship with Christ and at this point is not really interested. He has said he will not come to counseling if religion is pressed.

GRETCHEN JACOBS, MA, MS, CHAPLAIN

The following dialogue is recent. It occurred after he had another relapse because he was caught by his girlfriend texting another woman. He says they did not go any further but admitted that he may have if the texting had continued.

"Jack, I know you have issues with talking about your faith. I get that, but can we talk about why you feel the way you do for a couple of minutes?"

"OK."

"Do you believe in God?"

"Yes, but not church—not organized religion."

"I can understand that. Have you considered that church is a place to refuel your values and be reminded about what is important? Sort of like an accountability partner. Can you see that?"

"Yes."

"Another thing about church is that you get to know people who you might be able to help out sometime. (His girlfriend said that he likes to help people). That's a nice thing to do and is more meaningful when you know the people, yes?"

"I can see that."

"OK, just some food for thought."

(I did not want to alienate him because he isn't comfortable [yet] talking about faith issues, so I moved on, hoping I had made one beginning point.)

"So how has it been going?"

"Not good. I slipped up with a customer, and I got caught. I tried to lie about what happened, but after a few minutes I told Jill the truth."

"What happened with the customer?" (He then explained.)

"So you see that you took the bait. What were you responding to?"

"Her compliments to me."

"Do you feel Jill doesn't give you enough attention, sex, or compliments?"

"No, she is great at all of that."

"So what is it? Do you like giving compliments as much as getting them?"

"I like giving them more."

This is significant because it reveals he may be a people pleaser who pleases people to get attention for himself. (See chapter 24, "Codependency.")

"Would you say you're a people pleaser?" (He seems intrigued but comfortable with the label.)

"In the flirting/affairs area only."

"Did anyone in your family ever put you down at any time that makes you long for attention now?"

"No, only the bullies at school." (Pursue this later. Potential lack of control issues that lead him to take control by having affairs.)

"Because you so easily slipped into deep water when you were intent on being on your best behavior, do you think you have an addiction?"

"Yes, because with a little bit of flirting, I move right along."

(I gave him the analogy of a woman who was on a diet and was not able to go into a bakery or an alcoholic who cannot go into a bar. He got the concept that he cannot flirt since he drowns quickly…and its inappropriate for a married/committed man to do so.)

"So your setup for your tipping point begins with flirting, either you or her. [He nods.] *If you don't flirt back, and you don't initiate flirting, you won't find yourself in deep water, right?"*

"Yes, I see that."

"You have choices. You can be in control."

"I see that."

"What did you say to the woman when you ended this last slip?"

"I told her that I'm in a relationship, and I was stupid for texting her. She texted something about my girlfriend being a lucky girl, and I could sense she was still interested. I told her I had to go and didn't answer the couple of texts she sent after that."

We talked about what to say when someone flirts with him. He did not know what to say to kill it right there. I reminded him he was in control. I suggested he keep it short and direct, not "You're hot, and I would really like to be with you, but I've got a girlfriend." He saw how his original response just adds fuel to the fire and is a mixed message. I suggested he say, "I'm in a committed relationship and am not interested—period." No other explanation is needed. If the girl persists, say, "It's not my value—period."

He liked that response and promised to try it the next time he was flirted with, and he also would not initiate the flirting. That was his first homework assignment until we met again in a couple of weeks.

Build Up His Self-Perception

We talked about how he appreciated the attention, and I suggested one strategy to start. Get appropriate attention from other sides of himself—so that he can see that that he is more than a "sexual" man. Because he is a father, I asked if he would value a compliment about what a great dad he is, and he said, "Yes." A great husband? "Yes." A good friend? "Yes." A great player on his sports team? "Yes." A great coach to other parents' kids? "Yes." Through this strategy, he understood there are other areas in which he could strive to excel and receive quality recognition in order to build his self-esteem.

Creating Empathy

Next, we talked about how he comforted Jill when she found out. His response was about him, and he did not validate her feelings. He saw that he needed to do that by reminding her that this is *his* issue, and it has nothing to do with her or that she is somehow deficient, suggesting he tell her she is tremendous, beautiful, and so forth.

He said she has full access to his phone.

Taking Care of Your Own Business

I asked if he knows how to be social without being flirtatious. He said yes and gave examples. When I asked what he would do if his friend's girlfriend flirted with him, he said he would tell him. I suggested that he talk to the girl first, and only if it happened again, tell his friend.

To his astonishment, I mentioned how the Bible is the basis for our legal system and told him how it says that the offended person should go to the guilty person alone and talk about it. If they continue the behavior, bring another witness, and then on the third time take it to the church leaders for action. That is the basis for him approaching the flirter himself and taking care of his own business first. He saw that.

We talked about his support system, and he says he knows a few men who have good values.

Clues to His Behavior

I switched back to his addiction. "Is flirting enough or is sex essential?" He said he wants to sustain the relationship once involved, that one-night stands were not his thing. He likes to get to know someone.

I asked which was more important: his getting to know someone or the other person getting to know him? He likes to get to know someone. This indicated he longs to be able to trust enough to let others know him. I talked about the trust and emotional connection exclusive to a marital union and that he could have that with Jill. He saw that.

We followed up on a previous conversation about his getting a promise ring for his wedding finger (as a deterrent and as a reminder for him). He said he still wants to wait to do that until they are closer to getting married.

Homework
Another homework assignment was for him to keep track of flirting opportunities and his responses and share them with me during the next session. (I should have reminded him to think about the other roles he plays and to work on excelling at those to build his self-esteem.)

I prayed after he said he did not want to, and we ended the session.

Accomplishments

- He realizes he has an addiction.
- He sees that he is not in control—that he is swept along quickly and easily.
- He sees that he needs to be more direct and serious about responding when someone flirts with him.
- He sees that he needs to pay more attention to validating his girlfriend.
- He sees that he has other abilities and that he needs to get his value from those aspects of himself.

I hope that he will reflect on why he has needed the flirtatious/sexual attention and will figure out how to get healthier attention by acknowledging and growing his other roles.

Note: Previously, I discussed Jack and Jill's potential marriage and noted that they are unequally yoked. If Jack surrenders his life to Christ, major hurdles will be crossed. They will be closer to being equally yoked. He needs a lot of growth, and she needs to continue her faith journey.

They have been together for eight years, have two children, and both Jack and Jill want to be married. If Jack's addiction is surrendered to Christ, God will give him the victory. Right now, they are not ready to marry, but when Jack puts his life in God's hands, they will be on the right path. At least Jack is allowing some teaching. I encouraged Jill by reminding her that God wants everyone to come to Him and Jack is no exception. She is keeping her mind on Christ as she prays for Jack. They talk about Jack honoring her faith journey. I am hopeful that he will come to Christ.

Addiction and Recovery—Thoughts and Encouragement for Your Clients

Share the following information and teach clients and his or her partner to use the tools cited.
Recovery is learning to live your life differently—new routines, friends, and so forth. For the addict and partner, with insight comes a choice about the impact of the addiction: resentment or empathy. Remember that resentment is a sin and empathy is a godly virtue. Always try to be in God's will and not bring on God's discipline.

God speaking: "Then I will make up to you for the years that the swarming locusts has eaten" (Joel 2:25). Give God your life, and He will restore what has been taken away.

"For I am confident of this very thing, that He who began a good work in you will perfect it" (Philippians 1:6). Be assured. God will continue His work in you.

Jesus speaking: "The things that are impossible with people are possible with God" (Luke 18:27).

God speaking: "Moreover, I will give you a new heart and put a new spirit within you; and I will remove the heart of stone from your flesh and give you a heart of flesh. I will put My Spirit within you and cause you to walk in My statutes, and you will be careful to observe My ordinances" (Ezekiel 36:26–27).

- Learn to live with unsolved problems. It is life.
- "Pain is inevitable; suffering is optional."
- Having a pity party? Focus instead on what is OK about your life. Focusing on the negative will never make you feel better.
- Sometimes when we realize we are too weak to face life on life's terms, we stop relying on our own strength and seek the strength of God. Perhaps God used an illness or addiction for you to find Him.
- Meet your own needs and do not blame others when they don't meet your needs.
- Learn self-awareness by doing a daily inventory—reflect on your character defects and how you fared. (See chapter 30, "Spiritual Issues and Personal Growth for Counselors and Clients.")
- Do not compare—especially yourself to others. It is not godly because you will see yourself as "better than" (which is prideful) or "less than" (which is self-defeating). Both are sins. God wants you to be content with how He made you, and He loves you unconditionally *however* you are.

Managing Urges

Urges (of most sorts) last nine minutes. Teach clients to try to delay indulging in the urge for ten minutes and it should pass. While waiting for the urge to pass, do a healthy substitutional behavior like drinking water instead of eating, praying instead of getting on the computer to look at porn, or calling an accountability partner.

Improve your self-control. Slowly delay acting on your desire a little at a time. You may need to say to yourself that you are not denying yourself but instead delaying gratification (and that will help build your self-control).

Teach Clients to Manage Their Thinking

Teach clients that one's thinking can make matters worse. Challenge any faulty assumptions. Repeating negative thoughts just embeds them in your mind. As they say in AA, "Quit the stinkin' thinking."

Suggest they transfer the thoughts and feelings of love and compassion they have for someone they care about to someone who has harmed them. Encourage them to practice it every time a negative or hurtful thought comes up about that person. Suggest they think about him or her the way they think about someone they trust and respect.

If the client is willing, have him pray for God to change his own heart daily, as well as the heart of the person who harmed him. God *can* change hearts.

Ask of yourself, "How important is it?" This often defuses anger.

They Do Have Control
Teach them to ask of themselves, "Where is *my* control?" It probably is only in *their response*.

Triggers
Have clients identify their triggers (people, places, and things) so they can take care of the anticipated pain/discomfort/anxiety.

(See "What I Offer a Partner" worksheet in the appendix.)

Try a Twelve-Step Program
When they try a twelve-step program and are hesitant to return, one option members suggest is, "Give it at least six weeks. If you're still not sure, we'll give you back your misery."

Abstaining versus Recovery
There is a difference between sober (abstaining) and recovery (working on issues *and* abstaining). If you abstain but are not in recovery, you will probably just trade destructive behaviors and be a high risk for a relapse.

Keep It All in Perspective
Be careful not to focus on the behavior or the substance, as it is a setup for failure.

Remind clients to take it one day at a time, stay in recovery, and keep asking themselves what they can do to grow spiritually and emotionally—and make *that* their focus.

Relapse is not failure—it is a mistake.

A slip does not negate the work you have done. Relapse is falling out of the *recovery* process, but you are still *in recovery*.

Do not give a slip more meaning than it deserves because that will foster shame. Do not catastrophize shame—that is, view a situation worse than it is. That can lead to relapse. Remind clients that they may *have made* a mistake, but *they* are not a mistake. Remind them to be careful, as an acceptance of a slip (that is, giving yourself permission) is minimizing and justifying.

Keep humble—it helps prevent a relapse.

Remind them that when one slips, it does not mean one's progress was not real or that one did not grow. Clients need to acknowledge how far they have come—they may be arguing less with their wife, working steadily at their job, taking better care of their health, and so forth.

Remind them that when they fail, they do not go back to the bottom but to the top of where they left off.

> **"For what I am doing, I do not understand; for I am not practicing what I would like to do, but I am doing the very thing I hate" (Romans 7:15).** Even Paul struggled.

> **"For You have rescued my soul from death, my eyes from tears, my feet from stumbling" (Psalm 116:8).**

> **Jesus speaking: "In Me you may have peace. In the world you have tribulation, but…I have overcome the world" (John 16:33).**

Have Accountability Partners

Remind your clients to have God be their primary accountability partner. It will grow their relationship with Him, and He will convict them of any wrong thinking. He will open their eyes and give them strength.

Having one or two people support the clients in this work is very helpful. Every few days, encouragers will ask, "How is it going with counseling and your homework?"

When people do not have godly encouragers, they just hear from the discouragers who may be offering bad guidance, such as they should leave the relationship or retaliate.

Clients need to be ruthlessly honest about what they are or are not doing and be accountable.

Secrecy will not happen if they are serious about their recovery.

Stalled Progress

When clients are not working on goals or dedicated to participating in a twelve-step program, confront them on why they are not invested. There are many potential reasons:

- Fear of the physical withdrawal
- Fear of leaving a known social situation and fear of being accepted and enjoying a new one
- Fear of not succeeding for themselves and those needing them to succeed
- Fear of succeeding and then relapsing
- Fear that the internal emotional pain that has been stuffed with the addictive substance will be overwhelming and unbearable if exposed, and so forth.

If you have done your best to unwrap all of these areas to no avail and know that this will most likely take many months, then ask the client what he suggests should be done next.

If he cannot come up with anything, then say that unless he changes at least one thing, counseling will no longer be an option because all you would be doing is enabling. The one thing could be to go to a meeting weekly, stop his addiction for at least a week or month (depending on the addiction), get in a support group, meet with an accountability partner weekly and speak with that person daily, and so on.

CHAPTER 24
Codependency

What Does Codependency Look Like in Action? What Is It?

- Parents who repeatedly bail out the son who never gets his act together and still lives at home
- Couples who have been married for years but function more like roommates
- The woman who is at church every time the doors are open, neglecting her family
- The girlfriend who lets her boyfriend use her credit card, even though he doesn't pay her back
- The guy who stays with his girlfriend who cheats on him but always says she'll change
- The man who works fourteen hours a day and weekends to keep his title as the top salesman
- The husband who doesn't discourage his overweight wife from eating, so no one else wants her
- The woman who rescues cats, going out in a storm to feed them at the garbage dump
- The general's wife who stays married to him only for the perks of being a general's wife
- The pastor who won't share the lectern with his assistant
- The unwed fiftysomething aunt who has made her nieces and nephews her life
- The daughter who lives with and has cared for her mother for twenty years and rarely takes a break or asks for help
- The woman who changes an outfit she likes because you didn't
- The author who has to have a huge picture of herself on every book cover
- The grandmother who lives for her grandchildren and neglects her husband
- The grandparents who raise their adult children's kids while the parents aren't committed to getting their act together
- The daughter who constantly rolls her eyes while listening to her mother on the phone tell her how to raise her children but doesn't say anything

There may be other things going on in these situations, but one thing is probable—codependency. Do you recognize codependency in others? In your clients? In yourself? That list is some of what codependency *looks* like. Another way to recognize codependents is by their *names*: they are the people pleasers, family martyrs, the ones who mother, the meek husband, the doting wife, the enabler, the approval addict, your bossy friend, and so on.

These people are insecure, controlling, self-centered, and more, and these character traits typically show up as a *significant* part of the person's personality and behavior.

Each person finds a **payoff** in his or her dysfunctional relationships or situations. The payoff is something that fuels good feelings about themselves, maybe even makes them feel self-righteous. God, who hates pride and idolatry, does not approve of that kind of payoff. Codependency is often all about idolatry, making someone or something your excessive focus, your source of gratification. We all probably have some of it in ourselves, and some of us have so much that it is dysfunctional.

A Note on the History of Codependency

In the 1980s when the self-help movement was in full swing, twelve-step programs were flourishing for all kinds of programs besides Alcoholics Anonymous and its sister organizations for supporting partners of people with addictions (for example, Al-Anon, Gam-Anon).

Melody Beattie was the primary driver for codependency, and her classic book, *Codependent No More*, is still the bible on codependency. She has written other related books, which are all worth reading. Therefore, like the other twelve-step programs, CoDA (Co-Dependents Anonymous) groups, as they were and are called, sprang up nationwide using the twelve-step format for groups.

(See chapter 25, "Twelve-Step Recovery Groups: An Overview.")

Broadening Your Perspective

Attend a CoDA meeting, where you will learn much about this very common problem. For codependents, CoDA meetings are very helpful because everyone there has various traits of codependency, so you will get a good education and perspective. You can hear and see yourself in the group share time.

In Celebrate Recovery, the small groups are usually not large enough to have a special group just for codependents, so you will want to take that into consideration. However, in a mixed group, you also get a good education about life and may see a character defect you did not realize you had.

What Codependency Is, How It Shows Up, and What to Do About It

What Is Codependency?

There are many definitions, but basically it is an **inordinate reliance** or dependency on someone or something that consumes us. We lose who we are and what we believe to accommodate the person or thing on which we are dependent. We do whatever it takes to assure the relationship/attachment is maintained. We may not realize that our behavior is destructive, and sometimes we are in denial about our true motives. Four primary areas that codependency shows up in codependents are in their denial, low self-esteem, compliant behavior, and controlling patterns.

Denial

Codependents have always yielded to or been concerned with others, so they deny or minimize how *they* feel. They get lost in other's feelings and deny their own. A healthy response is to be concerned. However, we need to let others feel their own feelings, and grow from their grief and pain, because this is how we mature and learn. Codependents in denial need to face reality as well as honor their own feelings, decisions, and actions and not yield to someone who is controlling.

Codependents see themselves as unselfish and concerned about others. They are in denial about their motives. A healthy response is to check your motives: are you trying to buy a relationship through doing or giving? Are you trying to make yourself feel needed and useful at the expense of the other person's opportunity to grow and be independent?

Low Self-Esteem Patterns

Codependents have a hard time making decisions because they do not have self-confidence. If they grew up in an alcoholic family, depending on whether the alcoholic was raging or not, kids learn to switch-hit and do whatever it takes to keep the peace as a coping mechanism. That forfeits their practice at making healthy decisions.

Because they have low self-esteem, they judge themselves and decisions they have made harshly. In recovery, they accept that they did their best at the time and moved on. They learn to accept themselves as larger than their perception of themselves. Group members validate their strengths and assets.

Compliance Patterns

Codependents compromise their own values to avoid rejection by others. They stay in harmful relationships too long out of loyalty that is often not deserved and is not healthy. They feel sorry for others and compromise their needs, time, and self-attention for others. They have a hard time expressing their opinions and become swept away with other's behavior, goals, and dreams, leaving their own behind or even unidentified. In recovery, it is inspiring to see codependents break out and tap talents they never knew they had and interests they never acknowledged.

Control Patterns

This pattern shows up regularly and is easily recognizable. There may be some of this in many of us. Codependents believe that most people are incapable of taking care of themselves, and they need to do it for them. "Let me help. I'll do it myself; it will look better." They have a better way of doing everything—that party, that class, that reunion, that meal you made, this book, and so forth. They tell you that directly and are typically very critical. Nothing is ever good enough to meet their standards. They always have a better way.

You will hear things like this from couples: "He even criticizes the way I talk on the phone" or "She is never satisfied with how I do any chore; she always has to complain and do it over."

This is the person who comes over and organizes your cabinets while she babysits for you—without being asked. This is the person who says, "Oh my, you don't want to wear *that*, do you?" This is the person who buys you gifts you don't want or need, who tells you what to order in a restaurant (as opposed to the low self-esteem codependent who orders whatever you order), who refolds towels after you folded them, who asks, "So, what are *you* going to do today?" as if you have to report to her.

They "Know How You Feel"

Codependents attempt to convince others how they should feel as well as what to do. "Oh, you don't mean that; you are just saying that you have something you want to do by yourself. I know you really want to go shopping all day with me again."

"I Was Only Trying to Help"

The codependent has something to say about whatever the other person does, wears, buys, or says. A codependent's motto is, "I was only trying to help," and he or she truly believes this. Codependents do not see it as controlling or manipulative. Their need to control has distorted their objectivity.

Codependents become resentful when others do not want their help. They feel threatened by others who do not need them. They believe they are only trying to help and do not see themselves as interfering or caretaking or controlling. In recovery, they come to see that taking care of themselves is healthy and that "letting go and letting God" should be the rule. In addition, they need to accept that others need to reap what they sow.

Codependents freely give advice (and directions) without being asked. This flaw is common. They try to fix a problem when it is presented instead of patiently waiting to be asked or being content with just being a good listener. (We know that men like to fix problems and mostly women just want to be listened to, but that is not what the point is here.) This is a listening issue—men learning that there is value in just listening, not in fixing. When a codependent tells you how to drive and always decides where to sit in the restaurant, he or she is being bossy/controlling—period.

For codependents in recovery, it is agonizing to not fix, help, or give advice. They are dying to be asked for their opinion or help. As recovery progresses, they build their self-esteem by being disciplined and shutting up and recognizing that they did the right thing one more time. This builds their confidence and frees them to take care of *themselves*. They often are amazed at how much they enjoy not having to take care of or fix others.

Needing to Be Needed

Another control pattern with codependents is needing to be needed in a relationship rather than being in a relationship that has equality and a healthy balance. From a Christian perspective, that would mean equally yoked in ways larger than just faith. Codependents sometimes will link up with someone "beneath them" to be more in control, to have the upper hand, to believe that they are doing that person a favor by being with them, providing for them, doing for them, and so on.

Is Codependency an Addiction or a Dependency?

An addiction is a physical and psychological reliance that grows to be all consuming, and other facets of one's life become compromised. Therefore, this question is dependent on the severity of the behaviors. Codependents are not necessarily addicts, but they have dependencies, and some have relationship addictions that consume them. Is a workaholic an addict or codependent? Perhaps both. Is a she-never-says-no-when-asked volunteer a super person or a codependent? She is probably a super person who is codependent.

Relapse
It is easy to see when an addict or alcoholic relapses, but when one's issues are emotional/psychological, it is harder to measure the intensity or the amount of codependency when you fall off your wagon and slip. Some offer the criteria of breaking your own growth goal. For example, when your goal was to not lend any more money or not tell people what to do, you count it as a relapse when you do those things. You need to look at what happened that caused the slip. Was I manipulated? Was I not being careful? Did I not care about the consequences? Did I not pray an emergency prayer and ask the Holy Spirit to guide me?

Incidentally, any *physical* addictions need to be cleaned up before you can deal with any codependency issues. The addictive thinking masks emotions, so you cannot truly combat codependent behavior until the addictions are under control.

Dependency in and of itself is not necessarily a problem. It is, however, when it rules our lives. It is a problem when it rules the relationships involved. For example, a disabled parent may be dependent on her daughter for her care. That is not a problem. If the parent insists on the daughter's care exclusively, or the daughter will not hire outside help because the mother would not like it, there is a problem. A dependency can be or become an addiction as in a relationship addiction.

How Prevalent Is Codependency?
It probably has touched everyone, but not all of us have *dysfunctional* dependencies. Some of us have scars from a relationship or relationships where we lost ourselves or were controlled and manipulated by someone. That is codependency.

A local codependent group wears a T-shirt that says, "If you don't think you are codependent" written on the back, and "You're in denial" on the front.

Why It Happens
Insecurities, dysfunction, trauma, and drama in childhood can birth codependency.

Fractured relationships in the teen, adult, and even in our elder years (because of the growing insecurities about life, health, money, and so on) can give rise to codependent tendencies.

When a healthy dependence gets misguided, we need to renegotiate the relationship, distance ourselves, or leave entirely. It is a choice.

When you will not make a healthy choice, you are probably codependent. Often, people who cannot make decisions have grown up with conflicting situations where the parents were not consistent in how or what they expected from the kids. The kids grow up not knowing the right thing to do and are fearful of doing the wrong thing, so they do not make *any* decisions. (This is particularly true where the parent[s] were alcoholics, and their behavior was unpredictable.)

Behavior that may have been a part of a person's childhood will not be changed unless she allows herself to *feel the pain* of her past and that of her current situation, discovering the futility of her wrong thinking.

Relationships

Codependents often stay in relationships when there is no longer satisfaction. Sometimes one of the two partners will make the other partner feel guilty for taking a stand or for the problems. This is a manipulation—one of the most harmful tools codependents use and take advantage of. In many codependent relationships, both people are codependent and may switch roles as to who is dependent and who is depended upon.

Redefining the relationship can be terrifying for some and incomprehensible for others because *they have no idea* what a healthy relationship should look like. So they struggle to fix it. As a counselor, educating clients on what a healthy, godly relationship looks like is critical.

What Is the Payoff?

Sometimes out of fear, manipulation, or ignorance, we compromise and rationalize to find a zone we can live in. In denial, it feels like the right thing to do.

Codependents may be so attached to a relationship that abuse is more bearable *than the thought of being alone.* They do not or won't see that they have a choice.

Codependents panic at the thought of leaving a relationship. They also panic when they think they will have to live without that person.

This is not the feeling of sadness we all feel for the loss of someone close to us. Rather, it is the *inconsolable grief of people experiencing the loss of themselves.* They just cannot do it. That kind of codependency is also idolatry, which is a sin. When this is revealed to a codependent, it can be his or her wake-up call for change.

Characteristics of Codependents

There are a few major characteristics codependents may exhibit. One or more may apply.

Anger and Resentment. These may be present in codependent relationships. It can be blatant or masked.

Defensiveness. Sometimes it can be appropriate to defend oneself, but when a person is constantly trying to justify one's own or someone else's behavior, it is called defensiveness. Defensiveness is a weapon codependents use when they cannot bear to face the reality of their situation.

Identity Issues. People who lack self-worth attach themselves to people they see as necessary for their existence and become totally absorbed in their occupation, goals, or needs—just for the value of association and identity. An example might be grandparents who make their grandchildren more important than their mates, because perhaps they fill a need for attention and recognition. A person may associate with a popular person to share the attention.

Romanticism. Controlling codependents often pledge undying devotion and want the relationship to move forward quickly to secure the person. Being swept away may also fulfill a romantic fantasy for both of them. These are people who propose quickly, within days, weeks, or a couple of months.

Manipulation. This is often softer than sarcasm. It can take the form of claiming hurt feelings, tears, and comments such as "You really should have…" and "If you cared, you would have…" Frequent bouts of feeling bad and even chronic lateness can be tactics used to control someone.

(See the section "Emotional Manipulation" in chapter 7, "Assessing the Problem: Understanding Clients' Feelings and Reactions.")

Bondage. No doubt you have witnessed relationships in which someone obviously should leave and doesn't/can't/won't or does and then returns. This can happen because he or she is in emotional bondage to that person. The partners often switch roles, so they alternate times of being fed up and leaving the other. Why is this? The predictable drama can fuel their need for excitement. One or the other may feel stuck financially; the manipulative partner may have so browbeaten the partner that there is no self-confidence or hope of finding anyone else, and so forth. Therefore, they stay. There are relationship addicts and love addicts, and there are twelve-step groups to address these issues. Go online. Also, see the "Suggested Reading" section in the appendix.

Control. This can show up where there is a strong person and a weak person dynamic, but the roles can flip. Each person, although dependent, can flip his or her role to whatever is needed to keep the relationship intact. This dynamic is about the needy one and the helper. Other relationships are seen as threatening, so they are discouraged or not allowed, including relationships with parents and siblings, friends, and coworkers. The controlling manipulator tries to convince his partner that the other people in her life are using her, are a bad influence, or take up too much of "our" time. Manipulators say whatever they can to end or limit the relationship that threatens them.

Guilt. See the section on "Emotional Manipulation" in chapter 7, "Assessing the Problem: Understanding Clients' Feelings and Reactions."

How Codependency Shows Up in Our Lives

Parent-Child Relationships

Children, regardless of age, long for parental approval and love. If their parents are emotionally or physically unavailable, they seek ways to get approval and love elsewhere or wallow in feeling undesirable and unlovable. Some people become overachievers and try to be the person their parents would notice or approve. Others retreat emotionally and never feel worthy of being in a relationship.

We need to face the truth about our relationship with our parents if they were or are not emotionally available to give us what we want. Only then, when we honestly appraise the situation, can we begin to heal. This lack of acceptance from parents can be what causes clients' dependency and need for approval and can be the reason people stay in abusive relationships as adults.

Approach-Avoidance Relationships

These are the relationships that are on and off a lot. The players may well be codependent. What is essentially going on is as one person moves closer, the other person may feel suffocated (perhaps reminding him of his overprotective or controlling parent or a previous relationship) and backs off. The other person continues to pursue. They may go back and forth until she feels it is not going anywhere and leaves. He then feels conflicted and pursues, and the dance continues.

Look up "approach-avoidance relationships" on the web, and you will learn more. Ask your clients to read up as well if you think they may be in such a relationship in either role. When they read about it, they frequently claim that this is *exactly* what is going on. Their self-discovery and confirmation makes recovery easier. Your goal is to find out the following:

- If there were parental influencers
- If this approach-avoidance has been a pattern for them and for how long
- What happened
- What their fears are about being in a relationship
- What they feel they have to contribute (so you can assess their self-esteem)

(See "What I Offer a Partner" worksheet in the appendix.)

When codependents are dating, alert them to watch for pitfalls. Watch for red flags: people who want to mother you, fix you, do too much too soon, do things for you beyond being courteous, and want to get serious too soon.

The Christian Perspective on Codependency

Christians can become codependent in an effort to be generous, giving, and helpful—all things we as believers are called to be. The traits themselves are not the issue; rather, it is when we take our strengths and go beyond appropriate boundaries.

For example, being generous is a godly virtue. Being so generous that we become financially needy is inappropriate. If we swing the other way and become so tight that we squeak, that is also inappropriate. Giving our time and talents to doing God's work is also biblical, except when we neglect our spouses, children, parents, and ourselves. In addition, helping others is a godly virtue, but not if they can help themselves. Then we are enabling and being controlling.

Christians are particularly vulnerable to a controller's cry of "If you were a *real* Christian, you would [fill in the blank]." Being a Christian does not mean you have to be a doormat, a bank, or a maid, or do things in an intimate relationship that you are not comfortable doing because your partner says you have to be submissive. That is control, not love. It is manipulation—period.

Recovery Strategies

Teach all of the following material to clients, and assess your own vulnerability in any of these areas.

Depend on God

Teach your clients that change comes from the Holy Spirit's guidance in us with love, joy, gentleness, and the patience of Christ. Remind them to seek God repeatedly to help work through these land mines because it will help cultivate dependence on God. Teach clients to reinforce their mind with scripture and to give God their problems a thousand times a day if needed.

The emotionally dependent person, like the chemically dependent person, has a sense of incompleteness that can only be fulfilled through his connection with God. When He is first, basic emotional needs are met, and cravings for people, sex, food, drugs, and so forth diminish. Our relationship with God is reflected when we make Him our Master. It is not reflected when we are slaves to anything or anyone else.

Move from being codependent to being God dependent.

Ask God for insight and strength. Pray that God can begin your transformation. Pain is a great motivator for change.

Pray earnestly for healing, grace, wisdom, and timing before you discuss your concerns about a client. For clients, remind them to let the Holy Spirit dominate and overcome any feelings of coldness and bitterness about being controlled with the love, joy, gentleness, and patience of Jesus.

Lean on How God Sees You—Teach This to Clients

A relationship with Jesus Christ will bring security and comfort that no other human relationship can bring. If God finds us acceptable, that is all that should matter to us; the acceptance by others is not important or necessary for emotional contentment. Tell this to codependents who are people pleasers.

> "Though my father and mother forsake me, the Lord will receive me" (Psalm 27:10 niv).

Many codependents have their issues rooted in parental relationships. These issues can be healed in the codependent's heart with the comfort this scripture provides and a reliance on God. Remind them to tell themselves the truth: they are a valued and loved person, even if their mother and/or father fail to accept them and are critical of them.

Focus on scripture verses that tell you how acceptable you are to God:

> "This I know, that God is for me" (Psalm 56:9).

> "Therefore there is now no condemnation for those who are in Christ Jesus" (Romans 8:1).

Build Self-Esteem
This happens one brick at a time. Teach clients to celebrate successes, however small. When a people pleasing codependent says, "Sorry, but I can't help you at this time," that is huge; just saying no under any circumstance is a milestone for many, as is walking away from an argument, walking away from a gossip session, not sending Christmas gifts when you can't afford them, and so forth.

Recognize your worth in God's eyes. Because God forgave you for your sins, you surely are not above God to still carry them. Therefore, it is how God sees you—not how you or others see you—that matters.

Build self-esteem based on growing the characteristics of Jesus.

Get Educated
Read, read, and read about codependency. Go to meetings. Codependency is an insidious character weakness that is difficult to see in ourselves. Reading about codependency and going to meetings can help us see others, our relationships, and ourselves in a new light.

Define and Honor Your Boundaries
Being aware of healthy boundaries is essential, and our boundaries require constant monitoring.

Have clients make a list of what they want, need, and know is healthy for a relationship. Then tell them to screen out anyone, male or female, who does not fit those criteria. (See the worksheet "What I Want in a Partner" in the appendix.

Get a Sponsor (and/or an Accountability Partner)
The desire to go back to old habits and relationships and the emotional pain of leaving an unhealthy relationship can be excruciating—especially in the beginning—so clients will need support.

Resist Manipulation
Do not let the manipulative behaviors continue. Remember that it is not healthy for either the client or the client's spouse. Resisting manipulation will help clients be more tolerant to the child in them, who does not want to risk parental disappointment and disapproval.

Confront
When the time is right, tell clients to calmly and lovingly talk with their manipulative other about how the manipulations make them feel.

Clients need to take action. Nothing changes when nothing changes.

Face the Truth
Help clients acknowledge the pain of their experiences and losses, which will help them see the futility in their behavior and thinking.

Dealing with Parents
Instruct clients to pray and try to talk to the others in their dependent relationships—parents, partner, coworkers, and so on. Clients should limit the time they spend in person and on the phone with these people, if necessary. In the case of parents, they should continue to honor them, but they should stick to their recovery plan. Tell clients to have patience with their parents, to try to understand their behavior and their frame of reference. Forgive them.

CHAPTER 25

Twelve-Step Recovery Groups: An Overview

There Is a Twelve-Step Group for Every Need
Go online and search under most any behavioral issue and you will find a twelve-step group for it (Co-Dependents Anonymous, Emotions Anonymous, Gamblers Anonymous, Overeaters Anonymous, Sex Addicts Anonymous, and so on). Each group uses the same twelve-step format adapted from Alcoholics Anonymous' (AA) steps of recovery and twelve traditions that serve as rules of the group. Each group substitutes its issue-specific material in the AA wording as applicable (with permission from AA to do so).

Sponsors
Sponsors (seasoned participants who have been in recovery a long time) mentor and support others as mutually agreeable. The sponsor or accountability concept is crucial to *any* recovery program, secular or Christian.

Types of Meetings
Each group has open meetings, which are for anyone interested in learning about the organization, meetings, and issues, and most also have closed meetings, which are only for those who have that particular issue.

Check Them Out
So that you can confidently refer clients to applicable groups, it is suggested that you attend both options and appreciate the difference between a twelve-step secular group and a Christian twelve-step group like Celebrate Recovery. All twelve-step groups have websites and material about the issue they treat and recovery strategies. There are some conditions to copying/downloading the information.

A Higher Power and God
A secular twelve-step group speaks of a "higher power" instead of Christ or God intentionally. It is so people, who are uncomfortable with the concept of God or religion, or with men or fatherly images, can put their spiritual toe in the water and not feel threatened.

The men who started AA were Christians but also recognized the need to meet people "where they are" and not push religion or God.

Are there Christians at twelve-step meetings? Sure. Do they say God or Jesus Christ instead of "higher power"? Depends on the meeting. Some meetings are strict and will not allow it; others do. Some people say, "My higher power is Jesus Christ."

Some Christians attend secular meetings because there is not a Christian recovery group nearby or the Christian group is so small that the groups are not issue specific. Additionally, sometimes the language at non-Christian meetings is offensive to some.

Many people in recovery try to attend multiple times a week (or daily) in the beginning of their recovery and then weekly as they recover. Some people have multiple addictions/issues and attend a variety of meetings.

Meeting Format

In Celebrate Recovery (CR), there is Christian worship first, followed by a testimony or a teaching lesson. Then everyone breaks into small groups divided by gender and issue. In secular twelve-step meetings, there is no music, but there is a testimony or teaching on one of the twelve steps or traditions. Depending on the size of the meeting, they may or may not split into groups (typically not). This is because each meeting is already geared for a specific issue, and they generally feel mixing the sexes is OK, although there are separate meetings for men and women in some locations.

Talking

In both types of groups, attendants speak in turn, if willing (when unwilling, one says, "I'll pass"), about the large group presentation, the testimony, or whatever is on their heart. There is no cross talk, which means when someone is talking, no one interrupts him or her or comments on what that person is sharing. This is to give the person the freedom to share without feeling judged, which could happen if someone corrects the person's thinking or behavior.

This rule against cross talking is especially important with codependents because they so often deny or minimize their own feelings and take on everyone else's. In addition, codependents are often fixers, a trait that is not appropriate at these meetings, because attendees are not there to fix others, only themselves. Additionally, sometimes codependents with low self-esteem have a very difficult time talking or feeling that what they have to say is worthy of being said or heard. They may come a long time before they have the courage to speak.

Socializing

Everyone gathers for refreshments after the small group. That is the place where an attendee can approach someone and *ask if* he or she would like feedback on something he or she said. One asks because it is respectful and because attendees do not want to cross that person's boundary line. Additionally, asking allows that person to exercise making a choice, something many codependents need to practice. Lastly, sometimes codependents have a hard time saying no, so being approached can be upsetting and conflicting. Some people have such a hard time just talking that to hear feedback afterward is too overwhelming.

CHAPTER 26
Grief and Depression

Teach Clients about Grief
Grief is the internal feeling we experience from a loss. Losses come in many forms:

- Loss from a death
- Loss from divorce, of one's reputation, use of the body, sexual purity, family connections, a romantic relationship, friendship, a pet, childhood innocence, and so on.

Everyone grieves differently. Different cultures have different traditions for grieving and mourning, and the time it takes to heal is unique to each person and circumstance.

If clients find they are stuck in preoccupation about a hurt they have experienced or about someone who has died, and especially if they are trying to cover their hurt with potentially harmful behaviors (for example, isolating), or addictive behaviors (for example, alcohol, drugs, shopping), then maybe you and they need to look closer at their recovery. See if there are things you can do to help them get through it in a healthy way. Clients need to transform what was once "normal" to a *new normal*.

Grief is

- an expected, natural, and normal reaction to a loss;
- a feeling of sadness over what was or could have been (different, better, more); and
- a heaviness about the inevitable and sometimes unknown changes that lie ahead.

Grief can come in small doses that are easy to manage. For example, one may grieve because a vacation has been canceled. Although this is disappointing, this kind of grief can be easily managed. Grief can also come in large doses that show up in a thousand ways, making it harder to manage. How one manages grief depends on the type of grief and how the grief impacts us: grief can impact us very personally (a death), our friendships (betrayal), relatives (who moved away), as well as those impacting our community (a changing population), or the world (calamities).

Some of this grief will affect us directly; other types of grief we may not take in emotionally, at least on the face of it. We need to be aware of the compounding impact all of these losses have on our health, heart, and faith. If we do not take the time to process our grief, we can build up anger, resentment, fears, and other mental, physical, and spiritual health issues. As a result, we will not be as content as we could be.

How Grief Manifests Itself
Grief may show up as any of the following:

- Forgetfulness
- A sense of disconnectedness
- Sleeplessness or sleeping too much
- Unpredictable emotions—sometimes intense or seemingly absent emotions
- A change in eating patterns
- Anger

Knowing what "normal" emotions to expect when processing grief helps anxiety if clients are questioning their reactions.

Do not confuse the *stages of dying* (denial, anger, bargaining, depression, and acceptance) that were proposed by Elisabeth Kübler-Ross with the impact of grief. There are various ways to grieve, these stages go in cycles, and some stages are skipped. No order is right or wrong. Sometimes it is a year or two later until the impact is truly felt, and a trigger can set off new grief reactions anytime. Each individual is different and processes grief uniquely. There is usually only a danger when there are extremes in how grief is processed.

Kinds of Situations That Can Cause Grief

Losses that Can Cause Grief
Death of people or pets

For health issues: prolonged illness, disability, or chronic pain; loss of mobility or cognitive function

Aging: a change in appearance, abilities, social options, interests, possible loss of a longtime home and independence

Life-Cycle Changes that Can Cause Grief
Marriage and divorce, a change or loss in family and in-law ties, proximity of loved ones, a shift in loyalties, your new role

The birth of children, which can bring on changes in or loss of privacy, personal time, time for one's partner, and sexual energy; and a shift in finances and priorities

Empty nest, which brings a change or loss in roles, worries over building a new relationship with one's spouse, sometimes a downsizing of one's home, changes in how and where holidays are celebrated

Midlife crisis that results in a change or loss in expectations and behaviors of oneself and one's partner that were once familiar and are now sometimes unknown and threatening

Financial Changes that Can Cause Grief
Job loss can result in a change or loss of self-image, lifestyle, and spending patterns

Moving and Transitions That Can Cause Grief
Leaving friends, favorite places, the graves or memorials of deceased friends, family members, pets, schools, neighborhoods, lifestyle, and one's church community

Milestone Changes that Can Cause Grief
Graduations, necessitating leaving friends and a familiar environment behind
In a lifestyle or relationship
Self-image connected to a change in one's job status, age (turning eighteen, forty, fifty, sixty-two), looks, status (being labeled an adult, middle-aged, or a senior)

Trust Challenges that Can Cause Grief
Betrayal by a spouse, friend, business partner, or government (frustrating medical care options for veterans, for example)

Faith Challenges that Can Cause Grief
One's relationship with God, clergy, other believers
Contradictions in one's faith and reality
Shifts in one's worship/prayer/participation routine or place

Moral and Legal Injustices that Can Cause Grief
Changes in laws that threaten one's values and security
Changes in the political arena that impact one's patriotism, party affiliation, and civic involvement

Calamities that Can Cause Grief
Natural (earthquakes, tidal waves, tsunamis)
Human induced (war, terrorism)

Helping Clients Cope with the Holidays

- Help clients with their questions about managing the holidays after a loss or if a loved one is in a fragile state of health and is expected to pass on anytime.
- Help them learn how to face relatives and friends, who are not in as much pain as they are, without upsetting others' holidays.

- Help them explain to others without hurting them that sometimes they need companionship and sometimes they just want to be alone. (See the "Oreo Cookie Strategy" in the appendix.)
- Help them learn to take care of themselves through all the expectations.

Start with the problem of their expectations first. Help them understand each point below. Say,

"Whether your loved one has died or is dying, you need to do what feels comfortable for you. That means different things to different people—you cannot control others' expectations nor should you have expectations of others. Everyone grieves differently, and for some, the holidays are a reprieve from worries when grief can be put on hold. For others, their grief is intensified, as their heart and mind are flooded with memories. So let's give you permission to get through the holidays the way you need and give each other the gift of respect for how we each will manage our holiday time."

"Remember that the first time you go through the holidays and anniversaries will be the hardest."

"Be comforted knowing that you will go through them and come out a little more healed; otherwise, if you avoid the holiday, you simply postpone your holiday grief for another year."

"Time is a great healer (as long as you work on your recovery) as are tears, laughter, and memories."

"Choose to celebrate how wonderful and loving someone was and the memories of that love."

Healing
Say,

"Honor the surges of grief that come over you. Cry if you wish and spend some moments reflecting on your loss. Surges will come at unexpected times, like in the grocery store when you see his favorite cereal or when you hear a song on the radio. You might come unglued. This is normal. It may happen on and off for years."

"Honor your grief. It is part of healing to cry or just to be sentimental."

"The measure of healing or recovery is when the original emotions (sobbing, anger, hopelessness, and so on) attached to the source of grief are transformed/healed so those feelings become facts that you have come to accept with your emotions leveled. This means you may still have tender moments but not uncontrollable sobbing and intense sadness."

"You will go from blaming to acceptance, from excuses to honesty, to acknowledging your part. The original emotions will be transformed, and you will be healed."

"My soul weeps because of grief; strengthen me according to Your word" (Psalm 119:28).

> "For I consider that the sufferings of this present time are not worthy to be compared with the glory that is to be revealed to us" (Romans 8:18).

Grief Share and the **Grief Recovery Method** are two excellent grief recovery programs.

Clients who are grieving over a death are usually direct about why they feel they need to see a counselor. They are having a hard time because it is so new, or it has been a while but they are stuck and are having a hard time moving on. Or they feel they are managing their grief OK, but family members are worried about them.

When you ask someone who is grieving after a death, "How may I help you?" she will generally respond by telling you the story of the loved one's death. She will typically give details of the loved one's illness and how she was there with the loved one through it all. Just listen. It is healing for a client to have a new person to whom she can tell her story. There is healing in simply being listened to. You rarely have to ask anything, and when time is up, the client will express gratitude for your presence.

Grief counseling is all about presence. It is a time for you to listen with a compassionate heart and know that is the best gift you can give them. Your goal is to do the following:

- Ask questions to have the person talk as much as she can about the deceased—how they met, their life together, raising a family, retiring, and so on. She will evidence many emotionally expressive changes as she reflects on the life she had with her spouse.
- Move in and out of feeling questions to head questions to give her a rest, if needed. Your genuine interest in her and her loss is comforting.

Reminiscing

Ask if the client would bring some pictures of her deceased husband and their wedding and/or vacation albums, if possible, to the next session. She will do this most excitedly and will obviously enjoy sharing her memories. This exercise is very healing, personal, and rewarding for the client and the counselor.

- You want her to be reminded of the wonderful memories and to replace the more painful ones of her partner's illness or last days.
- Have her walk you through each album. (I use a whole session for this.)
- Listen to the stories and affirm the "good times" and apparent happiness.
- Ask questions to encourage her to keep talking.
- Validate often the apparent happiness they brought each other and their family. This helps with any guilt she may have for whatever they did not do or if she felt she didn't do enough.

In the next session, focus on the here and now.

- Ask what has changed for her on a day-to-day basis since the death, and ask how she is managing those changes. (Use only the applicable questions that are listed elsewhere in this section.)

Setting the Pace
Concerned family members sometimes push for busyness for the griever, thinking that will get her to "move on." That is not true. People who were not busy before the death of a loved one will only be stressed if they try to venture into a lifestyle that is not typical for them.

A griever needs to resume her life at a pace that is comfortable. When she begins to socialize and gets more active and gradually returns to doing what she enjoyed previously, the family will say, "She is getting back to being herself; her true personality is returning." (That is comforting and a valid measure of recovery.) She may have taken on new and different activities and even new friends, or maybe she has been working at fulfilling her dreams of traveling.

It is all healthy as long as she is doing that for herself and not to please others.

Explaining What Is Normal in Grieving
One helpful task you can provide is helping the client know what is "normal" (or not) and some things to expect and how to handle them.

- The beginning months are saturated with consoling rituals like visiting the grave and sorting through clothing, memorabilia, or paperwork. If pushy relatives insist on discarding clothes or mementos or suggest that the person move, this can cause the griever anxiety.
- Help her set boundaries to protect what she wants protected and to hold fast to her needs and wants rather than cave under pressure.
- The rule about not making any decisions for a year after a death is a sound one, and she may need help enforcing it.

Fears

- Explore any fears she may have about disappointing others by disagreeing with them. Remember the "Oreo Cookie Strategy" tool/technique in the appendix, or wrap hard things to say in love and grace. She can tell pushy relatives or friends, "I know you love me and are concerned about me. Thank you. [She is validating.] I am feeling competent to take care of things myself, including my social life. I am carving out a new life that works for me. Please know that I will ask for your help if I need it. Thank you for honoring my request."
- When grievers are not showing signs of healing after a couple of months, pursue what is holding them back. It may be the fear of change or that it would be disloyal to their deceased spouse to be happy and start living again. Correct this thinking. Their loved one would want them to be happy, not sad, to be living and not waiting to die.
- Having a relationship when they feel ready is not a betrayal to the deceased person; it is a recognition that she appreciated marriage. Widows and widowers often establish new relationships or even find a compassionate mate at grief support groups.
- Again, waiting a year is a good time frame for major decisions.

Managing Family Members and the Client's Assets

You may also need to help the client with contrary or jealous family members who do not want her to share her financial assets. Sometimes children of the deceased have a very hard time accepting a parent's new "friend." She may have fears about disagreeing with them, fearing they may not help her when she gets ill or needs assistance.

Teach Them Not to Compare

Help the griever by acknowledging how we all grieve differently, and only when it is extreme is there cause for concern. Otherwise, it is a personal journey and not to be compared. That comparison is troublesome mentally for many grievers who receive unsolicited comments from family and friends. Be her voice of reason and encouragement, and coach her with responses to relatives and friends who might challenge her about her choices.

Guilt

One common complaint grievers have is their feeling of guilt.

- Explain that true guilt is a result of hurting someone intentionally. Regret, however, is sadness over something you wish would have turned out differently and there is no malicious intent. This explanation usually allows grievers to concede that they have regrets, not guilt, and it is a huge relief.
- You can ask if they have regrets about how they treated the deceased. They may, but they will also probably concede to your inquiry if they were a good wife most of the time with a yes, that 80 percent of the time they were a good wife, daughter, son, and so on. Remind her that 80 percent is a great score. We are human. No one is perfect all of the time.
- Help her to let go of any regrets. Remind her of the wonderful times they shared and the joy they brought to each other that she revealed in the albums you saw and the stories she shared.

Grievers over a death may only need to come one or two times, especially if they just need to realize what is and is not appropriate in their grieving, but several times is more typical. If they are experiencing extreme sadness for more than several weeks, then counseling will take longer—months, probably.

Grievers are clients who are especially rewarding to work with. You can see their emotional growth from grieving to acceptance and healing. It is clear and mutually rewarding when they realize they are ready to graduate and no longer need to come.

Share the following counsel:

For Widows or Widowers

> *"Transforming a life you shared with someone for years, maybe decades, into a life you could still look forward to is a daunting dream, but it is doable. First, honor your grieving and grieve as much as you feel you are able for the first few months."*

"If you are naturally a social person, you may long to talk and share and feel comfortable getting back into your routine quicker than a more introverted person. Your return to socializing is no reflection on your love or commitment to your deceased partner, so guilt is not appropriate."

"Less social people may have anxiety about talking or socializing because they are used to doing things with a partner. These people need to ease back into life. Take small steps. Invite a friend over for tea once a week. Enlarge the number of people you invite if you can so that it becomes something of a new tradition. Try planning an outing together, like going for a drive and to lunch or a bus ride to a tourist destination. Visit a friend's church to have a new experience. Join a Bible study. Offer to make encouraging phone calls to the homebound for church or a social service organization."

The point is, grievers need to put their toe in the water in order to get back into society. As they venture out, your encouragement and eager listening about their progress will be of great help.

What Is NOT Helpful to Hear or Say to Someone Who Is Hurting

- "I know how you feel." (No one's *pain, feelings, circumstances,* or resulting impact is the same, although you may have had the same *experience*. It is just frustrating for the hurting person to hear that and may build resentment.) The Living Bible translation says in Proverbs 14:10: "Only the person involved can know his own bitterness or joy—no one else can really share it."

Look him/her in the eye and say instead any of the following:

"I am so very sorry."

"I can't imagine how much this must be hurting you. I am so sorry."

"I don't know what to say [and give him/her a hug or shoulder hug or a hand touch]*, but I am here for you"* (and then *be there for them* to listen).

Just listen, listen, and listen. Do not tell your story. Let the time be about them.

- "Don't cry." (Why not? Because crying is a natural emotion. Tears are for both men and women as one way to let out and relieve our pain.)

Look her in the eye and be silent. Just let her cry. Tear up with her if you feel like it. If she says, "Now I made you cry," you can say,

"Yes, and it feels good" (and you two can smile about it).

"It's OK to cry. I am so sorry."

- "Don't be sad. You can [marry again, have another baby, find another romance, job, family, and so on]." (Replacing a loss is not the same—ever. The hurting person is hurting right now and is focused on getting through today, and that is the pain you can help with. Thoughts of future opportunities may only bring anxiety about it all happening again.)
- "You'll feel better in time." (Time alone does not help us get better; it is the changes we make in our lives and the way we learn to accept what life brings that heal us. People can be sad for decades, and time will not make a difference unless they have an intentional change of their heart.)
- "He or she (the deceased person) is better off now/is in a better place/his or her suffering has ended." (Again, the hurting person is concerned about *his* own pain right now and, yes, *where* his loved one is matters to him (and he may even say so), but *his* pain today is real and that is what he needs comfort for. To focus on where the other person is may feel like you are dismissing or minimizing the client's pain.)
- "Keep busy." (Why? Because if a person was not the busy type before, it only stresses him to be around people so much or doing so much. Also, keeping busy sometimes just distracts us from the pain.)

Instead, suggest the client do one thing a day or week to serve *someone* else to help keep her hurts in perspective and to help her count her blessings. For example, the client can send a card, volunteer for an hour or two a week, visit someone who is in a worse situation (a homeless shelter, nursing home, a prison, a rehab, and so on) and keep her personal grief to herself for that time.

- "God needed them in heaven more than you did." (This thinking may lead to resentment toward God, and in truth, we do not know why God takes people when He does, especially when He takes someone prematurely.)

Trust in God's promises of comfort: **"The Lord is close to those whose hearts are breaking" (Psalm 34:18 tlb).**

Restore Your Life

Help clients see the need to make the effort to manage all that happens in one's life, good and bad. They can face the pain with help, or drown it with abusive behaviors, or in some other way simply stuff the hurt. One's life is a choice, and one can have healing and hope through a relationship with God and following the ways of Jesus. God has promised that.

Depression and Grief

When clients say they feel depressed, more often it may be intense sadness they are experiencing. Clinical depression is characterized by prolonged (at least two weeks) behaviors such as isolation, lethargy (not willing to do anything), a marked change of appetite (usually eating less, not more), a lack of interest in their regular activities, excessive sleeping, or lack of interest in personal hygiene or appearance. People with these symptoms need to see a professional.

Intense sadness best describes what many people go through at times. It resembles the characteristics of depression but on a much smaller scale, and the person may have good and bad days. These moods may last days or sometimes weeks, but when they seem to last months, people are usually encouraged by family and friends to seek help, and they probably need to see a professional.

You can say that you will do a brief assessment of their depression and determine if you are the right person to help them or if they need a referral to a professional. Sometimes that is terrifying to people, and they may want to backtrack on their self-diagnosis.

Here is one option. Gently (so it is not seen by them as your minimizing their problems) suggest that what they are experiencing may not be depression but an intense sadness. Clients may be relieved to hear this, or they may argue with you because they *want* the label of depression. If they argue, let it go, and just say,

"I understand what you are saying. Let me ask you some questions to assess what is going on."

"What is the source of your sadness?" (If they have come to you for grief counseling, they will easily identify the source, so your work is cut out for you.)

However, if they cannot put their finger on it, you need to probe. There are many possible reasons for their intense sadness besides grieving over the loss of a loved one. It may also be the consequence of the loss of their daily routine and their uncertain future, loss of a job, infidelity, a moral conflict (an undeclared addiction), boredom, aging, and so forth.

For clients who can't put their finger on why they are depressed, ask,

"What has changed recently in your life?" (This usually reveals the source.)

"How long have you been this sad?"

"What have you done about it so far?"

"Have you seen your physician recently?" (See the section on "Health" in chapter 6, "Assessing the Problem: Potential Contributing Causes of Problems.")

"Have you told him about your sadness/depression?"

"Did the doctor mention antidepressants?"

"What are your thoughts about taking them as a temporary measure?"

"Are you taking any prescribed or over-the-counter medications?" (List)

"Do you think any of the medications you're taking may have side effects that contribute to your intense sadness? What did your doctor say?"

"Are you attending any support groups? Talking with friends?"

"Are you eating sufficiently?"

"Are you sleeping too much or too little?"

"Are you getting out of bed, showering, and dressing in street clothes every day in the morning?"

"Do you exercise? What could you do for exercise?"

"What do you think would help bring you out of this sadness?" (You ask this because sometimes they can tell you.) Their answer(s) might be:

"I need to move back to where I used to live."

"I need a job."

"I need to be busy and feel useful."

"I need to make new friends."

"I need to stop worrying about things I can't change."

"I am tired of being sick/in pain."

"I need to move on."

These may reveal only part of the truth, but they will give you direction to work. Grievers, however, are typically able to say directly, "I miss my husband. I'm having a hard time without him."

When it is not an admitted grief over a death issue, it may be something that is hard for them to admit or disclose—resentment over having had to care for the deceased and the impact that had on their life, relationships and finances. Or it may be an addiction, an affair, embarrassment over their weight, a lack of friends, or having to take medications for a disorder they have. On the other hand, they do not even realize they are very mad at someone or something and are taking it out on others, themselves, or their routine by being sad.

If the potential solutions they identify seem reasonable, ask,

"Is that what you want help achieving?" (Sometimes people do not want to change because they get attention and sympathy or are able to use their "depression" as an excuse to eat, drink, or shop.)

You need to ask,

"If your routine has changed, are you doing any of the following things more or less than usual: eating, drinking, shopping, or isolating?" (If they are grieving, it is helpful to know what they are doing differently since the death.)

A basic solution is to help them to

- take baby steps toward their goal;
- do something for others in need and get their mind off themselves, as this has been proven to be very helpful with clinically depressed patients (tell this to clients); and
- get them *started* on recovery by having them *change at least one thing a day and keep on doing it.*

Suggestions for change follow. See if they will do some or ideally all of these and tell you about it at the next session:

- If they are isolating, ask if they would sit on their front porch, in their apartment's lobby, in the game room, or the library in their complex for a while each day and try to greet at least three people.
- Write a "Just Thinking of You" card each day to cheer up someone from his or her family, church, or neighborhood. (A store where everything costs a dollar has plenty of boxed and traditional cards.)
- Turn off the TV for at least an hour and make at least one phone call a day to someone *to see how he or she is*. Encourage your client not to talk about herself.
- Commit to eating a little bit at each meal if they are not eating or cutting down and only eating at mealtimes if they are snack bingeing.
- Take a shower/bath daily and get dressed (in street clothes) each *morning*.
- Walk five minutes a day and build it up to more time. If they cannot walk, do a stationary exercise, if their doctor approves.
- Pray and/or read the Bible at least ten minutes a day (preferably more) or watch a reputable Christian speaker (Charles Stanley, Joyce Meyer, and so on; attend or view the mass on television).
- Write down five different blessings every morning or evening and bring them to the next session.

They will appreciate structure and having something to do. Too many goals might overwhelm them, so let them commit to the number they believe they can achieve. You may need to write them down or ask them to write them down. After you or they pray to close, say you look forward to seeing them again and hearing about their progress (be positive). If they reply negatively, remind them this is a new day and a new beginning to their recovery. Therefore, have a positive attitude, and make that a part of their homework.

SECTION VI
Closure Material and Strategies for Growth

CHAPTER 27

Encouragement

Initial and Ongoing Reminders for Your Clients and Counselors

Work Hard and Be Patient

Remind your clients that counseling is like working out, being in training, or being on a diet. They cannot be off and on about it. They have to work hard for at least a few weeks to begin to see a change.

Our behaviors have been with us for years—sometimes decades—and it takes work and time to change them. Can God take away an issue overnight? Yes, and He has, but that is not typical. It usually takes time to change. If clients look beyond their problem, they will be able to endure it. If nothing else, they can remember their situation is temporary. Clients should consider themselves "in transition". Things *will* change.

If they work hard and still do not see any changes after a few weeks, then you both need to assess the following:

- If the goals are right
- If you are a good team working together
- If some issues are not being mentioned
- If there is something in the way that has not been discussed
- If money/fee is an issue

Recovery

Remind your client that sometimes the best thing to do is the hardest thing to do. It is not what happens to you that is important, but how you perceive and process it.

Recovery is learning to live your life differently with new routines, friends, and goals.

If God can deliver Shadrach, Meshach, and Abednego from the fire (see Daniel 3:17), surely He can deliver us from our trials. Notice that someone (it is presumed Jesus) was walking with them in their trial in the furnace. Jesus will be with us.

God speaking: "Then I will make up to you for the years that the swarming locust has eaten" (Joel 2:25). Give God your life, and in His time, He will restore what has been taken away, like your love of life.

"For I am confident of this very thing, that He who began a good work in you will perfect it" (Philippians 1:6). Be assured. God will continue to grow us.

(See also chapter 23, "Addiction and Other issues" for more encouragement.)

Encouragers and Accountability Partners

Having at least one or two people supporting the clients in this work is very helpful. Every few days, encouragers will ask, "How's it going with counseling and your homework?" Then they encourage them to be patient and to keep trying until they have a breakthrough—an insight that lifts the load they are carrying. When people do not have godly encouragers, they only hear from the discouragers, who may offer bad guidance, such as leaving the relationship or retaliation. Accountability partners are helpful for respectful confrontation and are a resource when clients are feeling vulnerable.

Pray and Seek God

If clients do not have a prayer life, help them build one. Start by asking them to pray at night, thanking God for any blessings He provided that day. Thanking God at every mealtime is a good reminder of God's faithfulness. Suggest they ask God to be their strength in meeting their goals and enable them to be patient and godly in their response to any conflicts.

God's Power and Promises

Get encouragement from reading about God's power and promises in the Bible. Believe that God is powerful and that He will honor His promises. That is fundamental for your faith. Be aware of when you are thinking in human terms and not God-size terms. Instruct clients to do the following:

- Distract themselves from their issues by prayers and petitions to God.
- Strive to have a personal legacy of faith and obedience to God. This will break toxic family patterns.
- See themselves as God sees them.
- Give up defeating thoughts and behaviors. "Give up and God gives."
- List those things for which they are grateful every day.
- Remember that sometimes the best thing to do is the hardest thing to do. Recovery is hard work.

Jesus speaking: "In the world you have tribulation, but take courage; I have overcome the world" (John 16:33).

Words of affirmation to give your clients:

"Good observation." "Good insight." "Well said."

Relapse Is Not Failure—It Is a Mistake

Let your clients know that a slip does not negate the work they have done. Relapse is falling out of the *recovery* process, but they are still *in recovery*.

Do not give a slip more meaning than it deserves or it may foster shame. Do not make shame a catastrophe or it can lead to relapse. Your clients may *have made* a mistake, but *they* are not a mistake. However, be careful because an acceptance of a slip may give license or justification or may minimize it.

Remind them never to think they can never slip—it sets them up for failure.

Humility

Keep humble; it keeps you from relapsing. It takes time to change.

Abstaining versus Recovery

There is a difference between sober/sobriety (abstaining) and recovery (working on issues *and* abstaining). If one abstains but is not in recovery, he or she will probably just trade one destructive behavior for another.

Clients should be careful not to focus their thoughts on their behavior or the substance; it is a setup for failure. Focus on the replacement behaviors and the rewards of following those goals.

Therefore, instruct clients to take it one day at a time, be in recovery, and keep asking themselves, "What am I going to do to be growing spiritually and emotionally?" Make that their focus.

Encouragement for Counselors/Servants

Besides some of the entries above that can apply to anyone, be affirmed in the following thoughts.

Depend on God, not a method. Always turn to the Bible for your source of wisdom.

Do not feel rushed. Remember everyone has problems, and most cannot be resolved immediately. God will provide. Many people want a "quick fix" and not have to deal with the root of the problem or have to change to fix the problem. Have patience.

> **"Hold fast to Him and serve Him with all your heart and with all your soul" (Joshua 22:5).**

God will build our character by the assignments He gives us.

> **"We do not know what to do, but our eyes are on you" (2 Chronicles 20:12 niv).**

> **"How blessed is he who considers the helpless; the Lord will deliver him in a day of trouble" (Psalm 41:1).**

"**The Lord will give you understanding in everything**" (2 Timothy 2:7).

As we allow God to work through us, we can be **"a vessel for honor, sanctified, useful to the Master, prepared for every good work"** (2 Timothy 2:21).

Offer hope with those things you know *you can* do:

- Listen so they feel cared for and heard.
- Pray so your faith will be inspirational and consoling for them.
- Be patient so you model that things can be sorted through.
- Have basic, current resource information handy for distribution.

Honor Your Boundaries

It is not your job to fix or change anyone. It is up to the Holy Spirit to convict them in His time. You are to enlighten them about other options, show them another way to look at the situation, and help them clarify options and their feelings and fears about them.

Your responsibility is to do your job and that only, and respect your job's boundaries and limitations.

Do not make promises you cannot keep. Say,

> *"I know you are anxious about your situation, and I will help you as best as I can. Please know, however, that our resources may be too limited to assist you with all of your concerns. These concerns take time."*

Be discerning. Be on guard for manipulators. Emotional manipulation is a survival response or at least an inappropriate coping skill that has served many people well over the years. If their first manipulation failed, they will come at you from another direction.

(See the section on "Emotional Manipulation" in chapter 7, "Assessing the Problem: Understanding Clients' Feelings and Reactions.")

Prayer

It is not your job to convert anyone. However, it is OK to ask if you can pray for that person and then do just that.

CHAPTER 28

Our Need for Confession

Choices

As an intervention, faith-based counseling may include teaching clients about personal confession. Teach clients about their choices. Tell them that as soon as God reveals our sins to us, we have a choice—to confess or to ignore His prompting. If we value our personal relationship with God, we will feel convicted to repent and never be out of His will. That conviction honors God. He will reward us, and our faith and personal relationship with Him will be strengthened.

Be a Confessor

Understand that you are not assuming the role of a Catholic priest. Encourage Catholics to have a priest hear their confessions, and if there is resistance to or shame about doing that, help them overcome their fears or issues so they can return to their faith practices and sacraments. If they need more help with their issues, encourage them to seek a professional counselor or a priest as well as an accountability partner.

Scripture says, **"Confess your sins to one another, and pray for one another so that you may be healed" (James 5:16).**

There is tremendous healing in sharing and in being heard without judgment. If clients say they confess directly to God, suggest that they do that regularly (perhaps daily or weekly) so they can see the patterns of their issues—what they are and are not making progress on correcting.

Remind clients of the limits of confidentiality if they share their sins with you as part of a healing process.

Sometimes clients hold onto sins even after confessing them to God (or a priest), or they have not trusted God with their confession. If they are Catholic and won't go to a priest, and you can't help them over this hurdle, you can offer to be their temporary confessor, a trusted person they can share their sins with, knowing they will not be judged. You will walk alongside them toward repentance, accepting God's forgiveness, and finding God's peace and healing. Your helping can apply to non-Catholic Christians as well.

As an aside, when I returned to the Catholic faith in 2015, I prepared to go to confession after reading pertinent books and pamphlets and carrying my very, very long list of sins accumulated over my forty-five-year absence from the faith. I opted to be face-to-face (rather than behind a screen) with the priest in the confessional. He heard my long list, which I wept all the way through. He encouraged me to talk, without judgment and with mercy. At the conclusion of my list, he gently said, "Welcome home, dear one." Then I really cried. Confession, or reconciliation as it is now called because we are reconciled or restored to a right relationship with Christ, was for me a beautiful, cleansing, and healing experience. Confessing for me to a holy man who is acting in Christ's stead had more meaning than just confessing to another man or woman, however godly that person may be. Yes, I told those sins also to God, but for me, I wanted the experience of admitting my sins in humility to a holy man. Those are my thoughts based on my experience, to give you another personal perspective.

Create a Safe Place
To encourage people to confess, you need to create a *safe place*. This means they see you as someone who is not judgmental, who understands, who will respect their confidentiality, and who will appreciate that they are in a battle. To evidence your presence as being a safe place, do not react with any alarming facial expressions when they tell you their sin, regardless of how outrageous or horrific or unfair it is. If they are sincerely confessing a sin, they will just share it with you and maybe cry, weep, or show great frustration or humility.

When We Do Not Confess
God created us with a longing to be in relationship with Him and to be at peace with Him. When we have sinned, we are unsettled emotionally, and this can show up in anger, bitterness, sadness, and physical ills.

Sharing our sins with another is healing, and often we feel like a burden was lifted off our back. That is the beginning of healing. The person we confess to can become our accountability partner, our go-to person when we feel vulnerable to committing that sin again, the one we go to for prayer, encouragement, and restored conviction against temptation. (Counselors should not necessarily be accountability partners as they then might be called and contacted often between sessions. It is not realistic timewise.)

Repentance
Repenting of our sins to God and committing to not sin again are essential to restoration. Until we have come humbly and sincerely before God, we will not have full restoration. That is why helping clients develop or grow their relationship with God is critical.

(See chapter 30, "Spiritual Issues and Personal Growth for Counselors and Clients.")

Sorrow can lead to repentance and repentance to a truly changed heart to be obedient to God.

Paul says, **"For the sorrow that is according to the will of God produces a repentance without regret" (2 Corinthians 7:10).**

There will be fruit when someone is truly sorry and a willingness to do whatever it takes to get back on track. If there is resistance, call him or her on it and address the cause of the resistance.

When They Test You
If they are testing you for your reaction and to see if you are judgmental, they may make up the sin to test you. If they are not fully sincere, they may sensationalize it—spice it up to lure your imagination and curiosity. Be on guard. If you do not need the details to get their point, say so.

Encourage Their Getting an Accountability Partner
After they confess to you, thank them for trusting you. Tell them they would benefit from having an accountability partner to go to when they feel vulnerable, and ask them to set that up as soon as possible. They may need to go to a twelve-step group, preferably a Christian twelve-step program like Celebrate Recovery, to find an accountability partner.

Confess to God
Then gently ask if they want to confess and repent to God at this time, or if they would want to do that privately in prayer later or see a priest. Sometimes it is just too much for people; they want to tell God even more now that they see how much better they feel, or they want it to be very private and personal.

Affirm in Prayer
Whatever they decide is good. If they decide to confess to God or a priest later, pray for them at session's end for healing and growth in their faith. When they leave, tell them you will be praying for them today for when they talk with God or a priest.

CHAPTER 29
Forgiveness

Unforgivingness is the root of many emotional problems as well as some physical ailments. Sometimes, we can admit our unforgivingness: "I'll never talk to him again!" Other times, we have buried the hurt so deeply that we do not realize how hurt and upset we are: "I am past even thinking about my childhood and what happened to me." Alternatively, "It's in the past; nothing will change what happened. I am over it."

When someone expresses or admits unforgivingness, begin there.

"I am hearing a lot of anger/pain/sadness/shame about what you're telling me about your/father/wife/boss/and so on. Would you be willing to tell me more about what happened?" (Healing comes in sharing and venting.)

"I appreciate that you shared the details with me." (You are validating.)

"What feelings did you experience during that incident/argument/discussion?"

Validate if their feelings were normal under the circumstances, and wherever they weren't, ask,

"Is that typical for you?" (If so, ask,) *"Under what other circumstances?"*
What other circumstances push your buttons or are triggers?"

"It's good when you can admit you have a problem with anger (or impatience or unfairness or being disrespected, and so on). We can work on that. Let us talk a bit more about your unforgivingness and your values about that. Is there a time when you were not forgiven for something, not given grace, and made to feel embarrassed or wrong or stupid?"

"Would you tell me about one of those times?"

"Were the feelings that came up back then similar to those you reacted to in that argument/situation that you mentioned at the beginning of this conversation?"

"Were you responding like you did then or perhaps like the person who hurt you responded?"

Wait in silence to see if the client sees the connection. Keep silent. She may see the similarities in the two situations. Stay silent, praying she makes the connection. Let the Lord wrestle with her heart.

"So you see the connection—old wounds driving a repetition in current behaviors. It has become about paybacks. Do you see it?"

"When we are hurt, it is in our sinful nature to retaliate. However, God has another way. First of all, do you believe that God is who He says He is, and that two of His many traits that we need to talk about are His forgiveness and His being a just God?"

"In a nutshell, God unconditionally forgives us when we go to Him with a repentant heart, wanting to change. As a believer, you accept that Christ's death on the cross took away all your sins and everyone else's, but we need to believe that and come to Him and accept that forgiveness. So that means we are called to forgive others as God has forgiven us."

"Does forgiveness sometimes take time? Yes, but if you pray regularly for God to change your heart to forgive genuinely (and keep praying daily until God changes your heart), in time it will happen."

"God is a God of love, and He responds to our efforts to love. While you are doing that, God is freeing you of the emotional attachment you have to the hurt rendered to you by the other person. God will give you a heart of compassion for that person, and you will sincerely pray for a changed heart for them rather than thinking about revenge. This heart transformation is supernatural, and is a great testimony to others about how God works."

Wait for a response.

"One option is for you to seek revenge, by wishing that something bad will happen to that person. Revenge can take many forms: ignoring the other person (although sometimes this is an appropriate boundary), not talking to or associating with him (perhaps adding to tension at family events), or opting not to attend a family event (which can cause heartache and disappointment), or maybe being angry with God for permitting the incident to happen. This is not a good way to practice your faith."

"When we hold in anger, it shows up as bitterness, irritability, or a bad attitude, and those around you have to listen to your negativity and complaining. Complaining is a sin. Do you know that? Do you forbid others to associate with the person with whom you are angry, thus frustrating them, too? Do you see how your choice progressively influences many others besides yourself?"

"When we have had disappointing relationships, we sometimes learn to trust only ourselves, so it is hard for some people to then trust God."

*"God says He will repay. **'For the LORD is a God of recompense, He will fully repay'** (Jeremiah 51:56). Do you believe that? He will take care of the person in His time and in His way. It is guaranteed to be better than anything you can do because God's ways are perfect, and He has the perfect and just solution. You may see it or you may not. Sometimes years later we learn of how someone who has hurt us was transformed. Others have been punished or they may have turned sincerely to God."*

> *"So now that you have awareness, you have choices. Heal from the old wounds through forgiveness or not. We can talk more about how to do that, or you can keep carrying the painful baggage and reacting the same way when you are triggered."*

Gently ask her to pray for whatever she has on her heart. It may well be a turning point for her spiritually and emotionally.

If she chooses not to forgive herself or the other person, that is a choice. Gently ask,

> *"What is the payoff?"*

She might be offended and self-righteous, thinking you do not see the outrageousness of what has been done to her. Her payoff might be sympathy, attention, or an excuse for her addiction(s). Remind her:

> *"Forgiveness is a choice—a hard choice sometimes. Forgiveness is also a command. Again, you are facing another choice: Be unforgiving or not. Be in God's will or not."*

Guilt is self-imposed. God does not make us hold on to guilt; we choose to. Making amends will dissolve guilt. When we have intentionally done something wrong, guilt is a predictable response that is nevertheless still redeemable. Regret is when we have unintentionally hurt or done something to someone. What people often label as guilt is really regret. Once they understand that, they have an easier time releasing it.

It has been said that God is more offended by our not accepting His forgiveness than the sin we committed. Think about that.

Words That Heal

Sometimes the very words that can heal lifelong hurts are the hardest to say. People cannot say them because of resentment; not knowing how, what, or when to say things; embarrassment and discomfort in saying words they have never said or only sometimes heard; or fear that the words will not be appreciated and worse, not returned.

Remind clients that if we can get past our fears by trusting God and asking Him to open our hearts to the person we need to talk with, we can find the courage to speak.

Practicing with someone or writing out what you want to say and reading it to someone is helpful and healing. Sometimes just saying the words in practice gives such a relief that it lessens the anxiety of speaking the words to the person.

If the person is deceased, there still can be healing.

(See chapter 26, "Grief and Depression.")

Ask clients,

> *"What are the words you long to hear?"*

> *"What are the things your partner can do to show his wanting your forgiveness?"*

If they say "Nothing," then work with them on what the payoff is for not forgiving.

As previously mentioned, *The Five Love Languages* by Gary Chapman is a classic book on what men and women need. Chapman thoroughly shares how each partner can fulfill each other's needs and gives examples and inspiration. He addresses the love behind the oil change for your wife, and why she wants a long conversation instead of roses. Read it yourself, and suggest that clients buy it and read it together.

Apologizing

Apologizing needs to happen as soon as possible—before words that are more hurtful are spoken and before you say more things you will regret and can't take back. In Ephesians 4:26, the Bible says, **"Be angry, and yet do not sin; do not let the sun go down on your anger."**

Is it OK to be angry? Yes, it is OK to honor your emotions, but not in a way that will hurt yourself or others. This is good wisdom, and you will not have any real peace until you clear your conscience anyway.

"Sorry" does not cut it when you have hurt anyone. Nor does "*If* I have hurt you."

A truly repentant heart is a humble heart. Make that apology believable by saying, "I'm sorry for [name what you have done]" or "Will you forgive me for [name what you have done]?" And, "What do I have to do or say to make it right?"

Naming what you have done acknowledges it, and makes you own it. It is a confession. Asking for forgiveness is even more humbling and surrenders your control to the other person. It also frees you. The other person can say you are forgiven or not, but you have done your part and can let it go without guilt. The other person may be so hurt or flabbergasted by your apology and request that she may say she needs time. That is OK. Again, you did your part. Just say, "I understand."

(See the section on "Apologizing" in chapter 21, "Managing Arguments.")

Forgiving and forgetting are often difficult. Some people can let things go easily; others hang on and may hold a grudge for decades and bring it up whenever the opportunity arises, so you never pay off your dues or complete your penance in the accuser's mind.

Sometimes the one who does not forgive and the one who does not forget dumps his junk on you, using it to feel in control. If he had been hurt and did not have control at one point in his life, he may take it out on others. Whether that is the case or not, we are still responsible for our actions today, in the here and now. Apologizing, forgiving, and forgetting are values we all need to embrace without excuse.

Our model of forgiveness is Christ, who forgave as He was being persecuted. He also forgave us while we were still sinners (Romans 5:8). The Bible tells us that God has removed our transgressions "as far as the east is from the west" (Psalm 103:12). (That is, He does not hold them against us, but God never forgets anything because He is perfect.) That is the standard. It is a hard one, but it is a godly one.

The biblical admonition stands: **"Forgiving each other, just as God in Christ also has forgiven you" (Ephesians 4:32).**

CHAPTER 30

Spiritual Issues and Personal Growth for Counselors and Clients

How Do You and Your Clients Know If You Are Growing Spiritually?

First, you will have an increasing awareness and uncomfortableness of your sins and character weaknesses. In addition, you will have a greater sensitivity to the Holy Spirit, especially when He convicts you. Your eyes and conscience will be opened.

> "For you were formerly darkness, but now you are Light in the Lord; walk as children of Light (for the fruit of the Light consists in all goodness and righteousness and truth), trying to learn what is pleasing to the Lord. Do not participate in the unfruitful deeds of darkness, but instead even expose them; for it is disgraceful even to speak of the things which are done by them in secret" (Ephesians 5:8–12).

When we realize we have grieved the Holy Spirit, we are inspired to confess our sin quickly and repent.

> "Therefore, strengthen the hands that are weak and the knees that are feeble, and make straight paths for your feet, so that the limb which is lame [your sin weakness] may not be put out of joint, but rather be healed" (Hebrews 12:12–13).

Second, you will see life from a new perspective. You will begin to see trials through God's eyes. You will genuinely see hardships as opportunities to learn about your weakness and grow. Therefore, you will view trials differently.

> "Consider it all [not some] joy, my brethren, when [not if] you encounter various trials, knowing that the testing of your faith produces endurance. And let endurance have its perfect result, so that you may be perfect and complete, lacking in nothing" (James 1:2–4).

Third, your desires will change to be in line with the Lord's.

> "I delight to do Your will, O my God; Your Law is within my heart" (Psalm 40:8).

Fourth, you will hunger to spend time with God. Prayer and Bible reading will change from being a duty to a longing. You will guard your time with Him and sense His presence and love.

> "O God, You are my God; I shall seek You earnestly; my soul thirsts for You, my flesh yearns for You, in a dry and weary land where there is no water. Thus I have seen You in the sanctuary, to see Your power and Your glory. Because Your loving kindness is better than life, my lips will praise You" (Psalm 63:1–3).

"When you become a Christian, your life is radically oriented to God. In His sovereignty, He ordered that relationship. What you do after you put your faith in Jesus Christ's atonement will reveal what you actually believe." (Anonymous)

The turning point for healing is when you experience any emotional unrest and you are willing to surrender and ask for God's help.

Do They Truly Believe?
If clients can believe that God is who He says He is, that the Bible is true, that Jesus rose from the dead, that the miracles are true, and that the promises are true, it is amazing, and it is hard not to believe. Remind them of the character traits of God, and have them look them up in the Bible. They will be encouraged to surrender their life to Him and be confident that He can change them.

Do not argue theology with them. It may be an excuse clients use to avoid other counseling work. Instead, give them an assignment to research their questions, and promise you will do the same so you can discuss it the following week. If the questions are too much for you, refer clients to a pastor or priest.

"If you only have a hammer in your toolbox, you treat everything like a nail." Learn, study, and expand your Bible resources, so your spiritual (and counseling) toolbox is full.

You can only take people spiritually as far as you have grown, so it is important to be a good role model in your lifestyle and Christian practices. Sometimes you will point the way, and they will surpass you. Joyously share your enjoyment of honoring God with your faith walk. Be an inspiration. If you can, share how you willingly sacrifice to make time to pray for others, read the Word (ideally the Bible all the way through yearly), go to Bible studies, retreats, honor the sacraments, read about the church's fathers and saints and others who have made a dramatic and inspiring contribution to the Christian faith. Say how these things affect your journey. You probably will earn their respect and perhaps be a seed planter (someone who has influence in someone's spiritual development at some level). The Holy Spirit's job (not yours) is to convert them and bring them to Jesus Christ.

Solutions for Excuses
When they give excuses for their faith walk, you can supply them with practical solutions because you have worked through those excuses and made time to spend with God.

For example, when people complain about distractions when trying to tread the Bible I share my routine. When I read the Bible, I have a notepad and a piece of scrap paper nearby. The notepad/binder is to write down whenever God speaks to me and opens my eyes to a verse. I date the entry in my note pad, write the verse down in full, and ask what the application to my life might be or why God pointed out that verse to me *at this time*. Sometimes, I know right away and write it down; other times, it comes later. Sometimes after writing the verse, I write a prayer to God. Rereading these faith journals every few months reminds me how often God has coached me, especially in times when I wonder where God is or how He is working.

The purpose of the scrap paper is to write down thoughts the devil uses to distract you. Instead of interrupting your time with God, just jot down the thoughts, such as "take meat out of the freezer," "call Mom," or "take your pill." Rebuke the devil and attend to your list later.

Assess Your Clients' Spiritual Walk

It is critical to assess where clients are in their spiritual walk. They may be uncomfortable when discussing faith matters because many do not have a firm walk with God; their church attendance may be irregular; and they will not pray daily or read the Word or even say grace at meals. Many do not see how essential God is as THE change instrument in their recovery. So be gentle when asking and not judgmental. Be patient, and you will be able to teach them helpful faith practices and build their personal relationship with God.

Take a reading on their faith practices frequently by asking these questions:

> *"Did you pray this week?"*

> *"Would you tell me what you ask for?"*

> *"Was that what God wants for you?"*

> *"Did you surrender anything to God?"*

> *"Did you trust that He would provide?"*

Some other questions to ask:

> *"Would you share what faith means to you?"*

> *"Would you share your thoughts about God with me?"*

> *"Would you tell me about how you were raised regarding faith?"*

> *"Are faith and God important to you?"*

> *"What are your thoughts about going to church or reading the Bible?"*

No matter how they respond, remember not to be judgmental. Just accept what they say and ask,

"Will you take a few minutes and talk a bit more about it?"

If they say, "Not really; I want to talk about my issue," tell them you will honor that.

If they say it is OK to talk about it, then gently ask where they are in their faith walk. Then you will know how to proceed strategically to help them grow.

It has been my experience that some people who call themselves Christians have a very shallow walk. Hence, striking a balance of counseling and encouraging the client's spiritual growth is a necessary but delicate task. Ask God constantly for wisdom and openers to help them grow.

Use the following explanation with clients to help them understand the relationship between spirituality and behavior. They may not have thought about the connection, yet it is critical.

God Is Real; See Him in the World and Inside of Us

The Bible tells us that God created each of us with an awareness of Him in our hearts and a longing to have a relationship with Him. God evidences Himself in His magnificent creation—the heavens, the physical properties that govern our lives like the seasons, gravity, our bodies, the ability to reproduce, and so on. God gives all of us a conscience so we know good from evil. For example, everyone knows that it is wrong to murder, lie, and cheat whether or not you were exposed to any religion. God puts that in everyone's conscience. (Nevertheless, people with certain psychiatric disorders do not acknowledge this.)

Move from Selfishness to a Morally Exemplary Life

We are exposed to many religions, and we make choices about which ones we are comfortable with and what we choose to believe. Sometimes we want to ignore our religion and consequently make behavioral choices out of our own selfish desires, like wanting to be romantically or physically involved with someone who does not belong to you. Perhaps it's wanting to indulge in your wants to excess like overeating or overdrinking. Our selfish choices can cause havoc in our relationships, health, and responsibilities. That is why we all need a foundation to build our morals and behavior on, and the Bible is the best resource for that because it is God's instruction.

Our Choices as Adults, Whether Christian or Not

Depending on how you were raised, church, prayer, or values may have different levels of importance. Those raised in a "Christian or Catholic-Christian home" were usually well versed in church, prayer, and the Bible, but as they became adults, they may have opted to no longer participate as before.

Others, having been exposed to a Christian faith, may choose what they want to follow or not—for example, choosing to live with someone prior to marriage, having sex before marriage, or practicing homosexuality.

Values and Religion

People seeking a Christian counselor have an expectation that the values and guidance provided are biblically based. (See chapter 9, "Assessing the Client's Experience with Counseling.") Clients may claim to be "Christians," but you will soon see the depth of their faith and commitment to biblical teachings. Accept where they are; do not challenge them yet.

First, try to understand where their values are from, and ask them in a gentle, noncritical way. They may say, "From my parents," "It's what everyone does and that's OK with me," or "It just works for me." Do not voice anything critical at this point. You do not want them to be defensive or feel ashamed. You will have time to talk through issues.

You can ask if they ever have any conflicts within themselves about what they are doing. If they say, "Sometimes," you can remind them that is God trying to teach them a better way. You can explain that God gave us all a conscience and that the war going on in our heads and hearts when we are struggling is God guiding us. (Some will say that guidance is the Holy Spirit for those who have accepted Christ as their Lord and Savior. Others claim that until you have accepted Christ, the Holy Spirit is not available—it is just your conscience. Discuss this with your pastor.)

You can ask, gently,

> *"Do you care what God has to say about what you are doing and how your behavior is affecting your responsibilities and relationships in life?"*

Losing Touch with God

God tells us what to do, but sometimes we just do not want to do it. If we defy God repeatedly, our heart gets hardened to hearing Him, and we slide down that slippery slope to trusting in ourselves because we cannot hear God.

God speaks to us. Like the "look" from a parent when we have misbehaved or a desirous look from a partner, we learn the meaning of looks over time. We also need to recognize God's voice, like the "look," and that takes time with Him. There are no shortcuts.

Help with Decision-Making

When we make a good/bad and strengths/weaknesses lists in trying to decide about something, add another column and name it, "What God would put on each line for the positives and negatives."

For example, in assessing whether to date a certain man, a plus might be that he is a good person, but a negative is he is not a Christian. God says to not be unequally yoked.

In assessing your list about finances, as another example, on the positive side, giving generously is biblical and God says He will reward us. On the negative is you will have to step out in faith while still being reasonable with your responsibilities. (It is one place in the Bible where God says to test Him.)

Does God Say Yes, No, or Wait?

It has been proposed that God sometimes answers the requests of His children with yes, no, or wait. However, what seems like a "yes" could be God testing us to see if we ask Him for His will even when something looks like a go. A "no" may mean God wants to cultivate our persistence and perseverance to see how much we truly desire our request. "Wait" may mean we need more information or more insight to make an informed decision. Ask God to show you what He wants and why.

God is always building our character to be more like Christ. Ask God what He is teaching you in your circumstances—patience, forgiveness, trust?

God Can Do the Impossible

The problem may be in what we believe about God and His ability to do the impossible. Bottom line: if we believe God is who He says He is in the Bible, we have a promise that He will provide. Rest in that.

As a faith-based counselor, your responsibility is to lead clients to healthy options that God would endorse. Often, this will mean asking them to take baby steps. Even when they know they are not doing the right thing behaviorally, they

- may not be ready to change,
- may not have the moral fiber to change, or
- may fear the change.

Sometimes they do not return to counseling because they do not want to disappoint you or themselves. That is why a desire for change has to come from them, and you have to be an encourager. Let them know that God will help them, although sometimes failure happens repeatedly.

> **"No temptation has overtaken you but such as is common to man; and God is faithful, who will not allow you to be tempted beyond what you are able, but with the temptation will provide the way of escape also, so that you will be able to endure it" (1 Corinthians 10:13).**

Opening Clients' Eyes about Values

For people who have not really thought about their values and, more importantly, how their lack of values has affected others, hearing that faith offers them another way of behaving is encouraging. This arouses their curiosity, and if they have left a trail of damage or if they feel hopeless, they become more curious and hopeful. Feed them gently but confidently, knowing that God can change their heart if they surrender their will to Him. Tell them that the power to change comes from God's Word and the Holy Spirit. Pray with them aloud about what God wants to do.

Spiritual Warfare

Ask clients about spiritual warfare and what they believe about it. It is real and they need to guard themselves against it. Pastor Tony Evans has written great material on spiritual warfare. Go to his website—www.tonyevans.org. (I gave my life to the Lord in 2000 when listening to a Tony Evans tape on spiritual warfare. I had been convicted, as I had never been before.)

Additional Ways to Grow Spiritually As a Counselor

Sacrifice

Ask yourself daily: What did/could I offer in sacrifice to the Lord today? Then write it in your journal. It will build your self-esteem as a giving person.

Keep a Daily Inventory

Do a moral inventory daily of your progress on your weaknesses. Confess regularly.

> "The spirit of man is the lamp of the LORD, searching all the innermost parts of his being" (Proverbs 20:27).

Read the Word on a Schedule

Make a commitment to read the Bible in a year. The web has a variety of options. This act of discipline will also increase your self-confidence as a representative of Christ.

Read one entire book in the Bible *daily* for a month. You will be surprised with each reading how God reveals new things to you.

Memorize Scripture

Memorize a favorite verse from each book of the Bible.

Keep Humble

You are an instrument of God, so be humble that He is using you.

> "So then neither the one who plants nor the one who waters is anything, but God who causes the growth" (1 Corinthians 3:7).

SECTION VII
Considerations for Helpers in Noncounseling Settings and Situations

CHAPTER 31

How to Handle Problematic Situations Outside of a Counseling Office and Case Examples

Not all of you will have a counseling office and provide nonprofessional counseling in a structured, scheduled situation. This chapter addresses the needs of people serving in ministries such as food box distribution, shelters, support groups, and so on. This would include anywhere volunteers may be used; where volunteers interact with staff; or where you are faced with people's/customers'/clients' personal, emotional, or behavioral problems and are expected to manage them, at least initially.

As a foundation, it would be helpful to read this whole book. However, minimally read the following chapters and the selected excerpts identified. This will prepare you and give you confidence.

Introduction (and disclaimers)
Read all the information

Chapter 2   Strengths and Characteristics of a Counselor
Read the entire chapter

Chapter 3   Qualities of an Effective Counselor
Read the entire chapter

Chapter 4   Vulnerabilities of a Counselor
Read the entire chapter

Chapter 5   Who Seeks Help and Whom to Accept
Read the entire chapter to understand who you should and should not help

Chapter 6   Assessing the Problem: Potential Contributing Causes of Problems (Health, Heart, and Fear Issues)
Read the entire chapter

Chapter 7   Assessing the Problem: Understanding Clients' Feelings and Reactions
In particular read the sections on "Some Exaggerated Reactions," "Entitlement Mentality," and "Emotional Manipulation"

Chapter 9 Assessing the Client's Experience with Counseling
Read the entire chapter to learn how to see what has been tried and to correct any biases about counseling

Chapter 10 Understanding Clients' Coping Mechanisms and Boundaries
In particular read "Boundaries," "Emotional Boundaries," "Crying Clients," and "Boundary Violations"

Chapter 11 Understanding Clients' Defenses
Read the entire chapter

Chapter 12 Preparation
In particular read the sections "Make It a Safe Place," "Listen," "Body Language," "Etiquette," "Language," "Introduction and Greeting," and "It's Not about You"

Chapter 13 Getting Started and Setting Goals
Read the entire chapter. This chapter emphasizes numerous essentials to know and practice: respect for the client (customer), creating order, attentive listening, open body language, and a section on identifying the real problem. Know that so often what people claim to be upset over is not the real problem. For example, it is not that a client does not understand the policy that each person gets one bag of food. Or that the food choices are lousy, or that the food bank is only open particular hours, and so forth. It is that he is humiliated having to ask for help, embarrassed about not being able to provide for those in his care, and is feeling helpless and dependent. Read between the lines of what he is saying and what he may be feeling. You do not want to have him feel you pity him or feel sorry for him. That will make things worse. Start right off with showing him respect.

See also the case examples at the end of this chapter.

Chapter 14 Counseling Strategies and Tools for Clients
Read the entire chapter so you can use the techniques even in short conversations or if you have a few sessions or conversations with an individual or couple. These are tools anyone can use to improve his or her communication skills, social rapport, and personal character growth.

Chapter 15 Types of Questions to Ask and a Strategy to Ask Them
In particular read the sections "Expressions to Encourage Continued Talking," "Opening Their Eyes," "Payoffs," "The Christian Perspective," "The Past," and "Visualize Forward"

Chapter 16 Sexual, Physical, and Emotional Abuse, and Anxiety
In particular read the section on "Emotional Issues—A Quick Assessment" and "For Generalized Emotional or Anxiety Issues"

Chapter 17 Why People Stay in or Return to Abusive Relationships
Read the entire chapter

Chapter 18 A Perspective on Our Family of Origin's Influence
In particular read the roles people played and often play now, and the section on "Values"

Chapter 19   Marital and Relational Issues
In particular read the sections "Letting the Past Go," "Love Is a Choice," and "Start Over"

Chapter 21   Managing Arguments
Read the entire chapter

Chapter 22   Anger Management
Read the entire chapter

Chapter 23   Addiction and Other Issues
Read where applicable to the problem.

Chapter 24   Codependency
Read the entire chapter

Chapter 26   Grief and Depression
Read what is applicable to your client.

Chapter 27   Encouragement
Read the entire chapter

Chapter 29   Forgiveness
Read the entire chapter

Chapter 30   Spiritual Issues and Personal Growth for Counselors and Clients
Read the entire chapter

Chapter 31 How to Handle Problematic Situations Outside of a Counseling Office and Case Examples
Read the entire chapter

Seven case examples follow with typical situations and proposed dialogue to help you manage problems.

Case example **#1 Someone angry at your policy**

Case example **#2 An accusation that you are pushing religion**

Case example **#3 Offensive language**

Case example **#4 Someone tries to talk to you about a personal, complicated, or controversial issue when there isn't privacy or time**

Case example **#5 Someone is emotionally broken (crying, tearing up) and wants attention when there is not privacy or time**

Case example **#6 A volunteer is noncompliant**

Case example **#7 A volunteer or customer/client/coworker who talks too much**

Case example **#8 A volunteer/employee/coworker is not performing and is absent a lot due to drama in her life**

The Case Examples

Case example #1: Someone angry at your policy

An infuriated customer is angry about not being allowed to get two food bags and is causing a scene at the food bank.

"May I ask your name, sir?" (You are showing respect.)

If he just says his first name, use that. If he gives his full name, honor it.

"Thank you, Jack (or Mr. Wright). I agree that the policy we have of one bag per family (or whatever he or she is disagreeing with) may seem unreasonable and is frustrating. (Repeat) I agree."

Then be silent as he digests your surprise response of agreement.

"Would you take a minute and talk with me about it inside where it is quieter?" (You are giving him control, a choice, and getting him off stage.)

If he is hesitant:

"I value your thoughts; please consider talking with me." (He sees he is valued and would not be backing down in front of others because you are inviting him.)

He agrees. Show him the way by extending your arm in the necessary direction, but gesture that he should go first, ahead of you (as a courtesy).

"Please sit down. Thank you for giving me a couple minutes of your time." (His time is seen as valuable.)

"We are always looking to improve the way we do things. I value your thoughts. How can we make the system better?"

He may not realize all the factors that play into a policy. Listen respectfully and silently to his thoughts while giving constant eye contact, and say,

"Thank you, Jack (or Mr. Wright)" (regardless of the practical value of the suggestion).

If it seems helpful, say,

"I would like to share some inside information about the number of boxes that go out on a daily, weekly, and yearly basis, the approximate cost, and the number of volunteers helping here." (You are not defending; you are trying to bond through the sharing of special information. Then share what is helpful to your case.)

Share also how volunteers are needed and welcome, and say,

"I'm wondering if volunteering here is something you might consider."

He may be willing, or practical matters may prevent him from participating. Either way, remind him, and say,

"We would certainly appreciate your help."

If he asks about a paying job, share about any support/employment prep service you have or know of, if that is something that he would be interested in (always give choices). Give him your card and suggest,

"Keep in touch. May I pray for you if you have any requests?" (not "needs").

He may well say he has some right there. If so, pray for him and his requests. Thank him again, and walk him out. Sign him up as a volunteer if that is applicable.

Case example #2: An accusation of pushing religion

Your requirement for recipients of food, money for bills, and so forth, to attend a church service is infuriating a potential recipient. He is in a cubicle separated by a desk from the volunteer/ministry worker. He has already given you his name and filled out his request. You have learned that having people fill out the information first is advantageous as you have a name to respectfully call them by, and you can assess the financial situation in case there may be exceptions made or other options considered. You just explained the policy to assure that he understands the conditions of receipt. He explodes.

"Pushing religion is not OK! Forcing people to go to church in order to get help is why organized religion is a joke. You aren't helping people; you're setting them up so you can convert them!"

Do not defend your policy. He may be disappointed with God, or his personal experience with religion has been hurtful. Or his embarrassment of being needy is making him angry at himself, and he is taking it out on the system and religion.

> "Mr. Smith, I can see you have strong feelings about religion. You're right. Organized religion can have many problems. I agree with you, and I'm sure Jesus would, too" (opening the door to some words about Jesus).

Be silent as he digests your response. He may jump to side with Jesus or ignore your comment. If he mentions anything about Jesus, ask,

> "Would you share more of your thoughts about Jesus? I value your thoughts."

If he does not pick up on talking about Jesus, you can add,

> "I liked how Jesus chose to lead a simple life of poverty and sacrificing and to be on the go all the time. He chose a very hard lifestyle."

This is your potential opener to ask,

> "Because you don't like organized religion, what do you think about anyone living a life that reflects the teachings of Jesus?"

He may say something like he thinks it is only important to be a good person. You agree and say,

> "But we all fall short; we all mess up. Then what? How do we get to heaven if we mess up?"

Or you can say,

> "One of the things I like about Jesus is how He can forgive our mistakes and give us a clean slate to start over. I know I have a past that is a train wreck, and I am so grateful I got to start over. Do you like that about Jesus?" (not "believe that" about Jesus; assume he may already know that but may not necessarily believe it for himself.)

See what he says (anything is imaginable). Remember to pray during the silence for his surrender. Follow with saying,

> "I would welcome your company anytime over a cup of coffee to talk more together about Jesus or your life if you'd like" (hoping he would welcome some friendship).

Hopefully, you have planted a seed and also defused the tension. Do not push for his surrender. Let God lead the way in His time. We are here to be a light, by being an example.

Case example #3: Offensive language
A volunteer is using offensive language despite two polite requests to watch her language.

> "Martha, may I speak with you in the office, please?"

She may ask, "What's up?"

"Let's go to the office and talk, please."

Show respect by asking her to please sit down.

"Do you know why I wanted to see you?"

She may say her "mouth" and defend herself with some explanation that she is trying to work on it, and may apologize. Work toward the larger issue.

"Martha, we all have our junk we are working on, and I appreciate how hard it can be to change patterns."

(This is the top layer of the "Oreo Cookie Strategy" tool in the appendix.)

"We have several volunteers who are new believers in Christ and are trying very hard to change a number of things in their lives. They need encouragement and to be around good role models. You are in a position to be a role model to others and to help them become better Christians.

"We really need your help in being a role model and encourager for others. We need you to be controlled about your language, and if you slip, quickly apologize with sincerity. I see you having the potential to be a good influence in what you say rather than a person who uses offensive language."

(Middle layer of the Oreo—that was your pitch.)

"I am hoping you will honor yourself and others by taking on this new role. If not, we may have to part ways. Thank you for considering our request and helping out."

(The bottom layer of the Oreo—affirming your request.)

Then stand up, acting like it is a given that she will comply, and *thank her again for helping out.* Walk her back to her work site saying,

"Thank you again, Martha" in earshot of those nearby (giving her grace, respect, and having her feel no shame).

Bad language is a tough pattern to break, but it is a choice. As is said elsewhere in this book, if I were to give you $1,000 for not swearing for a day, you would do it. Remember to validate/praise her efforts regularly.

Case example #4: Someone tries to talk to you about a personal, complicated, or controversial issue when there is not privacy or time

Sometimes people are spontaneously motivated to share something, they have finally worked up the courage, or they may be being controlling, as examples. Either way, a simple solution is to use the Oreo tool.

> "Mrs. Gabriel, excuse me. What you have to say is important and deserves my full attention."

(Top layer of the Oreo—affirmation of her feelings.)

> "Please give me a few minutes and then I can take time to speak with you in a quieter place."

Or "I would appreciate it if you would call me, and let's set up an appointment as soon as possible."

(Middle layer—your request.)

> "Again, I care and want to hear what you have to say and will find the best time for you and me."

(Bottom layer—affirming your need.)

You are taking care of yourself and your immediate agenda, without leaving her with the feeling of being dismissed. If she persists, repeat your initial statement.

Case example #5: Someone is emotionally broken (crying, tearing up) and wants attention when there isn't privacy or time

You may have callers or in-person situations where someone is emotionally unglued and wants your immediate attention. (See chapter 26, "Grief and Depression.") His feelings may have been triggered by a sermon, sitting in church alone after the death of a spouse, or seeing someone in church, or he may have been upset and came to church or the support group hoping to be able to stay composed but couldn't.

First, it is your priority to affirm that you care. Perhaps touch his shoulder, have constant eye contact, and then maintain your plan per case example #4. He may start or keep talking/crying, and it feels awkward to interrupt him. It is OK to do that with grace, as you are teaching him that sometimes *we need to and can* manage our feelings even when they seem overwhelming and out of control. Repeat that you care and want to talk privately with him.

If he dismisses himself ("Oh, I'm OK; I don't want to bother you; I know you're [too] busy [for me])," that is a manipulation. Do not feel guilt-tripped into yielding. Gently repeat your position and say,

> "I need to take care of what I am doing, and I will see you shortly."

That is all you can do. Imagine pastors who perform hundreds of funerals and make innumerable visits to the sick. These people or their loved ones could take up all of a pastor's time. This attention seeking and/or genuinely wanting to thank their pastor or update them on their loved one can occur as they greet the pastor after the service or happen to run into him or her out in the community. It is not good timing.

Ministry leaders, counselors, and really anyone who has a relationship with someone he or she has ministered to are sometimes approached at awkward times. People think that because you have had a shared experience, they have special privileges to take up your time.

It is an impossibility to live up to everyone's expectations. Set your boundaries ("We can talk about this at your next appointment"; "Please call me at the church, and we can talk about this") and pray for the Lord to help the person understand and receive your offer to talk at a better time.

Case example #6: A volunteer is noncompliant
As stated elsewhere in this book, sometimes people exercise control in areas where they *can*. This often happens when there are areas in their lives that are out of control—things they cannot control (like someone in their life who is an addict, or a job loss, a tragedy, a betrayal, and so on). It is like the person who kicks the dog when angry at his boss.

Or the noncompliant person may be seeking attention or not feel socially adequate in interacting with associates in his assignment. Or he may not know how to do the task correctly and is avoiding it. If he is overwhelmed and too busy to do the task, he may have an attention deficit disorder. Or he may be fearful of not doing it right and then being criticized (perhaps as an impatient or critical parent may have done with him instead of being politely and patiently corrected). Or he may be bored.

Therefore, first you have to assess a potential reason for his noncompliance. For example, did he understand the directions he was given? Check out his environment (Is it overstimulating?), his social interaction with coworkers (Does he seem to fit in?), his skill level (Does it match his apparent ability? Perhaps he has never used a dishwasher, or a washing machine, or painted anything and is embarrassed to admit that).

A rabbit trail detour I will share from my own experience: I did not grow up with a dishwasher and had no idea how to load or operate one. After college dorm living, I took a room with two flight attendants who were intimidating in their beauty and knowledge from world traveling. They asked me to load the dishwasher before they left early one morning. I was very embarrassed to admit to them that I did not know how to do that. I panicked and moved out while they were gone. Really. Need I say more? I still panic sometimes when I am given instructions and fear not getting it right. (We all have our junk, as I said before, and sometimes our old fears will resurface.)

Be patient and do not assume someone's competency. Many people have a fear of criticism or disappointing others; it is very commonplace.

Take the person aside. Then with gentleness, first say you care about him and are concerned about his investment in his responsibility. (Top layer of the Oreo.)

You wish to know if there is anything going on that is hindering him from giving the responsibility his best—that it is your goal to take care of any problems if you can. (The middle of the Oreo—your pitch.)

Say you are encouraging him to be truthful in helping you fix the problem with a solution that is mutually rewarding so he can remain part of the mission. (Bottom layer of reaffirming your pitch.)

Review chapter 13, "Getting Started and Setting Goals," especially the sections on "Fear" and "Motivation Issues."

Case example #7: A volunteer or customer/client/coworker who talks too much

We have all observed the workers huddled near the department store's sales desk chatting rather than doing their work: the person who stands in your office doorway asking questions while ignoring that you are obviously being busy; the volunteer who talks incessantly and is distracting to others trying to work; or the person in a meeting or audience who is talking to his neighbor and is rude and distracting.

How we respond is telling. Some make a scowling face at the talker, some make a sarcastic remark, and some are intimidated and do not want to hurt his or her feelings so they try to still work and listen. That is being codependent—sacrificing your responsibilities for others out of fear of what they will think, also known as people pleasing. (See the "Oreo Cookie Strategy" in the appendix and read chapter 24, "Codependency.") Some give up and listen but rage inside with resentment (a codependent trait), and some have learned to respond with grace and love.

> *"Jenny, I would like to talk another time when I can pay more attention."*

> (Top layer of the Oreo)

> *"I know you understand that I need to give what I am doing my full attention."*

> (Middle of the Oreo)

> *"Thanks for understanding. Catch you later"* (and go back to work).

> (The Oreo's bottom layer of affirming your position)

Case example #8: A volunteer/employee/coworker is not performing and is absent a lot due to drama in her life

Some people drawn to drama are so used to it that they think it is normal. Either they share their drama to get attention or that is all they have to talk about (little time or focus to be truly invested in others); they feel victimized and want prayer, advice, sympathy, or whatever. They feel that because they have all of these "situations," exceptions should be made for them. They have an "entitlement mentality." Say,

> *"Peter, I am concerned about you."*

> (Top piece of the Oreo)

> *"There is a lot going on in your life, and it is impacting your performance, which in turn is impacting your coworkers' performance and the mission of our church (organization/business/and so on). I need you to do two things to help manage this situation: one, please keep your personal life to yourself and do not discuss it at work. Two, I suggest you see a counselor to get a perspective on your situations and see if he or she can help you get stability in your life."*

(Middle piece—your petition)

"Peter, I know you want to be healthy and to thrive in your work and social life. I believe that keeping your personal life to yourself and seeing a counselor are two effective ways to improve your life and your work performance and keep you in good standing here. Thank you for your understanding and anticipated cooperation. Let us talk again in two weeks about your progress. Thank you, Peter."

(Bottom layer—affirming your stance)

If a problem returns, read the section on "Managing a Relapse" in chapter 13, "Getting Started and Setting Goals."

Understanding the reasons will help with any drama in your environment.

SECTION VIII
Professional and Liability Concerns

CHAPTER 32
Administrative and Legal Reminders

Supervision

There must be supervision for the counseling services provided. A designated supervisor is responsible for the following:

- Ensuring the counselors are in a safe setting
- Ensuring counselors know who the supervisory contact is 24/7 in case there are off-hour emergencies
- Intervening in emergencies for behavioral problems or when clients are in serious emotional distress
- Periodically reviewing how cases are handled
- Periodically randomly reviewing client files
- Providing support and encouragement
- Providing, or ensuring the provision of, initial and ongoing training
- Ensuring there is a support group for counselors
- Attending the support groups run by counselors and their own support group and observing the strengths and weakness of counselors, and discussing with them in group or privately, as appropriate
- Adjusting the training materials to include anything identified that needs to be included

Some constructive advice or coaching can be given in group, while other times, because of the counselor (he or she may be new, insecure, timid, not knowledgeable, having a hard time grasping some of the concepts, and so on), it is best to address any concerns privately. Hopefully, if the private critique is done well and received well, you can ask if the counselor will share what he or she did and learned with the group from his or her triumphs and mistakes.

Options for Supervision and Support

One option is to contract with a professional counselor to provide supervision, and/or run a support group for counselors, as well as provide initial and ongoing training. A professional may do this as a volunteer or for a fee.

Pastors and usually others in church leadership are a resource for offering godly ways to manage a case if needed, but time constraints may be a barrier.

Peer-led support groups for counselors have merit, but it is preferable to have a leader who is a professional.

Support groups for counselors (or anyone providing counseling) are beneficial and can be used for supervision and training as well. Encouragement as well as case critiquing can be provided and serve as helpful teaching examples for others. Such groups would meet at least monthly, ideally with a choice of a daytime or a nighttime meeting for the convenience of all people providing counseling. Here are a few points to keep in mind:

- Client names are not to be used in supervisory support groups (first names only, if necessary).
- Everything said in group is confidential.
- Remember that these counselors are not such by formal training, so encouragement is golden.

Helpful comments by a supervisor or leader in group would hopefully reflect the skills and techniques mentioned in this book and their own expertise.

Problems

Some typical problems that may arise in group training and a supervisor's potential response follow.

- For boundary issues (a counselor is overinvolved with a case):

"I can see you are sincerely invested in this case." (validating)

"Do you feel like you have identified all the boundary areas that you need to be alert to?" (attempting to see if the counselor sees there are issues either with herself or the client)

"Are there areas you personally are trying to be conscious of?"

- For boundary issues (client appears to be taking advantage of the counselor):

"This sounds like a challenging case." (validating)

"Do you feel swept up in it?"

"Where would you say limits may need to be set?" (prompting)

"Are you comfortable stating those limits to the client?"

(If not) *"Where do you want help?"*

- For emotional manipulation by a client:

"The client sounds to me like he is a manipulator. What do you think?" (Suggesting, not telling, and inviting a potential admission that he has been vulnerable to manipulation rather than you being accusatory, which would be embarrassing and make him defensive.)

Encourage the counselor to reread chapter 7, "Assessing the Problem: Understanding Clients' Feelings and Reactions," the section on "Manipulation" and check the index.

- For irritating clients:

"I think anyone would be frazzled by that client." (validating)

"What emotions were coming up for you?"

"Were you OK with how you handled yourself?" (preventing defensiveness)

"What might you have done differently?"

"Does anyone else have thoughts on how this client might have been handled?" (letting others support and then offer suggestions and comment on those suggestions or have the group chime in)

- For someone who is burning out, but he or she doesn't see it:

"I know your dedication, and it is appreciated. I am concerned that you are losing the balance in your life and have worked too hard at counseling. What do you think?"

"Are you allocating enough time for God's priorities: Him first (reading the Word and praying), then your wife, then your kids, then your job, and then your volunteering?"

"You know, sometimes we don't see how we start to slip down that slippery slope of an unbalanced life. I suggest you ask your wife and the people closest to you what they think and ask them to be honest."

"Meanwhile, I encourage you to pray about taking a few weeks off and relaxing. You are truly valued, you know that. However, none of us is irreplaceable. God will provide."

- For a counselor who "shoots from the hip" and doesn't apply strategies for first developing rapport and trust,

"There are advantages to taking a few precious seconds before responding in a conversation with a client. That is also a godly approach."

"Wait for the Holy Spirit to coach you and to draw on what you have learned as well as what you know already. We all came with our toolboxes, and part of this training is to teach us more tools, some of them better than the tools we have used."

"When clients see you taking your time to respond or to say something, it shows them you are being thoughtful, careful about what they hear. That honors them and builds trust."

"I am interested in your thoughts about what I have just shared."

- For someone who is defensive when the supervisor or peers critique him in group,

"I see you wanting to explain [rather than "are being defensive," so he is not embarrassed] *your position on how you handled that situation."*

"There are many ways to handle a situation as evidenced by the options others are presenting to you."

"I have found that conceding on a point, or even admitting that we can be wrong sometimes, is a relief for most of us. We don't have to always be right."

"Clients will also respect you when you can say to them, 'I see your point. My previous comments were not on target. Thanks for correcting me.' That honors them, makes you real, and shows you can give up the power, that it's more important to 'have it right' than for you to be right."

"Any thoughts on what I have shared?"

- For someone who wants to rescue a client:

"Much of the time, our helping a client isn't helping them. It is rescuing, and they need to turn to God for help and learn to depend on Him. God puts problems in our paths to grow us and to turn us to Him. Clients won't develop confidence in their ability to provide and do for themselves if they don't have opportunities to learn, grow, and see that they can survive mistakes."

"Do you believe that God wants us all to depend on Him?"

Record Keeping/Tracking

Keep track of the number of people you serve using a simple form noting the following:

- Date of contact
- Full name, date of birth, contact information
- Their basic problem(s)
- If/where you referred them
- Any unmet needs (for potential resource building and grant opportunities)
- What you provided (counseling, food, cash, bill paying, and so on)

Keep records for thirty days, or longer if space permits, because clients often return for service.

Keep a list of the handouts and homework assignments and the date given on the face sheet of a client's folder to help you keep track.

Legal Issues

There is always a legal vulnerability when providing any type of service, especially a personal one like counseling. Additionally, in counseling you are dealing with emotionally charged people and sensitive issues, so there is an added vulnerability. The organization should consult an attorney about numerous issues, including having necessary policies in place for forms, record keeping, confidentiality, same-gender consultations versus not, misquotes by clients, false accusations, and so forth.

Some clients or their attorneys will request that you testify or ask for your notes for court. It is a helpful safeguard against future misunderstandings if you have a form that the client signs that acknowledges your policy on providing client information. That is still no guarantee that your records won't be subpoenaed.

If you are permitted by policy to provide certain information, it will be more credible if you have that completed on standardized forms on letterhead, which keeps the information very brief.

Be careful when seeing clients of the opposite gender, especially if the issues are sensitive. Clients may project things onto you that are untrue, think you said things you didn't, believe you were flirting when you weren't, and so on. It is best to be extra cautious and to be on the safe side and see only clients of the same gender. Still, that is no guarantee that you won't be vulnerable to erroneous accusations and even legal action.

Be careful about "recommending" anything or anyone. It is better to "suggest," but even then, *it is not a counselor's job to tell people what to do.* You can present options and let the client decide what works, and never give "advice."

Clients may misquote you or misunderstand what you have said, so be very careful when you speak. It is very troublesome when a client thinks you "told" them to get a divorce or leave a situation. Choices always have to be the client's.

(Additionally, if clients do not or cannot follow your advice, they may not return to counseling out of embarrassment or frustration. Such a problem may have been avoided if you had made it clear that you will help them through their situation as best as you are able, but they are responsible for their choices. Also, to encourage their return as scheduled or later, tell them you will do your best to help them now or in the future in case things change again.)

Insurance

Most counselors have professional liability insurance, and it would behoove the organization whose umbrella any nonprofessionals are working or volunteering under to consult an attorney on how to handle this. It is difficult to acquire professional insurance if you are not licensed on some level.

Confidentiality
Tell clients that all information shared will be held confidential. (The agreement form could also state this.)

Client Contract
Many counselors use a contract or an agreement with the client that states the following:

- The parties the agreement is between
- The date of the agreement
- The counselor's credentials
- When the agreement will expire (for example, three-month intervals)
- What the counselor will provide (a fifty-minute session)
- The fee and whether insurance is accepted
- When fees are expected to be paid (at the end of each session)
- The client's liability to pay if there is an insurance dispute and if he or she does not show or cancel with less than twenty-four hours' notice
- The amount due for late cancellations or no-shows (for example, half the fee for the first incident, full fee thereafter)
- The policy on confidentiality and release of information
- The noncounseling work they may choose to provide (court appearances, letters regarding participation, and so on, for the courts) and the fee
- Any reasons for termination
- The after-or between-session contact policy (by type, conditions under which contacts are appropriate and accepted, the length of time—for example, very short conversations)

SECTION IX
Next Steps

CHAPTER 33
Preparations

Pray and ask God for confirmation of you/your organization venturing into a counseling ministry. Wait for confirmation.

While you are waiting, reread the entire book (again). Read any relevant books on the Suggested Reading list.

Take the Knowledge Test if you have not already. Address any personal weak knowledge areas.

If you have realized you have need of some counseling yourself, take care of that.

If God confirms you/your organization doing counseling, start preparations.

Identify who will provide your supervision and discuss training, accountability, counselor reviews, and support plans.

Develop a plan for emergency contact with a supervisor for managing crisis cases as well as handling crisis during work hours.

Develop policies about whom you will and will not accept, and the fee (if applicable).

Develop policies about clients' missed or canceled appointments without twenty-four hours' notice and the consequences.

If you have a fund for supplementing client fees, state the conditions for application/access.

Develop a resource list of area shelters, twelve-step groups, Celebrate Recovery Groups, licensed therapists, certified addictions counselors, their fees/insurances accepted, and so forth. Keep the resource list current.

Develop a policy on confidentiality as well as mandatory reporting requirements.

Develop a form for client information that also has your service expectations.

If you have purchased this book, make copies of the handouts for your use only.

Consult an attorney about any liability issues, insurance issues, supervision, the adequacy of your forms and policies, handouts, and so on.

Pray regularly for yourself, your clients, and your organization.

Appendix

Reader's Knowledge Test
Tools for Counselors to Use as Homework for Clients
    Oreo Cookie Strategy
    Getting Back on Track
    Communication Tool: The Table Meeting
    What I Want in a Partner Worksheet
    What I Offer a Partner Worksheet
    Ways to Improve Communication
    Life Lessons Learned
Suggested Reading
Reader's Knowledge Test Answers
Acknowledgements
Index
About the Author

Reader's Knowledge Test

Reader's Knowledge Test
(The answers are in the appendix)

This is a simple test of some of your recollection from the chapters. It is not intended to confirm your expertise or ability to counsel. Knowing the material and then competently managing dialogues with your clients takes much practice and prayer.

Complete The Entire Test Before Checking Your Answers
True or False

Chapter 1 (No test questions)

Chapter 2
__1. Servants honor others with humility, unselfishness, giving, and compassion.
__2. Counseling will grow in you the fruit of the Holy Spirit: love, joy, peace, patience, kindness, goodness, faithfulness, gentleness, and self-control.

Chapter 3
Effective counselors:
__1. Honor where clients are at regarding their insight, self-awareness, and self-honesty.
__2. Patiently wait as counseling, circumstances, and God open their clients' eyes.
__3. Assess their own failures and weaknesses and role model healthy recovery.
__4. Are willing to grow and learn, knowing they can only take others as far as they themselves have come.

Chapter 4
__1. Supervision is encouraged for both professional and nonprofessional counselors.
__2. Being compassionate is godly; being a rescuer is not.
__3. "Doing it all"/having a savior mentality may fulfill a need in your own sense of worthiness.
__4. Being overly involved as a counselor is a boundary issue and potentially an ethical one.
__5. Counselors need to be on guard for emotional manipulation and be alert to clients' needs and fears.
__6. "Projecting" is, essentially, when a client "dumps his/her junk on you," and "transference" is when he or she sees you as someone else.

Chapter 5
Nonprofessional counselors should refer clients with the following disorders/issues to a professional:
__1. Borderline personality disorder, bipolar disorder, admitted severe depression, those persons who have panic attacks, schizophrenia, obsessive-compulsive disorders, those who have a mental health inpatient unit history, have been traumatized, or are admitted cutters.
__2. Any client who speaks of suicide in any manner (past or present).

Chapter 6
__1. Expressed physical problems, including medication and sexual issues, may be contributing causes to mental health issues and need to be assessed by a physician.
__2. One's feelings can be deceptive and should not dictate behavior.
__3. Fear is the root of many emotional stressors.

Chapter 7
__1. Unspoken issues by clients can be more troublesome than those admitted.
__2. Having clients list their bad habits and their frequency as well as their wrong or unhelpful thinking can be eye opening for them.
__3. Clients often have minimized or ignored their feelings so frequently that they have a very limited "feeling vocabulary." Encouraging them to use other words and seeing them struggle helps clients realize this.
__4. Clients fear change, and fear changing themselves because of the unknown.
__5. Choices about our behavior are often dependent upon our circumstances and who is involved.
__6. Make every effort to understand a client's fears: where they came from, how the client has or has not managed them, what are their consequences.
__7. Teaching clients to *respond* rather than *react* is a quick learn and a very practical tool.
__8. Catastrophizing is thinking the absolute worst will happen.
__9. Forecasting is assuming the worst, predicting the future with many "but what-ifs."
__10. Emotional manipulation is a common controlling tactic. Teaching clients to recognize the tactic, respond with healthy control, and hold their ground is critical.
__11. "If you really loved me…" is a common emotional manipulation.
__12. "People pleasing" is one of the traits of codependency.

Chapter 8
__1. In assessing a problem, do the following: see how long the problem has been going on, see if any of the family history has or is contributing to the problem, and assess the historical or biological history.

Chapter 9
__1. In assessing the client's previous experience with counseling, your goals are not to repeat areas already successfully covered, but rather to see what the client's response to his/her previous experience was, and teach him/her what to expect with you so he or she is comfortable.
__2. One significant difference between secular and Christian counseling is that secular counseling attempts to change the thinking and behaviors, whereas Christian counseling does that and also recognizes that surrendering to God is the only permanent cure in recovery.

Chapter 10
__1. When a client is crying, do not hand him/her tissues.
__2. Boundary setting is essential for clients to learn as well as counselors.
__3. It is best not to hug clients as this may trigger past boundary violations, or they may not want to disappoint you and yield, while inside feeling controlled.

Chapter 11
__1. Be alert to a client's use of defenses as he or she tells you where he or she has fear and needs to protect him/herself or others.
__2. Counselors need to know the root of a defense.
__3. Examples of defenses are controlling behaviors, avoidance behaviors, being defiantly silent, retaliating, crying, detaching, and nonstop talking.

Chapter 12
__1. Making the client's time in your session a "safe place," and always treating him/her with respect is very important to establishing rapport and trust.
__2. Listening is essential for the counselor and should be done 90 percent (most) of the time.
__3. Praying before the session is good role modeling and shows your dependence on God.

Chapter 13
__1. Clients need to come up with their goals.
__2. There are "ideal" and "acceptable" goals, and the client needs to understand the difference.
__3. What clients initially share as their goal may not be the real issue, but that will likely be revealed in time.

Chapter 14
__1. Discernment is a careful screening of what you are observing, hearing, or reading to test the truthfulness or integrity of the content.
__2. Counselors need to be discerning to assess a person's motives and heart and to "read between the lines" of what clients are saying.
__3. Validating is an essential communication tool.
__4. To acknowledge the "performer" as well as the "performance" is a helpful way to build self-esteem and give genuine compliments to the performer.
__5. As counselors, it is essential to be a good role model of recovery. However, being ready to admit to a client where God has changed you takes discernment.
__6. Discipline is one of the primary keys to success with any addiction or unhealthy habit.
__7. Teaching clients about discipline and holding them accountable is essential.

Chapter 15
__1. Never ask questions out of curiosity; always have a purpose.
__2. Use the silence to pray silently and ask the Holy Spirit to guide you.
__3. Do not fill in someone else's words for him/her.
__4. Move between questions that engage emotions and questions that engage the mind.
__5. There are "thinking," "feeling," and "doing" types of questions, and all are important to ask.
__6. Counselors can give clients an emotional break by moving from a feeling question to a doing or thinking question.
__7. Asking about the "payoff" to a client's behavior encourages him/her to be honest about why he or she does it.
__8. As Christian counselors, encouraging and helping clients to know what God says in the Bible about their behavior is appropriate.
__9. Helping clients visualize what their changed life will look like gives hope.

Chapter 16
__1. Some clients will not label abuse (especially sexual abuse) as that because it is too horrifying for them.
__2. Families may go into denial about any abuse by trying to keep it a secret or pretend it never happened.
__3. A "scapegoat" is someone in the family who is labeled as the cause of problems, when this is typically not the case.
__4. Exploring a client's fears may be appropriate.
__5. Certain sexual, physical, and emotional abuse situations may best be referred to a professional.

Chapter 17
__1. There are many potential reasons why someone may not leave an abusive relationship, including addiction to the relationship and couples thriving on drama.

Chapter 18
__1. Our family experience may be the source of our unresolved behavioral issues.
__2. Family members may adopt roles to help them cope in a dysfunctional or problematic family situation.
__3. The role each parent plays in modeling gender-related behaviors is significant.
__4. Our parents' marriage may be the most influencing factor in how we handle relationships.
__5. Values learned by clients at home may need to be challenged.

Chapter 19
__1. There is a strategy for getting resistant partners into counseling that is effective.
__2. Observing the dynamics between couples gives a wealth of information.
__3. Teaching clients how to politely correct each other on admitted problem areas is helpful.
__4. Encouraging couples to use the romantic names they used when they were courting helps restore tenderness.
__5. Saying "I" statements rather than "you" statements is a basic help in communication.
__6. In premarital counseling, it is very helpful to teach couples to understand and respect each other's backgrounds and how they each got their values before criticizing any differences.
__7. The life cycles couples go through from premarital dating to growing old together can arouse emotional confusion. A counselor can help couples understand what is normal to help relieve anxiety.
__8. Discussing sex with clients requires prayerful consideration. These clients may need to be referred to a professional or at least someone of the same gender.
__9. Love is a choice.
__10. Separation is rarely helpful to marital restoration.
__11. Enlightening couples about the reality of the impact of divorce on the kids can be a wake-up call to working things out.
__12. Selfishness is the root of many marital problems.

Chapter 20
__1. Assessing parent and in-law issues will usually yield a wealth of problematic issues concerning roles, resentments, baggage with each person's own parents, boundaries, loyalty conflicts, and so forth.
__2. Being caught in the middle of parental or in-law issues can be a significant source of problems in relationships.
__3. Unrealistic expectations are a common source of relational strife.

Chapter 21
__1. The Table Meeting tool is a helpful communication builder for couples as well as families.
__2. Having clients say, "I love/care about you too much to argue with you" often stops arguments and subdues the tension.
__3. One issue per argument/discussion is a good rule.
__4. Apologizing is essential to emotional restoration even if one's apology is not accepted.
__5. Forgiving and forgetting is godly.

Chapter 22
__1. Anger may be a reaction from when someone has been in fear, hurt, pain, or has been disrespected, powerless, bullied, victimized, ignored, and so on.
__2. Getting to the root of anger is essential, and then correct any distorted thinking.

Chapter 23
__1. Addictions have a probable cycle.
__2. The brain can be rewired to combat the addiction.
__3. Finding the source of the pain and fear is helpful to healing and managing the addiction.
__4. There are progressive phases of the addictive cycle.
__5. Helping clients see the corruption in their values can be a wake-up call.
__6. A partner's enabling can be innocently done or calculated to manage the addict's reaction.
__7. Building up a client's realistic perception of herself and the many roles she plays in life helps her to see that she is more than just her problem (be it an addiction or a behavioral issue).
__8. Urges probably can be managed.
__9. Triggers must be identified in order to be managed.

Chapter 24
__1. One definition of codependency is that it is an inordinate reliance or dependency on someone or something that consumes us.
__2. Codependency can show up in denial, low self-esteem patterns, being overly compliant, and/or being controlling.
__3. Codependency is very common.
__4. Anger and resentment (blatant or masked) may be ever present in codependent relationships.
__5. Approach-avoidance relationships may be a pattern with codependents.
__6. One recovery strategy for codependency is to honor one's boundaries.

Chapter 25
__1. Attending "open" twelve-step meetings of various kinds would be helpful to counselors.
__2. Reading some of the issue-specific twelve-step books would be helpful to counselors.

Chapter 26
__1. Grief may show up as forgetfulness, a sense of disconnectedness, sleeplessness or sleeping too much, unpredictable emotions, a change in eating patterns, or anger.
__2. The loss of an addiction (through recovery, for example) can cause grieving.
__3. Milestone changes like a graduation can cause grieving.

__4. A betrayal can cause grieving.
__5. Grievers need to honor the surges of grief that overcome them.
__6. Grief counseling is all about presence.
__7. Helping a griever reminisce is healing.
__8. Educating grievers about what is and is not normal is important.
__9. Grievers typically have many fears.
__10. Helping grievers understand the difference between guilt and regret is helpful.
__11. Saying, "I know how you feel," "Don't cry," or "He or she is in a better place" to a griever is not helpful.

Chapter 27
__1. Counselors need to remind clients that they will have to work hard for several weeks to see changes.
__2. Sometimes stalled progress is because the goals are not right.

Chapter 28
__1. Confessing your sins or weakness to a priest (for Catholics) or a counselor is healing and should give you a sense of peace.
__2. Repentance means turning around, changing your behavior.
__3. Without genuine repentance, change is unlikely to be sustained.

Chapter 29
__1. Unforgivingness is the root of many emotional problems as well as some physical ailments.
__2. There are healing words that help relationships thrive.
__3. Apologizing is more than saying you are sorry.

Chapter 30
__1. People will know if they are growing spiritually when they have an increasing awareness of their sins and character weaknesses, they will see life from a new perspective, their desires will change, and they will hunger to spend time with God.
__2. As a counselor, you can take people only as far as you have grown.
__3. Counselors need to be able to provide challenges and solutions to excuses about faith issues.
__4. Keeping a journal or a daily inventory of progress is helpful.

Chapter 31
__1. The Oreo tool is helpful for teaching clients how to respond appropriately.
__2. Showing respect, even when someone is not deserving of it, is godly.

Chapter 32
__1. There must be supervision for the counseling services provided.
__2. It is predictable that counselors may have initial problems with boundary setting for themselves, being emotionally manipulated, finding certain clients irritating, burning out and not seeing it, talking without thinking or relying on the Holy Spirit for guidance, getting defensive, or trying to rescue clients.

__3. Accurate record keeping is essential for potential liability issues.
__4. Counselors should not recommend but rather suggest.
__5. Confidentiality is absolutely critical in counseling.

YOU HAVE FINISHED.

Tools For Counselors to Use as Homework for Clients

*R**EMINDER**: The following "Tools" in this appendix may be copied <u>by the original purchaser only for his/her exclusive use in his/her ministry or job and are not to be copied for others' use. Others are encouraged to purchase their own copy of the book to have their own personal access to the tools.</u>*

It is my request that a prayer be said that the "Tools" and the contents of this book contribute to both the user and the recipient to grow in devotion and obedience to Christ. Thank you.

Oreo Cookie Strategy

Oreo Cookie Strategy
(a.k.a. "Wrapping a Point with Love and Grace")

Purpose of This Tool

This tool teaches you how to say something effectively so it will be better received by the person hearing it, without him or her becoming as defensive as he or she might be if you simply blurted it out.

It is especially useful when someone needs to say something that is hard for the receiver to hear. It builds confidence in the speaker that he or she has control in conversations and situations instead of feeling like a victim. Think of the three-layered sandwich cookie when you are in the situation, and it will help you include all three points. People tend to forget the top layer, which is very important not to skip. It is another way of validating the other person—an essential communication tool.

Top Layer
<u>This is an acknowledgment of what the person was probably feeling behind the statement.</u> Look past the statement (and possibly the manipulation) and try to see his or her heart. Respond with something like any of the following:

"I can see that you are really upset about this…and I want to talk about it, too. Let's set a time to do that when we both are not upset."

"I know you care and just want to help."

"I appreciate your offer to take care of [you fill in the blank]*."*

"I love you and want our marriage/relationship to be the best it can be."

Then do not say "but." Just pause or, if you feel the need to say something transitional, consider saying "so" or "and." "So I [or "we" if you're speaking for your partner] want to say that—"

Middle Layer
<u>Make your point</u> in an even voice (not one of frustration), with love and grace with words like:

"I am not agreeable with [your coming home and ignoring the chores/kids/me, and so on]*."*

"I am not OK with your [using bad language/temper/spending money without asking, and so on]*."*

"We are committed to managing our problems ourselves and will ask you if we need your help."

"We want to make decisions as a team, so I want to discuss your request with my husband/wife."

"In our marriage, we handle things differently than your suggestion, and it works for us."

"Some things are not open for discussion outside of our marriage."

Bottom Layer

<u>You reaffirm your point</u> with grace. Keep repeating as often as you need to. Be patient; you are changing a relationship dynamic, and it is threatening to others. Be firm, as it will show your maturity and confidence.

"So thank you for understanding and respecting my/our viewpoint on this."

"So I/we appreciate your honoring where I/we stand on this and not discussing it anymore."

"So, as I said before, I thank you for your thoughts and for your remembering/honoring that this is a closed topic."

Getting Back on Track

Getting Back on Track

For: Backsliding, slips, bad choices, intentional indulgences, breaking your drug/alcohol/tobacco sobriety or food abstinence, losing your temper, using bad language, fantasizing, sex outside of marriage, looking at porn, and so forth.

Purpose: **There has to be a consequence to wrong behavior** or there will not be any incentive for correcting it, and *the consequence needs to be immediate and sacrificial*. A guilty conscience is not enough. Nor is knowing that you displeased God. You need *to do something about it*. So, as soon as you indulge in wrong behavior, take the following steps:

- **Admit your wrongdoing to God, with *humility*.**
- **Fast/abstain as a consequence to your behavior.**

You can fast the very next meal (no beverages or food whatsoever, except water). Be considerate if someone is preparing your meals and let the person know you will be sitting at the table with the family but not eating. If they ask why you are not eating, you might say it is your way of taking a "time-out" because you made a mistake. Kids may see self-discipline in a new way.

Or you can fast from some pleasurable activity for several hours (for example, watching or playing your favorite sport game—and don't record it—or all Internet and e-device use).

Whatever you fast from has to be *a sacrifice* and desirable enough that it is an incentive to not indulge in your wrong behavior. Wanting to honor God by our obedient behavior *should* always be enough to keep us on "the narrow path," but as humans, we may also need another incentive to stay on track.

Decide about how long you need to fast or abstain. That could be as short as a half hour if you are skipping a meal or a few hours if it is missing a sporting or "entertaining" event. *You* need to decide, *with integrity*, what would be sacrificial. Use that time to pray or read your Bible or some Christian literature. Do something godly. If others can see you doing something godly instead of your usual routine, you are being a witness for Christ, and that is pleasing to God. Replace a bad habit with a new one. Doing something godly will strengthen your relationship with God and fortify you against future slips.

Repent to God by stating how you will change your ways and then *do it* (trash that website, video, book, food, drug, alcohol, and so on). Get the problem out of sight and reach. Repentance means changing your direction, so that means dealing with the problem *aggressively* so you cannot turn back to it.

Apologize. Tell anyone you have offended by your behavior, if that is appropriate (for example, if you lost your temper, used bad language, or got drunk), that you are *sorry and ask for their forgiveness*. No excuses, no defensive responses, no justifying your behavior. Excuses nullify an apology. The Bible says to let your yes be yes, and your no be no. Keep it simple and sincere. Asking their forgiveness is an added form of humility and a deterrent to doing the wrong behavior. It makes an apology more sincere.

Receive God's forgiveness with thanks, humility, and joy. You do not have to *ask* God for forgiveness. When Jesus died on the cross for *all* of our sins (past, present, and future), *He took away sin for everyone, for* *all time*. However, *you have to <u>receive</u> His gift of forgiveness* by believing what Jesus did and who He was to have forgiveness. It is as simple as that.

Once you accept God's forgiveness, He forgets your sin as far as the east is from the west, so you should, too. Be done with it, and move on, with the joy of thankfulness. If you beat yourself up, the devil will build on your guilt, and you are likely to begin a downward spiral of indulgent behavior all over again. If guilty thoughts come up, just remember God's grace and dismiss the devil in the name of Jesus Christ, and pray and focus on something else. When you eliminate a wrong behavior, you need to replace it with something godly and fruitful or the devil will return and fill the void with something undesirable.

<u>Hold yourself accountable.</u> Find someone you respect and ask if he or she will ask you regularly (weekly is helpful) how you are doing with your issue. Then be honest and let that person encourage you and remind you to do all the steps to recovery. Thank him or her, and pray together.

<u>Build your self-esteem and discipline by acknowledging your progress.</u> Self-esteem is built one brick at a time, and soon a healthy boundary wall will exist to protect you from sinning. Self-discipline is a great source of confidence and strength. Be encouraged by your accomplishment of managing and overcoming a weakness, and praise God for His help.

Communication Tool: The Table Meeting

GRETCHEN JACOBS, MA, MS, CHAPLAIN

Communication Tool: The Table Meeting

The purpose of the table meeting is to allow each person an opportunity to fully express his/her thoughts and feelings in a safe place in order to promote problem resolution. This tool can be used with couples, a parent and a child/teen, entire families, or groups. The table meeting can build communication and relational skills, as well as empathy, respect, and patience. It is a very effective tool.

Typically, in arguments, some people are better at arguing than others. If someone feels intimidated, not listened to, or respected, then he or she may shut down and use the "silent treatment," or the arguing escalates and drama results (door slamming, yelling, pouting, following someone around yelling or pleading with him or her, not letting someone be alone to cool off, and so on).

If a table meeting is conducted by the rules, it can become a great resource for settling disagreements, and this will build hope that problems can be worked out. This is especially encouraging to children and teens who have witnessed parents fighting and not getting things resolved. Kids may then think that uncontrolled arguing is normal and to be expected, which is discouraging, untrue, and poor role modeling by parents.

Table Meeting Rules

Where
The kitchen table is a great place to hold table meetings. The kitchen table is often the "hub" of activity, and when successful table meetings occur there, it becomes a constant reminder that all things can be worked out. If, instead, you hold table meetings in various places or try to use the living room sofa or someone's bedroom, there *is not any healing tradition attached to other places* as they are used for other purposes like watching TV or "hiding," and the table meeting will not be as effective. In addition, the kitchen table is typically available anytime, so if a late-night table meeting needs to happen, it can, without disturbing others in the household.

When
Anyone can call a table meeting whenever there is a sense that tension is developing or there already is a problem. If you are in places like the car or a restaurant, out doing anything, or in your bedroom, someone just says, "We need to have a table meeting. Let's drop this subject and set a time today or tonight to have a table meeting. What works for you/us?" Try to have the table meeting as soon as possible.

If you do not resolve things with one meeting, or you just do not have enough time to work through all the issues, set another time and date for the next meeting. *Then do not discuss the problem issue at all until the table meeting—not at all!* If someone brings it up, just remind him/her to hold on and that you will talk about it at the table meeting. If it is an urgent situation, take a break (a few minutes or a day, but set the return time) and then resume.

Etiquette

Pray
When you gather, first pray for Christ to be over the meeting, and at the end of the meeting, close in a prayer of thanks.

Heads Up
Give everyone present a copy of this Table Meeting tool and allow time for each person to read it.

Someone Leads
Someone leads off by saying what the one issue on the table is. One issue per meeting.

Talking Time
Each person at the table gets a turn to talk for ten full minutes without interruption. Ten minutes to start gives shy talkers plenty of time to have the floor and helps anyone get a lot off his/her chest. If you do not need to use all of your time, you can say, "That's enough for me for now. Your turn."

Use Only "I" Statements
The person talking needs to use "I" statements ("I am not comfortable with how you talk to me") instead of "you" statements ("You are always rude to me"). No one can argue with an "I" statement as it is how the *speaker* feels. Any "you" statement just makes the other person defensive and incites him/her to attack.

No Past Issues
Nothing from the past should be brought up if you can help it. Deal with the current issue and what can be done about it and be expectant and confident that a new outcome can result. (Do not say, for example, "Well, *last* time you _____" or "You have *never* been able to _____, so I'm worried.")

If a previous issue is found to remain unresolved, schedule a table meeting to deal with it at another time.

This Is a Technique
This process is not a conversation; it is a communication technique.

Pay Full Attention
Whenever someone is talking, everyone needs to give him/her *full attention and respect.* This means *always* looking at his/her eyes and paying attention to what he or she is saying. Do not respond to whatever is

being said with dramatic expressions like eye rolling, making faces or noises, and so forth. Do not interrupt a speaker even to ask questions.

Keep all technology devices off (TVs, stereos, phones, and so on).

Validate *First Every Time* before You Speak
When it is your turn to respond to a speaker, first try to start with words that affirm the feelings of others at the meeting. Show that you appreciate how they feel and use words that are encouraging—for instance, "I can see this is very upsetting to you. I really want to get this worked out" or "I hear that you are really frustrated and out of patience with this problem. I do not want to see you upset. I want to fix it."

Apologize and Ask for Forgiveness
If you realize you need to apologize, make a genuine apology: "I'm sorry I have hurt you. Will you forgive me?"

Asking for forgiveness is a humbling experience and goes a long way—much further than just saying you are sorry. If the offended person says he or she is not ready to forgive you right then, say you understand, and just let it go. You did your part. Even if it was not asked for, an apology is a good place to start your turn to speak. An apology is your admission that you have contributed to the problem. Remember that apologies must be followed by changed behavior.

Notes
If you want to make short notes because you do not want to forget a point, that is OK.

Rotate Turns
Each person present gets a turn until everyone is heard and then the turns start all over, maybe for five minutes in the second round or whatever everyone agrees to.

Reach a Resolution
Keep going around the table until a resolution is reached. If you need to do research, need time to think some points through, or need time to pray about the next steps, do that. However, remember not to talk about the problem until the next meeting.

It's Done; Let It Go
Once an issue is settled, even if you are not entirely satisfied with how it turned out, do not bring it up again. It is history. Let it go.

Take a Look at Yourself
Take the log out of your own eye before you criticize others; it will prevent many arguments.

What I Want in a Partner Worksheet (Husband/Wife)

Name and Date:_____

What I Want in a Partner Worksheet (Husband/Wife)

The purpose of this tool is to help you think through what you desire in a potential mate. Assess if your responses are realistic and agree with what God would want for you. When you meet someone, measure him/her against what you wrote and objectively decide if he/she is truly a match. Do not compromise. Show your list to your counselor to get another perspective on your list.

Make a list completing each of the following categories:

The **Essentials** (These traits/characteristics I do not want to compromise on)

Preferred traits/characteristics (These would be desirable but are not essential)

Would be nice if he or she…(These are luxuries/fantasies about the person)

What I Offer a Partner Worksheet (or What I Bring to the Relationship and What My Triggers Are)

GRETCHEN JACOBS, MA, MS, CHAPLAIN

Name and Date_____

What I Offer a Partner Worksheet (or What I Bring to the Relationship and What My Triggers Are)

The purpose of this tool is for you to acknowledge your strengths and weaknesses objectively. This is not an exercise in humility for the part about what you offer. It is, however, an exercise in honesty. Please be open about all of your strengths as well as your weaknesses, likes and dislikes/triggers, and your reactions. Discuss this tool with your counselor to discern if you have an appropriate perspective on yourself.

What I offer a partner and what I bring to the relationship

As you think of what you offer, think about what your values are, and use them as prompts (for example, being honest, kind, considerate, thoughtful, respectful, generous, punctual, clean, caring, thrifty, supportive, sociable, or collaborative).

Include what you relate to or like to do as this is also what you offer (for example, keeping a clean house; cooking; shopping; attending activities with the kids, family, relatives, and friends; spending some time alone; eating out; exercising; taking care of myself; date nights; reading; TV; movies; camping; or gardening).

What my (little and big) triggers are and *how I react to them*

For triggers, think about all the little and big things that others do that set you off, push your buttons, or tax your patience. Examples are voices being raised, being talked down to, someone being angry, controlling, late, messy, inconsiderate, ignoring you, refusing to talk, walking out in anger, sharing your private information with relatives or friends, teasing, telling you what to do instead of asking, cheating, lying, getting drunk or maybe drinking at all, using drugs, spending money without asking when it's tight, pushing you into sex, and so forth.

For each trigger, write down how you react. Examples: walk away, yell back, curse back, give them the silent treatment, eat, drink, or take drugs. Bring the sheet to counseling to set goals in each area.

Ways to Improve Communication

(Including a Summary)

GRETCHEN JACOBS, MA, MS, CHAPLAIN

Ways to Improve Communication

The purpose of this tool is to develop healthy ways to communicate and enhance your relationship with your partner (or any others in your life). Find two things a month you want to work on and discuss your progress with your spouse/partner and your counselor.

"He" and "she" are used interchangeably, as all of this material can apply to anyone. Consider posting the summary on your bathroom mirror. Work on two of the suggestions for a month and ask your partner for feedback on how you are doing.

Don't Stuff or Hide Your Feelings
Always speak to each other with "emotional integrity" (meaning, be honest and tell the truth about how you really feel). Honesty at that level is what helps bind couples, allowing them to share what is not shared with anyone else, in a safe, trusting environment.

If you need grace to help you say something hard that might hurt someone's feelings, ask God for help. However, do not ever pretend about your feelings. Share them with grace and wrapped in love. However, if you have a negative feeling, think long and hard about how important it really is, how accurate it is, and how necessary it would be to share it, and then assess whether *you* have any faults that you need to take care of before you criticize others.

> "Help me, Lord, to keep my mouth shut and my lips sealed!" (Psalm 141:3 TLB).

Say What You Need
Realize that men are typically "doers" in their "love languages" and women are "expressers/feelers." To show his love, he changes the oil, while she constantly picks up his socks or dims the lights to set the mood for romance. Learn to appreciate how your partner expresses his or her love to you and accept it, without *your* expectations.

If you need something other than what he is doing, don't tell him what he is doing wrong—show or tell him what to do. Do not be mysterious and then have him "not get it." That will only set you up for a disappointment.

Be Affectionate
Foreplay for women starts in the morning with a tender embrace, a loving word, and nonsexual touches throughout the day. When it is bedtime, be sure to honor each other's needs. Ask God for help if you are tired or not in the mood. Then put your heart ahead of your will and please your partner, even if it is a sacrificial act. God will honor your obedience.

Be Patient
Physical and emotional intimacy takes time, practice, and prayer, especially if there has been discord.

Compliment
At least once a day, find something to complement each other on. Examples could be a meal, her looks, her outfit, her company, her conversation with company, the way she takes care of herself, her intelligence, her caring heart, her faith, her patience, and so on, or his helpfulness in keeping the yard nice, the car taken care of, or the bills managed; his manners; his intelligence; his common sense, and so on.

Rev It Up
Be affectionate throughout the day, and then when you are intimate, be passionate. Keep your mind in the moment and do not let the devil distract you with unrelated thoughts.

Be Polite
Always have *exceptional* manners. Thank each other for even the routine chores the other does (regardless of how many *you* do) whether you are alone or in public.

Watch your language especially as a godly man or woman with Christ in your heart. If you slip, apologize to both the hearer and to God.

Honor Privacy
Always honor your partner in private conversation and publicly. Never disclose personal information or make each other the butt of humor. If you do, quickly and, if appropriate, publicly apologize. There are only two people you have to please: God and your partner. Put God first, then your partner, and then your children. Respect each other's privacy, however it is defined.

Act Promptly
When you find yourself wanting to retreat into angry silence, catch yourself. Instead, say that you need to talk about whatever is upsetting you. Then, first ask God, as you pray together, to protect each other's feelings as you discuss the issue together.

Honor God
Keep God in the center of your relationship. Pray together at every meal; use it as an opportunity to acknowledge and be thankful for every person at the table.

Pray Together

Every night, pray together before you go to bed and clear the air of anything that is unsettled. Never go to bed with any tension. You can always say that you are sorry that you both are fighting and that you want to make up.

Pay Attention and Validate

Learn to listen to the other person with your full attention. Look her in the eyes as she is talking (no newspaper reading or glancing at the TV). Do not try to fix it if she has something troubling her unless she asks for help. *Just listen* and empathize by saying something like, "I can see you're really upset (or sad) about that. I am sorry. Let me hold you." Then just say, "It will be OK," "We'll get through this," "God will help you; let's pray," and so forth.

Be Invested

Every day, ask each other how your day was, and then ask some questions about what your partner tells you. Be sincere.

Don't Criticize

Do not be critical or judgmental of *anyone*. Only comment on the good and the positive. Keep any negativity and criticism to yourself. Ask God to take away any critical spirit in you. Mind your own business. It is not your job to fix or educate anyone, unless someone asks. This will make you more pleasant to be around and draw people to you.

Man Up

Men, be the spiritual heads of your households. Thank God for the privilege and honor to minister to your families in His name.

Minimally, say grace at every meal, ask God out loud to bless your partners' day as they leave, and thank Him at the end of the day. Then count your blessings and admit your failures. You can start out admitting your failures silently, but there is healing in confessing these out loud to your partner. God rewards humbleness.

> "I refresh the humble and give new courage to those with repentant hearts" (Isaiah 57:15 TLB).

Don't Keep Score

Be *more than* helpful; do *more than* your share. Don't keep score. Ask how you can help.

> "Whoever wishes to become great among you shall be your servant" (Matthew 20:26).

Honor Your Word

Keep your word. If you say you're going to do a chore, do it. If you can't get to it when you promised, recommit to another time that is not too far off, and then ask if the change is OK with your partner. That is how respect and trust are built. Be a person of your word and be definite about it.

> "Let your 'yes' be 'yes,' and your 'no' be 'no'" (Matthew 5:37 HCSB).

Give It Up

Love your neighbor (that also means your partner) as yourself. You are not more important than anyone else. Give up your rights.

> "The more lowly your service to others, the greater you are. To be the greatest, be a servant. But those who think themselves great shall be disappointed and humbled; and those who humble themselves will be exalted" (Matthew 23:11–12 TLB).

> "We can justify our every deed, but God looks at our motives" (Proverbs 21:2 TLB).

Accept Each Other Unconditionally

God uses the marital relationship as the personal opportunity to practice being like Jesus and loving as the Son loves the Father. Know and accept each other—warts and all. That is a yearning we all have: to be accepted unconditionally, and to have someone really know us and accept us, like God accepts us.

> God speaking: "I don't want your sacrifices—I want your love; I don't want your offerings—I want you to know me" (Hosea 6:6 TLB).

Don't Compare

Give this relationship 100 percent. Do not get distracted by the past (including people).

Repent

Repent (ask for forgiveness and then *change your ways*) to each other for all the things you are beginning to see where you have fallen short. Ask your partner to gently point it out to you when you slip, and then do not be defensive. Just thank him or her for helping you grow more like Christ. This will be very hard, but know that it is hard for everyone.

Forget the Past

Remember this is a new beginning, a new game, so be determined. Forget the past. Pray for each other. Ask God for help.

"**The beginning of wisdom is this: Get wisdom**" (Proverbs 4:7 NIV). In other words determination to be wise is the first step toward becoming wise.

"But all your feverish plans will not avail, for you never ask for help from God" (Isaiah 22:11 TLB).

"I will give you a new heart—I will give you new and right desires—and put a new spirit within you. I will take out your stony hearts of sin and give you new hearts of love" (Ezekiel 36:26 TLB).

Summary of Communication Tips from Ways to Improve Communication

Be honest and tell the truth about how you really feel.
Show or tell your partner what you want him/her to do.
Be affectionate throughout the day, passionate when intimate.
Practice these tools and pray to have them become part of your character.
Complement each other daily.
Always have *exceptional* manners.
Respect each other's privacy in conversations with others and in private.
Say you need to talk about whatever is upsetting you.
Keep God in the center of your relationship.
Pray together before you go to bed; never go to bed with any tension.
Learn to listen to him/her with your full attention, and then empathize/acknowledge his/her feelings.
Do not try to fix him/her.
Ask each other how his/her day was each day.
Do not be critical or judgmental of *anyone*.
Men, be the spiritual head of your household. Say grace at every meal. At bedtime, count your blessings and (both of you) admit your failures and ask for God's help.
Be *more than* helpful, do *more than* your share. Do not keep score.
Keep your word.
Give up your rights.
Accept each other unconditionally.
Do not compare.
Repent (ask for forgiveness and then *change your ways*).
Forget the past. Pray for each other. Ask God for help.

Life Lessons Learned

GRETCHEN JACOBS, MA, MS, CHAPLAIN

Name and Date: _____

Life Lessons Learned

Purpose of this tool

Life experiences can make us bitter or better, fearful or willing, suspicious or open, and so on. Where we hold on to negativity, it hampers our future and our relational opportunities. This tool reveals where your lessons learned left you discouraged, struggling, or perhaps in a place of understanding. Discuss your responses with your counselor to help you grieve your negative reactions and transform them into acceptance so you can move on.

Make a list of the most significant events in your life that have affected you and left you with a "life lesson" learned. Then write the life lesson learned *at that time*, and if it changed years later, write both.

Examples

I went through a terrible divorce. The life lesson I learned was to "not be as concerned about money as how all of the fighting was impacting the kids."

My dad was never around. The original life lesson at the time was that "life is disappointing." Now I would say my dad had issues and did not know how to handle stuff, so he stayed away. Therefore, the life lesson now would be "figure out how to cope with stuff at the time and don't avoid it."

Suggested Reading

For those clients or counselors who are not book readers, suggest they minimally go to the web and type in the title of any behavioral or emotional issue and read about it to get at least an overview. Some websites have surveys you can take to see where you stand on having an issue. People will often take the survey out of curiosity, then be alarmed at their rating, and seek counseling.

Abuse (Childhood, Sexual)

Bradshaw, John. *Healing the Shame that Binds You*. Deerfield Beach, FL: Health Communications, 1988.
Tracy, Steven R. *Mending the Soul: Understanding and Healing Abuse*. Grand Rapids, MI: Zondervan 2005. Area support groups and training are also a good resource.

Borderline Personality Disorder

These books are very helpful if you are interested in learning about people with this diagnosis. Books can help you assess if someone you care about or are working with might need an evaluation because he or she has intense mood swings and irrational anger outbursts—two of the various criteria of this disorder.

Kreger, Randi. *The Essential Family Guide to Borderline Personality Disorder: New Tools and Techniques to Stop Walking on Eggshells*. Center City, MN: Hazelden Foundation, 2008.
Kreisman, Jerold J. and Hal Straus. *I Hate You—Don't Leave Me: Understanding the Borderline Personality*. New York: Perigee Book, 2010.
Mason, Paul Mason and Kreger, Randi. *Stop Walking on Eggshells, 2nd ed.: Taking Your Life Back When Someone You Love Has Borderline Personality Disorder*. Oakland, CA: New Harbinger, 2010.

Codependency

Beattie, Melody. *Codependent No More: How to Stop Controlling Others and Start Caring for Yourself*. Center City, MN: Hazelden Foundation, 1992. This book is considered the bible on codependency and is a must-read for counselors and many clients.
The CoDA (Co-Dependents Anonymous) website (http://www.coda.org/) has good information for assessing one's degree of codependency as well as a list of area meetings.

Forgiveness
Stoop, David and James Masteller. *Forgiving Our Parents, Forgiving Ourselves: Healing Adult Children of Dysfunctional Families*. Ventura, CA: Regal Books, 1996.

Homosexuality
Comiskey, Andrew. *Pursuing Sexual Wholeness: How Jesus Heals the Homosexual*. Lake Mary, FL: Charisma House, 1989.

Love Addiction, Relationship Addiction
Carnes, Patrick J. *The Betrayal Bond: Breaking Free of Exploitative Relationships*. Deerfield Beach, FL: Heath Communications, 1997.
Mellody, Pia. *Facing Love Addiction: Giving Yourself the Power to Change the Way You Love*. New York: HarperOne, 2002.
Meyer, Joyce. *Approval Addiction: Overcoming Your Need to Please Everyone*. New York: Warner Faith, Time Warner Book Group, 2005.
Peabody, Susan. *Addiction to Love: Overcoming Obsession and Dependency in Relationships*. New York: Crown Publishing, 2005.

Marriage and Relationships
Arthur, Kay. *A Marriage without Regrets*. Eugene, OR: Harvest House, 2000.
Byock, Ira. *The Four Things that Matter Most: A Book about Living*. New York: Atria Books, 2014.
Chapman, Gary. *The Five Love Languages: How to Express Heartfelt Commitment to Your Mate*. Chicago: Northfield, 1995.
Eggerichs, Emerson. *Love & Respect: The Love She Most Desires; The Respect He Desperately Needs*. Nashville, TN: Thomas Nelson, 2004.

Mental/Emotional Struggles
Emotions Anonymous (Saint Paul, MN: Emotions Anonymous International Services, 2009) has a wealth of true stories of members' struggles and how the organization helped them. This book is a fascinating read, and it will sensitize you to the pain people with mental health issues endure. See http://www.emotionsanonymous.org/ for information and meeting locations.
Meyer, Joyce. *Approval Addiction: Overcoming Your Need to Please Everyone*. New York: Warner Faith, 2005.
———. *Battlefield of the Mind: Winning the Battle in Your Mind*. New York: Warner Faith, 2002.
———. *Beauty for Ashes: Receiving Emotional Healing*. New York: Warner Faith, 2003.
Stanley, Charles F. *Emotions: Confront the Lies, Conquer with Truth*. New York: Howard Books, 2013.

Pornography
Hall, Laurie. *An Affair of the Mind: One Woman's Courageous Battle to Salvage Her Family from the Devastation of Pornography*. Wheaton, IL: Tyndale House, 1996.

Sexual Addiction

Anderson, Neil. *Victory over the Darkness: Realize the Power of Your Identity in Christ.* Minneapolis, MN: Bethany House, 2014.

Carnes, Patrick. *Out of the Shadows: Understanding Sexual Addiction, 3rd ed.:* Center City, MN: Hazelden Foundation, 2001.

———. *Don't Call It Love: Recovery from Sexual Addiction.* New York: Bantam Books, 1991.

Earle, Ralph and Gregory Crow. *Lonely All the Time: Recognizing, Understanding and Overcoming Sex Addiction, for Addicts and Co-dependents.* New York: The Phillip Lief Group, 1998.

Schaumburg, Harry W. *False Intimacy: Understanding the Struggle of Sexual Addiction* Colorado Springs, CO: NavPress, 1997.

Sexuality

Ethridge, Shannon. *Every Woman's Battle: Discovering God's Plan for Sexual and Emotional Fulfillment.* Colorado Springs, CO: WaterBrook, 2003.

Reader's Knowledge Test Answers

All of the statements are TRUE. Now you can focus on learning the dialogue strategies.

Acknowledgements

With great thanks to J. Klundt, J. Enabnit, J. Baker, B. Carr, B. Bivens, E. Fleming, J. Jensen, and C. Goodson for their encouragement; E. Stumpf for her creative and business expertise; and my clients for giving me the privilege of serving them.

Index

(Also see the Contents and Suggested Reading section in the Appendix for material related to your search)

Addictions
alcohol, alcoholics, alcoholism 20,34,55,56,70,98,142,144,145,149,150,151,165, 166,168,169,175,254
drugs 20,30,56,96,98,116,140,142,143,144,145,147,149,150,151,172,177,266
eating disorders 104,151
gambling 142,145,150,151
pornography 20,93,116,120,152,153,154,278

Communication tools
apologize, apologizing 44,54,55,61,72,80,98,137,219,254,260,269
mirroring 55,74,75
Oreo cookie strategy 40,49,50,86,128,180,182,219,222,237,249,250
performance/performer 75,76
validate/validating 28,29,30,31,42,48,55,56,73,74,75,79,80,82,84,109,124,133,159, 182,198,228,229,250

Coping mechanisms
avoidance 48,49,126,171
blame 47,68,92,93,103,122,123,160
blaming 30,82,93,121,180
denial 20,29,55,91,98,99,102,146,165,166,168,169,178
detachment 48,53,54

Counseling tasks & skills
assessment, assessments 3,14,19,34,126,127,131,153,186
contracts 227,232
etiquette 43,60,214,259
forms 35,61,62,231,236
goals 7,33,62,64,66,67,68,69,70,99,11,113,114,162,188,191,192,193
payments 66

pray, prayer, praying 8,10,14,21,23,38,46,62,65,67,68,77,78,80,81,82,96,97,105,108,109,110,122,133,150,154,159,
160,161,169,172,174,179,188,192,194,195,196,197,198,199,200,203,204,205,206,208,217,
218,221,222,229,235,236,247,254,255,259,260,269,270,271,273
records 230,231

Counseling concerns
burnout 10
confidentiality 8,53,195,196,231,232,235
legal 92,158,179,227,231
insurance 37,231,232,235,236
supervision 8,227,228,235,236

Disorders, mental health issues
anorexia 14,151
anxiety disorder(s) 14
bipolar disorder 14
bulimia 14,151
borderline personality disorder (BPD) 14,33,99,100,277
depression 14,19,20,25,26,177,178,185,186,188
narcissism 32
schizophrenia 14
trauma 9,10,14,20,92,93,95,144,168

Family, roles
family history 34,35,150
family of origin 101
lost child 102
martyr 102,164
scapegoat 92,103

Life stages
empty nest(ers) 26,121
newlyweds 25,115,116,117
premarital 107,114,115
retirement 125
widows/widowers 182,183

Marital issues
affairs 132,134,144,147,153,154,155,157
children, kids 26,27,30,39,52,61,62,70,75,92,93,98,101,102,103,104,106,117,118,119,
120,121,122,123,127,127,131,132,138,141,146,148,170,171,178,203,258,269,278
divorce 27,30,103,110,122,123,124,147,151,177,178,276
in-laws 114,127,129,130
separation 110,122,123

Recovery issues, tools
boundary, boundaries 7,41,42,43,45,46,61,63,80,103,113,128,129,176,199,228,255
calming tools 23
daily inventory 160,209
discipline 4,10,26,54,72,78,118,140,159,167,209,254,255
intervention 148
journaling 76,77,205,209
repentance 77,122,195,196,254
triggers 43,68,95,139,150,161,198,265,266
urges 160

Relational issues, behaviors
anger 13,25,26,27,33,43,46,51,52,54,61,70,72,73,92,95,122,136,138,139,140,141, 148,150,161,169,177,178,180,196,198,199,201,266,277
approach-avoidance 171
arguments 49,51,116,131,132,134,135,258,261
bondage 170
codependency 14,22,33,65,149,152,164,165,167,168,169,170,171,222,277,
empathy 6,8,23,32,158,159,258
emotional abuse 95,99
emotionally conflicted 99
entitlement mentality 30
fear 9,Chapter 6, 20,21,22,24,26,27,29,31,32,37,38,39,47,48,49,53,55,79,93,94,98,105, 116,121,123,128,129,133,135,138,139,144,147,149,163,169,171,177,183,194,195,200, 208,221,222,276
lateness 48,52,53,170
love addiction
mind reading 29
minimizing 20,29,153,162,185,186
payoff (reward) 22,24,36,85,164,169,200,201
perfectionism 29
procrastination 49,50
projecting 9,22
rebound relationships 124
relationship addiction 98,99,168
silent treatment 48,50,51,134,258,266
wall of words 48,54,55

Twelve-step programs and related terms
accountability partners 7,111,156,162,163,173,192,195,196,197
enabling 21,67,81,148,151,163,171
higher power 175,176
meetings 56,149,151,155,165,173,175,176
sponsors 175,277

About the Author

After retiring from a thirty-two-year career with the state of New Jersey in human services, Gretchen secured a master's degree in Christian counseling and also became licensed and ordained as a chaplain. She has had a private, faith-based counseling practice in Mesa, Arizona, for more than seven years. She is a "returning Catholic" after a forty-five-year absence. Over the years, prison ministry, working with sexual offenders, and couples counseling have captured her heart as has working with teens. Gretchen is an avid reader and creative writer. Reach her via her website at gretchenjacobscounselor.com.

www.ingramcontent.com/pod-product-compliance
Lightning Source LLC
Chambersburg PA
CBHW080532170426
43195CB00016B/2543